Self Seeking

Finding a Modern Teacher of Advaita

Other Books by This Author

An Essential Guide to Sanskrit for Spiritual Seekers
978-8189320003

Back to the Truth
978-1905047611

How to Meet Yourself (and Find True Happiness)
ISBN 1-84694-041-9

Enlightenment: The Path through the Jungle
978-1-84694-118-4

The Book of One: The Spiritual Path of Advaita, 2nd Edition
978-1-84694-347-8

Sanskrit for Seekers
978-1-78279-227-7

A-U-M: Awakening to Reality
978-1-78279-996-2

Western Philosophy Made Easy
978-1785357787

Answers … to the Difficult Questions: For Spiritual Seekers
978-1789042207

Confusions in Advaita Vedanta
978-93-81120-29-3

Self Seeking

Finding a Modern Teacher of Advaita

Dennis Waite

London, UK
Washington, DC, USA

First published by Mantra Books, 2025
Mantra Books is an imprint of Collective Ink Ltd.,
Unit 11, Shepperton House, 89 Shepperton Road, London, N1 3DF
office@collectiveinkbooks.com
www.collectiveinkbooks.com
www.mantra-books.net

For distributor details and how to order please visit the 'Ordering' section on our website.

ISBN: 978 1 80341 889 6
978 1 80341 893 3 (ebook)
Library of Congress Control Number: 2024939936

A CIP catalogue record for this book is available from the British Library.

Design: Lapiz Digital Services

UK: Printed and bound by CPI Group (UK) Ltd, Croydon, CR0 4YY
Printed in North America by CPI GPS partners

Contents

Introduction

About This Book

Explanation of the Title

People often become dissatisfied with their lives, for all sorts of reasons. The reasons are irrelevant as far as this book is concerned (although, interestingly, many spiritual teachers will claim that they are very relevant, and they will devote most of their efforts to addressing them). The point is that, because of these reasons, people start to think about the meaning and possible purpose of their lives. Of course, they do this because they are looking for some relief, end of suffering, happiness etc. The precise way in which they rationalize this is not relevant. They want a way forward which offers some promise of fulfilment.

Unless such a person has been brought up in a religious environment, with their family and maybe even friends believing in a god or gods, they are unlikely to look to organized religion to provide their direction. Instead, probably by searching the internet, they will look at alternative offerings. In this way, they are likely to become a 'seeker.'

Probably the most frequently encountered way in which popular approaches talk about this process is as looking for (and hopefully finding) your true or real Self. Thus, the person may be described as 'seeking the Self.' Hence the title: 'Self Seeking.' Unfortunately, it does seem to be the case that lots of so-called spiritual teachers see this as a great opportunity to make lots of money at the expense of these gullible seekers. Thinking of it in this way, we might imagine the book to be more appropriately titled: 'Self-seeking.' The hyphen signifies a world of difference!

The intention was that this book would highlight those topics which are often misrepresented by some teachers and books, and examine all of the things a seeker should consider when looking for a teacher. The book would then conveniently split into two: 1) Teachers — what to look for and what to avoid; 2) Topics often misunderstood (by teachers as well as seekers).

Unfortunately, it became obvious before I completed both aspects that combining the two would make the book too long — probably approaching 200,000 words, when the publisher's guideline was an absolute maximum of 80,000. Accordingly, there will now be two books — one for the teacher aspects and one for the topics. This is the 'How to find a teacher' book, otherwise known as 'Beware of Teachers'!

The Mining Metaphor

Searching for the truth is rather like trying to find gold, or other rare metals. It is certainly possible simply to stumble upon a nugget whilst looking for something else entirely. One can also waste years sifting through silt on the bed of a stream, only occasionally finding a few particles of value. And then there is the 'fool's gold' of pyrites or iron sulfide, which may superficially resemble gold but is of zero value.

It is especially appropriate for Advaita, which is the metaphorical gold to be sought and sifted from the ore of the Vedas. As will be explained below, the larger portion of the Vedas relate to the actions — rules and rituals — to be followed by the seeker. These certainly promote a worthy lifestyle, respectful and sympathetic to others, and presumably give some sense of achievement and virtue to the performer. Since they also help to prepare the mind for the real task, they are certainly not without any value. But they are the mineral content only; there is no elemental gold here.

When someone decides to embark upon a spiritual search, trying to find the 'meaning of life' (however they might phrase this), they do not usually know where to look and certainly do not have the tools to undertake the extraction of gold from ore themselves. They probably do not even know quite what they are looking for, in which case they are reliant upon the 'stumbling' technique.

Slightly more aware seekers may know that gold can be found by panning, and they will visit satsang teachers whom they have been led to believe are productive streams. If they are lucky, they may even come across the occasional fragment, but not enough to assemble into a meaningful understanding.

It is likely that such a prospector will be aware that there are proven mining techniques, through which pure gold can be extracted from the ore. But they also realize that this requires special tools and techniques, as well as lots of scientific knowledge. Few wish to commit to the long-term studies that this will require; they want results now.

If they do investigate further, they will learn that the raw ores are the ancient Vedantic scriptures and the tools used are knowledge of Sanskrit and the traditional ways of interpreting and explaining the text. Gaining these skills for oneself is an almost impossible task. It would take many years of total devotion and this option is simply unavailable to most.

Consequently, the most reliable method — the one most likely to provide the results one is after — is to find a teacher who is proficient in the proven skills, who can use the methodology that has been shown to work; who can read the traditional texts in the language in which they were written and interpret them for someone who is ignorant of the messages contained in them. Such teachers are unfortunately rare, and one may have to travel unfeasibly large distances to find one. Since the traditional approach requires that one attend talks regularly for many years, this method requires implicit trust and total commitment — something usually lacking in new seekers. Reading books and listening to recorded talks is therefore the only way open to most.

If it were the case that the seeker had to *do* something, then the task would be much easier. In the 'panning for gold' metaphor, instructions could be given for finding the most likely stream, how to make a 'pan' and so on. But, as will be seen, discovering the truth is not about 'doing' anything. The 'truth' is already the case; it is not something that we bring about. Our present situation is one of ignorance about our real nature and the only way to remove ignorance is to input knowledge.

The classic metaphor is the one about the lady who thought she had lost her necklace. She thought that it must have fallen off at her friend's house, from which she had just come. Accordingly, she returned there and asked the friend if she had found it. The friend pointed out that it was still around the lady's neck, having slipped down beneath her dress. The question is: did the lady need to go the friend's house in order to find the necklace? The answer is that the lady did not realize that she still had the necklace and needed to be told this by the friend. Similarly, we do not realize that we are already 'perfect,' 'complete' and 'eternal' and this has to be pointed out and explained by the teacher.

The ways in which teachers attempt to point this out vary significantly and will be examined in detail later. There is a natural tendency to assume that all modern teachers are fully acquainted with the historical method and, having the benefit of modern science and technology, are able to bypass outdated and religion-oriented approaches and go straight to the bottom line. But actually, modern teachers are in no better position than ancient teachers when it comes to Advaita. We all apparently live in the world and see it as separate from ourselves. And the fact of the matter is that, even when we have realized the truth, this situation remains unchanged! The difference lies in the knowledge we have of what is *actually* the case, beyond the appearance. Simply telling someone that reality is non-dual makes no difference whatsoever. We have to approach the truth gradually, with deep understanding, not wishful thinking!

One final point regarding this mining metaphor. I will be promoting traditional over modern teaching throughout this book but traditional, too, is not immune from being confusing or misleading. If one thinks of the Vedas as being crude ore, the Upaniṣads, Bhagavad Gītā and Brahmasūtras have to be thought of as refined ore. These, too, have to be 'processed' by a skilled and qualified teacher in order to extract the pure gold of Advaita teaching. One can even consider that there are varying levels of purity here — increasing carat counts! It may even be true to say that there is no teacher who can deliver 24 carats! All are necessarily affected by the brilliance or not of their own teacher and the extent to which they themselves have overcome their own pre-realization conditioning.

But, in the presence of a qualified teacher, it is most likely to be your own qualifications that determine the outcome. If your mind is not prepared, you are very likely to reject even the purest gold.

The Dangers!

The prospectors of the Californian Gold Rush of the 1850s were presumably subjected to various scams by the unscrupulous. I am no historian, but I would guess that some were sold deeds to land known to be devoid of gold. And maybe they were sold fool's gold, in the belief that they would be made rich. Wherever there is a demand, one is certain to find people prepared to offer a supply of false or substandard product in exchange for profit. Such is the world we have always lived in.

The parallel is clear. There will always be seekers of truth. Some (probably very few these days!) may be prepared to give up their day-to-day lives and become monks so that they can learn from a teacher over many years. But most will only be prepared to buy a book or two (and maybe even read them!) or travel a short distance to attend an occasional satsang. They might delude themselves that, as soon as they start to see some positive effect, they will extend their commitment.

Since the advent of the internet, anyone is able to make themselves aware of the situation regarding such people. They can see how popular the various means have become and may just be tempted to take advantage of one or other in order to make some money. Cynical, this may be but, with even the best intentions, this signals a serious danger for seekers.

The qualifications for a good teacher are many and stringent. It has to be said that there are very few of those writing books or holding meetings today who have them all. (I do not, for a start!) Yet books sell and 'silent residentials' etc. are held, and well-attended. Lots of money changes hands along with, no doubt, some provocative ideas. But, I am confident in saying, some of these 'teachers' are not 'enlightened,' and maybe even do not know exactly what that means.

Regarding reading books, one immediately interesting point to note from perusing Amazon is that those titles containing the word 'Advaita' and giving the impression of being 'serious' do not usually have a large number of reviews. even where those are all 5*. It is those books with provocative, 'self-help-oriented' titles which catch the attention and clearly draw the readers. People want a quick and easy solution to life's problems. Not to escape life but to convert misery into happiness and start to enjoy life. They do not want to have to study dry scriptures or listen to what might be thought of as 'preaching.' I hope I haven't lost you already!

My Qualifications for Writing This Book

This section reproduces an article that I wrote nearly 10 years ago for my publishers' magazine (it was never published for some reason!).

Dreaming of God

A philosophically-inclined wit once inquired into the difference between having God speak to one in a dream and dreaming about God. This metaphysical query is the basis of this article on Mind-Body-Spirit books in general and my own writing in particular.

Let's assume for a moment that I am a 'successful' author (by which I mean that I have written books that are acknowledged as 'worthy' rather than that I have made much money from the pursuit!). There are effectively two elements to this success:

1. being able to write, and
2. being knowledgeable about the subject-matter of the books.

If I am deemed to have achieved those accomplishments, what were the principal factors?

Writing Ability

Three elements have influenced this: a deprived childhood, an enquiring mind and a good education. By 'deprived' here, I mean 'socially deprived.' There were no other children of my age in the neighborhood. I had to provide my own entertainment. This was mainly achieved by reading around three books per week from the library throughout most of my childhood and adolescence. Mostly SF, I concede, but I also graduated to some traditional and modern classics as well as a little nonfiction. This had the effect of developing a wide vocabulary (I always looked up new words in the dictionary) and an appreciation of how to put those words together in an interesting and informative manner.

This academic style of leisure activity both supported and enhanced my education and my attitude to it, so that I gained a scholarship to a prestigious school. There, I was obliged to study Latin. Although I did not at all appreciate it at the time, this provided an understanding of the underlying structure of words and the importance of correct grammar.

On leaving university, having spent the previous 10 years specializing in Chemistry, I got a job as a computer programmer. Some years later, I discovered that I had a hitherto unrealized skill for explaining difficult concepts, when I was asked to write a manual to explain the functioning of the software in a complex telecommunications system. Provided that I could fully understand the intricacies myself, I found that I was able to break things down into their fundamental elements and document this knowledge in such a way as to educate others. But, in order to reach that stage, I had to sit down with the authors of the software and get them to explain to me all of the interactions and functions until I understood everything for myself. This was an absolute requirement!

Knowledge of Subject

I also have my education to blame for this aspect, to some degree. Since it was an all-male school, in addition to the woeful social skills that I had gathered earlier, my ability to interact with the alien female of the species was virtually non-existent. This shortcoming significantly helped to bring about my general dissatisfaction with life and engendered an interest in philosophy and matters spiritual, to try to fathom some meaning and purpose.

I floundered for some years in the mass of miscellaneous material available before I finally became aware of Advaita. Again, it took some years even to find out what exactly this was about, since there was (and still is to some extent, in the West) a dearth of books on the subject.

Having decided that I sincerely wanted to understand this teaching, I soon discovered that there is actually only one process for achieving this. Śaṅkara, who is the principal historical teacher of Advaita and responsible for making it more generally available in around the eighth century CE, states it as follows: *Listen to the teaching (from someone who is qualified to give it); ask questions to remove all doubts; dwell on what you have learned until it is completely assimilated.* [Note that these stages are called śravaṇa, manana, and nididhyāsana respectively in Sanskrit.]

This poses an immediate problem: how does one find a 'suitably qualified' teacher? Such a person has to know the scriptures inside out, understand Sanskrit, and (most importantly) be able to explain it to a 'suitably qualified' seeker. This level of knowledge is really only available to someone who has studied for a long time with another, already-qualified teacher. I have received emails from seekers all over the world asking if I can recommend a good teacher in their area. I am rarely able to oblige. [This book is, in fact, an attempt to answer their question comprehensively!] If you live in India, there is no problem. If you live in one of the major cities of the civilized world, there is a possibility. Others have only two choices: relocate or resort to reading and the internet, as I had to do.

Experience and Knowledge

Writing about 'spiritual' matters is fraught with language problems. Many authors in the MBS category are presumably attempting to communicate their 'experiences' of whatever topic they write about. I say 'presumably' because I freely admit that I have not read any of those books that claim to use extrasensory means of acquiring information, whether from angels or crystals or any other source. This is not because I believe such books are entirely fictional. But, even if they are based on what the writer believes to be fact, it is simply not possible to communicate experience in an unambiguous manner. Experience is ultimately ineffable; only masters of fiction write about it with any degree of success.

To some degree, even 'objective' data suffer from these problems. After all, unless we are talking about the axiomatic or mathematically defined, even physical 'facts' are observer dependent or relative to the frame of reference. Attributes of objects depend upon the nature and acuity of the senses that perceive them, as well as on the individual's prior knowledge and experience. Thus it is that anyone attempting to describe or teach a system of philosophy needs to tread very carefully, as it were, when they speak or write.

I actually began my first book, *The Book of One* (Ref. 84), in a similar spirit to that with which I had approached the Technical Manual; I wanted to reach that level of understanding with respect to the teaching of Advaita. And the process was the same – read extensively, ask lots of questions of others more knowledgeable than me. I began in relative ignorance but acquired more and more understanding as I continued. I often encountered views that were mistaken but, over time, the correct views were reinforced by constant repetition from different sources and the erroneous ideas were discarded. There was the constant need to be alert to the dangers, cross-referencing every new source against previously read material, looking for reinforcing or contradictory views, and always exercising doubt and reason to question and validate new information.

The vast amount of research I conducted on *Book of One* enabled me subsequently to write *Back to the Truth* (Ref. 467), since I had collected hundreds of excellent references from other sources. This process has been the cornerstone of all of my books. *A-U-M: Awakening to Reality* (Ref. 379) is an exposition of a book I had read some 25 years earlier. I recognized its importance at the time but was quite unable to understand it, or to find anyone who could explain it to me. In researching it, I acquired virtually every book (in English) that had been written, including several that had extremely low print runs in India. And I listened to hundreds of hours of talks from acknowledged experts. The annotated bibliography in the book runs to 34 pages.

Without such background research, discovering the truth from those who already know it, it is impossible to write books such as these in other than a cynical manner. Of course, there are those who are perfectly aware that what they write is little better than fiction, but their livelihood depends upon persuading others through their books and lectures. Some may genuinely delude themselves also but there will always be complete charlatans in any field.

The advice I would give to any seeker-of-truth, whether via a proven path such as Traditional Advaita or via some of the more recent, questionable paths is as follows. Only accept and give credence to books that provide knowledge that seems to be authentic, and which include lots of references that can be checked. Such books must also not be contrary to reason and need to provide convincing arguments if they are to change one's views. If a book is constantly saying 'this is what I have found,' 'I believe,' 'it has been my experience' etc. — by all means read it (if you must) but take all that is said with a large pinch of salt and look for a book that does not rely on such tactics. Remember the premise of this article: Experience equips one to write fiction; knowledge equips one to write nonfiction.

Background to Seeking and Advaita

Why Seek the Self, and Why Advaita?

This is another article, previously only published in Ref. 531.

If you are reading this book, I suggest that there is a high probability that you are not happy! It is an undeniable fact that the majority of people today are dissatisfied with what they perceive as being a mediocre existence. They may feel that they are limited by an unattractive and illness-prone body or by a mind that is imperfectly educated and unable to make intellectual leaps of understanding. There are very many things that we want – objects, partners, lifestyle, jobs etc. – but few that we seem to be able to obtain. (And, even when we do obtain them, their rewards are invariably ephemeral.) Western society relies upon the media advertising all of these things, and thereby continually reinforcing the desires. Being repeatedly frustrated by this materialistic lifestyle, it should be hardly surprising that many turn towards the spiritual in the hope that this might bring about peace and a durable happiness.

The problem is that all 'paths' and 'systems' can only promise you a *future* happiness, so that we need to have some sort of reassurance that the commitment of our time and effort will prove worthwhile. Unfortunately, the majority of the 'new age' techniques bring with them no reassurance at all. Frequently, these systems are quite contrary to reason and often rely upon putting one's belief into something that is totally unbelievable. Cynically, one might think that the only reason that there are *several* books upon a particular topic is that the later authors realized after the first book that there was money to be made out of a gullible public.

A 'spiritual seeker' might be defined as the person who has realized that the attaining of 'things' does not, in fact, bring about lasting happiness. All it does is trigger the beginning of the next desire. This is what leads people to seek the magical, the fantastical that will shatter our mundane existence once and for all. Whether this be foretelling our future through tea leaves or crystals, or communicating with aliens or angels hardly matters; our minds make the leap from the worldly to the unknowable, other world where we are promised something that will truly satisfy.

But of course it doesn't, because such worlds are not only unknowable but also imaginary. The fact that this cannot be proven to be so allows such ideas to exist but makes no difference to the outcome. Desiring the illusory is even less satisfying than obtaining the desirable.

We need to think about what it is that we really want and then refine our desires; evolving from wanting mere gross objects to the desire to discover our own nature and that of reality itself. It is discovered that our desires develop from the gross to the more refined. There is a natural and a necessary progression involved here. We begin with wanting simply *things* in the outside world (of course these may be people or situations etc.). Then we realize that it is not the things themselves that we want but the happiness that we believe they will bring. The objects are many but the happiness is actually only one. Moreover, there usually comes a time when the object ceases to give happiness and you want to get rid of it!

The next step follows logically from the previous. The fact that things do not always give happiness means that the happiness is not actually in the object but in our self. It is never anywhere else! And it is this fact that deserves serious investigation. The suggestion is that happiness is our natural state and that this is revealed whenever a desire is removed (e.g., when we obtain something that we want and the desire for it goes away). Clearly, since we do not experience happiness all the time, this natural state must somehow be covered over. So the next startling realization is that nothing I can *do* could ever obtain happiness for me (since I cannot choose whether or not to have desires). Indeed, it seems that most of the things that I do bring unhappiness! Instead, what has to happen is that I must come to know this natural state, i.e., my true self. This true self is not something to be obtained but something I have to know. Accordingly, the penultimate refinement of my desires is from wanting to find my Self to wanting Self-knowledge.

And thus we come to Advaita. Advaita is a proven teaching methodology to give me knowledge of my Self. The knowledge is contained in the scriptures called the Upanishads, which were written down thousands of years ago, having previously been passed down by word of mouth from the ancient rishis.

Since they were necessarily in fairly dense form, and written in Sanskrit, they need to be interpreted and explained by someone who both knows the Self and is familiar with the techniques, stories and metaphors used to unfold these scriptures. These techniques have themselves been passed down from guru to disciple in a structured manner. Accordingly, the last refinement is from wanting knowledge, to wanting to hear these scriptures explained by a qualified teacher.

So, what does Advaita actually say? Very briefly, we presently experience ourselves as separate persons in a universe of objects. Despite this seeming duality, according to Advaita, reality is actually non-dual. This non-dual reality is called Brahman. As a matter of fact we do feel ourselves to be other than our body or mind. Advaita calls our essential self, which is beyond body and mind, the Atman. And the fundamental message of the Upanishads is that this Atman is Brahman.

[Important note: whenever I use the word 'Brahman' on its own in this way, I am referring to the non-dual reality, called 'nirguṇa Brahman' — Brahman 'devoid of qualities.' If I want to talk about the Brahman that apparently creates and governs the world, called 'saguṇa Brahman' — Brahman with qualities — I will use the word Īśvara. There is, of course, only 'Brahman' — the differentiation is only for the sake of teaching.]

There is an oft-quoted sentence which is said to summarize Advaita. This is:

brahma satyam, jaganmithyā, jīvo brahmaiva nāparaḥ (this is the Romanized equivalent of that Sanskrit sentence). Translated, it means: "Brahman is the reality; the world is not in itself real; the individual self is not different from Brahman." And the purpose of the teaching is simply to bring about this realization.

Unlike religions and most other spiritual systems, you are not asked to set aside reason and accept the unprovable as truth. On the contrary, you are encouraged to question everything until all doubts are satisfied. The only 'practices' you are expected to follow are those which promote self-control of mind and senses so that discrimination may operate in a still mind. Thereafter, it is simply a matter of listening or reading, clarifying confusion and reflecting until there is 'enlightenment.'

Advaita

[Note that some of the material in this section appeared in the earlier book *Back to the Truth*. It is simply a very brief explanation of what Advaita is in case any reader should be unfamiliar with the term.]

The literal meaning of the word 'religion' is 'to bind back' (from the Latin re-ligare); i.e., to return to the reality of our true nature. All religions have the same objective and, though most will deny this, the same truth. Reality itself cannot be spoken of, however (that would necessitate that we, doing the speaking, would have to stand outside of reality), and herein lies the ultimate problem and the root of all contention between the different teachings.

Philosophy is the secular approach that uses reason and logic to look for meaning in our lives and to explore the nature of reality. It does this without reliance upon faith in something that initially lies outside of reason. Nevertheless, the aim of both religion and philosophy is one, as Swami Nikhilananda has pointed out: *"The goal of philosophy may be Truth, and the goal of religion, God; but in the final experience God and Truth are one and the same Reality."* (Ref. 193)

Advaita is both a philosophy and a religion in the original meaning of the word. It is one of the few teachings that provide what is effectively a graded approach that is suitable for practically everyone, excluding only those who will not listen. For those who do not yet have the driving desire to discover the 'meaning of life,' there are preliminary practices intended to prepare the mind and promote the right attitudes. Whatever the nature or circumstances of the individual, there is a strategy to suit. Note, however, that *only* knowledge will take you all the way. Supposed 'paths' such as Karma Yoga and Bhakti Yoga etc. cannot themselves give enlightenment. Only knowledge can do this.

The teaching strategy of Advaita uses a number of models or metaphors. The novice spiritual aspirant is initially taught that the grossest level or approach represents the true situation. As her understanding grows, however, this provisional story is shown to be untrue and a new picture, which is more subtle, is given. Ultimately, each description has to be rescinded since none could ever be true in any objective sense, but the giving up of the grosser standpoint entails the sublation of the mistaken ideas which are preventing the intuitive realization of the truth. This method is fundamental to the teaching of Advaita and is called adhyāropa-apavāda. More will be said about this below.

The word 'ignorance' is usually used to refer to our initial lack of understanding but — let it be said at the outset — 'ignorance' is not a really-existent entity. It is simply the word we use to talk about not having sufficient knowledge about something. Lots of deeply philosophical texts on Advaita have been written over the past thousand plus years. Many of these speak of ignorance as though it were a real entity. They argue amongst themselves and end up writing virtually incomprehensible material that is thoroughly confusing!

Advaita, being the non-dual reality, necessarily points to the essential truth in all religions. For example, sayings from the bible such as those of God to Moses (*"I am that I am"*) or of Christ (*"The kingdom of heaven is within you"*) express the fundamental truth of Advaita, the non-dual reality of Brahman. The difficulty with books and teachers is that you need ones that speak to your current level of understanding. Begin with the simple, and graduate to the more sophisticated. Ensure that the sources that you use know what they are talking about! A teacher who does not understand the goal, and the means of teaching it, is obviously not going to be very helpful at explaining them! And the most serious problem of all is that, to begin with, you are not going to be able to differentiate good teaching from bad.

Sources of the Teaching

> *Access to the Vedas is the greatest privilege this century may claim over all previous centuries... In the whole world there is no study so beneficial and so elevating as that of the Upaniṣads. It has been the solace of my life and it will be the solace of my death.*
>
> Schopenhauer (Quoted in Ref. 140)

Advaita Vedānta is a philosophy that was systematized in India around the eighth century CE by someone named Ādi Śaṅkara. ['Ādi' means 'first.' There have been other Śaṅkaras since and some care must be taken not to confuse them.] In fact, the essence of the teaching had been around for very much longer than this, being derived from the material contained in the Upaniṣads. The Upaniṣads are a part of the sacred Indian texts called the Vedas, written around 1500 BC, though they are said to have existed in spoken form long before this. (Some evidence suggests this may have been prior to 6000 BC, with the written Sanskrit alphabet – Devanagari – in use in 3000 BC in Western India.)

The Vedas consist primarily of hymns and rituals. We are supposed to follow the instructions contained therein and behave in accordance with their ethical principles in order to attain our desires and fulfill our ambitions. The Upaniṣads are mostly found in the final sections of the Vedas, which are called Vedānta, i.e., end or culmination (anta) of the Vedas. They deal with the philosophical aspects regarding the nature of reality, the Self and the world, and it is from them that Advaita is derived.

It is a non-dual philosophy, which means that in reality there are not two (things). This is the literal meaning of the word 'Advaita' – *a* meaning 'not,' and *dvaita* 'two.' This is an alien and apparently meaningless concept to most people at first hearing and I will not attempt to elaborate further at this point.

The sources of this teaching, then, began with the Upaniṣads. Over the centuries which followed the writing down of those scriptures, other important works, which interpreted or attempted to summarize them, followed. Amongst these, perhaps the most famous is the Bhagavad Gītā, the 'Song of the Lord.' This is a book whose importance to the Hindu religion is on a par with that of the Bible for Christians. It forms the central part of a much larger, epic poem called the Mahābhārata, said to have been written by the same author – Vyāsa – who compiled the Vedas.

At the level of the story, the Gītā (as it is often called) speaks about the crisis of confidence confronting the prince Arjuna, as he faces his old teachers and members of his family, at the start of a great battle in which most of them will be killed. His charioteer is the lord Krishna and the Bhagavad Gītā tells of the conversation in which Krishna persuades Arjuna that it his duty and destiny to fight. It is, of course, very much more than this, effectively using the essence of the Upaniṣadic philosophy to provide guidance to the ordinary person as to how to live his or her life.

Sri Parthasarathy begins the introduction to his 3-volume *Srimad Bhagavad Gītā* with the words:

> *The Bhagavad Gītā, the 'Song of the Lord', begins with the word 'dharma' and ends with the word 'mama'. Together they mean 'my dharma' or 'my essential nature'. This phrase indicates the prime message of the Gītā, that the ultimate purpose of life is to realize one's essential nature. To discover It within and become one with It. One's essential nature is the supreme Self*

within. It is God. The philosophy of the Gītā guides one to the attainment of this supreme goal. (Ref. 387)

One of the clearest traditional books on the subject is called Vivekacūḍāmaṇi — the *Crest-Jewel of Discrimination.* It may have been written by Śaṅkara, although there are some good reasons for doubting this. But, nevertheless, it covers all of the essentials, from the initial assessment of the human condition to realization of the final truth of Advaita, in an eminently readable manner. Early in the text, the seeker lists the seven questions that he wants answered:

50. The pupil said: "O my Master, please listen to my question. My ends will be realized if I can hear the answer from your lips."

51. "What is bondage? How does it arise? What keeps it in being? How may one escape from it? What is the not-self? What is the supreme Self? How can one discriminate between the two? Please tell me that." (Ref. 388)

And the teacher answers all of these questions and more in the text that follows.

The sources for the teaching of Advaita are the following. The section on 'Recommended Reading' later indicates my personal recommendations from these. As a general warning, scriptural sources should never be consulted (other than for original quotations) unless they are accompanied by a recommended authoritative commentary. This should ideally consist of Śaṅkara's commentary (bhāṣya) with further clarification as needed by the translator.

1. **Original scriptures: prasthāna traya:** This simply refers to the 'three methods or sources' from which the teaching

derives. Śaṅkara has provided extensive commentaries on them:

a. **śruti** – the Upaniṣads, of which around 108 still exist from the many more original ones. Śaṅkara provided commentary on 10 of these, which are consequently referred to as the 'principal' or 'major' Upaniṣads. The word literally means 'that which is heard' and the texts were learned by heart down the traditional lineages (sampradāyas), from master to disciple.
b. **smṛti** – this is almost invariably used to refer to the Bhagavad Gītā, although other texts of this category exist. The word means 'remembered.' They comprise laws and guidance based upon the Vedas.
c. **nyāya prasthāna** – this invariably refers to the Brahmasūtra. Nyāya is the system of logic and reason used in Indian philosophy.

2. **Later Independent Treatises: Prakaraṇa Granthas:** This refers to stand-alone texts which cover particular aspects, or even the entirety of the teaching. The one which is certain to have been written by Śaṅkara is Upadeśa Sāhasrī, the 'Thousand Teachings.' Other classics not written by Śaṅkara include Aṣṭāvakra Gīta, Dṛgdṛśya-Viveka, Pañcadaśī, and Yoga Vasiṣṭha. (But note that one should beware of such post-Śaṅkara texts as there will almost certainly be statements which cause confusion and some which contradict Śaṅkara.)
3. **Historical Sages before Śaṅkara:** This is principally Gauḍapāda, who is generally thought to have been the teacher of Śaṅkara's teacher (Govinda). He wrote an extensive commentary (kārikā) on the Māṇḍūkya Upaniṣad (which is said to encapsulate the essence of the teaching of Advaita). [My book *A-U-M* (Ref. 379) was written to explain this text.]

4. **Historical Sages post-Śaṅkara:** There are quite a few of these, depending upon whom one regards as a 'Sage.' Refs. 380 and 381, for example, provide voluminous material from, and essays on, some 40–50 teachers between 800 and 1200 CE. Most names are unfamiliar to all but Advaitin scholars these days, but some left a legacy of specific ways of interpreting Śaṅkara. In particular, Advaitins in the post-Śaṅkara era started to analyze the logical implications of some of the concepts used to help the seeker remove Self-ignorance. (This is effectively in defiance of the fact that all these concepts are only interim and have to be discarded eventually.) In particular, scholars could not reach agreement over concepts such as māyā and ignorance itself (avidyā). This led to a split into two schools — Bhāmatī and Vivaraṇa. (Entire books discuss these differing views but a short essay on the distinction can be read at Ref. 528.) Key teachers and texts followed in both schools and further divergence of views have also developed. Sureśvara was a direct disciple of Śaṅkara, and his teaching with its slight differences is called Vārttika, in recognition of the mammoth text that he wrote as commentary on Śaṅkara's bhāṣya (commentary) on the Bṛhadāraṇyaka Upaniṣad. (The word 'vārttika' means an 'explanatory' or critical 'gloss' on another text.)
5. **Recent Sages/Teachers:** Ramakrishna and his direct disciple Swami Vivekananda are responsible for instigating what now exists as a network of centers and ashrams around the world, each with their resident monks and teachers who presumably pass on the message as taught by their teachers. (This teaching is known as Neo-Vedānta and does not always correspond precisely with traditional Advaita, although maybe 90% is common.) Swami Chinmayananda also established a

chain of missions and centers, and this applies also to Swami Dayananda, who was in part a disciple of his.

Other key teachers, responsible for inspiring many others, were Nisargadatta Maharaj, Ramana Maharshi and Atmananda Krishna Menon. Osho also has to be mentioned, although he incorporated material from other traditions and is nowadays regarded as a charlatan by many.

6. **Modern Satsang Teachers:** Most claim allegiance to Ramana or Nisargadatta but there are numerous 'independent' teachers who claim not to belong to any lineage but to have attained enlightenment on their own (usually after many years of searching and questioning). New ones also 'pop up' from time to time. A 'subsection' of this group are the 'Neo-Advaitins,' who effectively claim that no teaching of any kind is actually required.
7. **Other Teachers and Writers:** Advaita is not a 'popular' path in the West, as is attested by the paucity of books on the subject in the High (Main) Street bookstore. But many books *are* available, even if you have to order them from India. See the details of my own 'library' on the subject at Ref. 529. (Warning: I have not been keeping this up to date as I can no longer easily maintain the website.) Also, over the past 10–20 years, as the internet has expanded, increasing numbers of articles and blogs can be found. Some of these can be very good indeed. The problem for the new seeker is discovering which! And the same applies to the books, of course. Many of these are written by academics, who are studying Advaita as part of a course at university. Unfortunately, unlike most subjects, an academic is not the best person to consult! The extent to which Advaita can be treated as academic is limited. Ultimately, we can say nothing at all about reality. Since it is non-dual, it cannot be objectified. There is no 'subject' and 'object.'

The Content

Back to the Truth

This endeavor could be considered to be a follow-up to my book *Back to the Truth* (Ref. 467), published in 2007 — 17 years ago as I write this. There are two reasons why I felt I should do this.

Firstly, I have just received an email from the publisher saying that this book has sold another 500 copies — a total of 7000 so far. (This is very good for a book on Advaita. Most would-be seekers stop at Mindfulness or Eckhart Tolle.)

Secondly, I recently read a (15 page!) review of my last book (*Confusions in Advaita Vedanta: Vol. 1 Knowledge, Experience and Enlightenment,* Ref. 398) in The Ramana Maharshi publication *Mountain Path* (Ref. 468). This review criticized a number of points where I had pointed out that Ramana's teaching diverged from the traditional, and thereby was a cause of confusion in seekers. In particular, it made the point that:

> *The author of this book is extremely well read, pedagogical and has a deep knowledge about Advaita Vedanta but does seem to have little knowledge about other holistic aspects of Hinduism or the Indian context. He treats his readers as uttama adhikārīs* [highest-level seekers] *who are of course very rare. Further, one would guess these traditional Vedānta texts are read by less than 1% of the general population and this book caters to the top 1% of that 1%.*

Whilst I accept the praise and criticism of the first four points, I disagreed with the last point. I actually state in the book that: *"Both beginners and long-term seekers will have some difficulties with this book."* I point out that: *"The benefit is, however, greatest for the beginner because this will enable him or her to proceed more quickly, avoiding some potentially dangerous confusion later."* As regards the experienced seeker — the 'uttama adhikārī' of the reviewer:

> *He or she may have to let go of some cherished concepts that were believed to be sacrosanct. The benefit, however, is similar to that for the beginner. Ideas that were held erroneously may have been preventing further progress. Once removed, the way once again becomes clear for the progression to full understanding.*

However, if it is the case that the beginning seeker, or indeed anyone without Sanskrit or scriptural familiarity, is turned off by the approach of that book, then there is clearly a need for a more 'approachable' text to address these issues. In particular, many seekers' only source for this knowledge may be via Western teachers who themselves do not actually know very much about 'pure' (i.e., traditional) Advaita. Accordingly, there is a clear need for a book to remedy this situation. This, then, aims to be that book.

Back to the Truth tended to suggest that any of the various approaches could prove successful, presumed to be dependent upon the skills of the teacher; that one should look for a teacher whose approach best suited one's own outlook and background. Accordingly, I presented extracts and quotations from the widest possible range of sources. I selected them on the basis of how well they succeeded in expressing the teaching aspect that I was presently addressing, regardless of whether or not the overall approach of that teacher/writer could be recommended. I did not point out that even a poor teacher can occasionally make profound statements. And I overlooked the possibility that a reader might take an extract as being fully representative.

Since then, I have read much more, discussed topics with many others, and written another six books on Advaita. (And my library of Advaita-related books has grown to nearly 1500, not to mention the gigabytes of electronic documents!) My book *Enlightenment: The Path Through the Jungle* looked at the meaning of the term 'enlightenment' and the various 'paths' available to the seeker for reaching that objective. The relevant conclusion of that book was that most of the teaching available in the West today is unlikely to prove effective. The research that I have carried out for this book indicates that the situation is actually very much worse.

The proven effective method of teaching is that provided by Traditional Advaita. This consists of regular (usually weekly) series of talks on particular scriptural texts, carried out over many years by qualified teachers. 'Qualified' in this context means someone who is ideally enlightened themself, who has good general teaching skills and, most importantly, has learned these proven techniques from his or her own teacher. This entails that the teacher belong to a sampradāya, i.e., a lineage of teacher-disciple, stretching back for generations, in which these skills are passed down. Since the scriptures were all written in Sanskrit, excellent knowledge of that language is ideally also required. Śaṅkara warns us (Bhagavad Gītā 13.2) that *"One who is not a knower of the traditional interpretation is to be ignored like a fool, though he may be versed in all scriptures."* (Ref. 389)

James Swartz points out that teachers who claim to be enlightened, and teach mainly by talking about their 'experience' should be avoided:

> *An enlightened person is not necessarily a qualified teacher and a qualified teacher is not necessarily enlightened! If my teaching is nothing more than me and my enlightenment story – what I did, what happened to me — it is not going to work for you. My enlightenment and the conclusions I draw from it do not amount to a teaching because the problem is generic ignorance. The solution for self-ignorance is self-knowledge, and knowledge is not personal.* (Ref. 447)

This new book then will suggest that, if you want a truly reliable approach, well-proven to be successful, you are obliged to seek out traditional sources. In this way, you will find yourself going back to the *authenticated* Truth; far more likely to break through the habitual thought patterns of twenty-first century man, despite being 5000 years old!

And, just to reiterate, this 'book' is actually two books. The one in your hands — *Finding a Modern Teacher* — is specifically aimed at helping you to find a teacher or to decide which books to read. It will explain what enlightenment is and what you must do to 'get it.' Most importantly of all, it will give you a whole list of warnings, explaining what to look out for (and what to reject) when you are looking for someone or some books to explain Advaita to you. Many teachers either do not know or choose not to follow the proven path. There is much to discover on many topics before you will be convinced of the truth. It is the job of the teacher (or book) to explain all of these and remove any remaining doubts that you may have. The partner book — *Mining for the Truth* — will address all of these topics and show how most teachers fail to clarify the true situation, leading to your confusion, and either delaying or preventing enlightenment.

Note on Sanskrit Representation

Note that just a few Sanskrit terms will be used in this book where they are deemed necessary, since you are very likely to encounter them when reading other texts on Advaita. The actual Devanagari script will not be used, however, since few readers are likely to be familiar with it. Instead, they will be shown in IAST format (International Alphabet of Sanskrit Transliteration). I usually include a glossary of the words used and a guide to IAST or ITRANS (the other frequently encountered form), but because there are so few Sanskrit terms used, I have not done so in this book. Please refer to one of the other books if necessary (or buy one if you don't have any!).

The titles of scriptural texts, together with the names of Indian teachers and characters from the scriptures will usually be given in IAST rather than their English or 'Romanized' version. Both forms will be encountered in reading but, while the Anglicized version can easily be worked out from the IAST, the reverse is not the case! Thus, Śaṅkara will usually be written in the correct form – Śaṅkara – and Gaudapada will be written as Gauḍapāda. Similarly, scriptural texts such as Vivekachudamani and Bṛhadāraṇyaka Upanishad will be shown as Vivekacūḍāmaṇi and Bṛhadāraṇyaka Upaniṣad.

Quotations

Note that all quotations from other books will be *in italic font.*

In this book, I provide many quotations that I criticize for one reason or another. Those seekers who claim the originator as their guru will probably argue against my condemnation. (I know because this has happened many times on my website!) A typical argument is that the quotation was not intended to be taken literally or is taken out of context. And they may be right. Perhaps it was intended as a metaphor or even, in an extreme case, as antiphrasis (a rhetorical device of saying the opposite of what is actually meant in such a way that it is obvious what the true intention is).

But no arguments of this nature can provide an adequate defense. The bottom line has to be that the purpose of any teaching is to reduce confusion, not add to it! If simple, common-sense reasoning shows that what is said cannot be true, then it has to be rejected, whoever is claimed to have said it.

When I give 'negative' quotations from books or other sources, I will still aim to give a reference. (Otherwise, it might be claimed that I am inventing it for the purpose of my argument.) But I do not want to criticize any author unjustly. Mistaken or misleading statements can appear even in otherwise good books. It may be that, for whatever reason – lack of editing or language skill for example – what one reads is not quite what was meant. This, of course, is the positive interpretation. It may also be that the writer simply did not understand Advaita. Whichever the case, my aim is to indicate the apparent confusion and not to damage the author's credibility. That is, I am criticizing the statement, not the author. It may have been many years since a book was published and the author's possible misunderstanding then may now have been corrected. Such quotations serve to illustrate how a seeker may be misled and should be taken in that way without further criticism.

Here is an example of how this will work. In the Preface to *Back to the Truth,* I said: *There is a path for those who wish to use only the clearest reasoning to approach an understanding of the nature of reality and there is one for those who merely want to surrender all of their day to day worries to a personal God.* Yes — I said that! And it is misleading, although I could argue that, since I used the word 'path,' it is pedantically correct.

The fact of the matter is that there is only one means of 'becoming enlightened' and that is to gain Self-knowledge. Karma Yoga is the path of surrendering actions to a deity. It is 'helpful' to do this because it eliminates selfishness and thereby lessens the influence of the ego. It therefore helps to discipline the mind, perhaps enabling commitment to study with a teacher. All other 'paths' are *only* useful in this way — preparation of the mind. Only Jñāna Yoga — the path of knowledge — can bring enlightenment.

So, having criticized my own writing first, I feel less guilty about what is to follow!

The 'Truth'

The book is aimed at readers who are looking for the 'Truth' — the truth about who we are, the nature of the world and reality — and the ways in which the teachers of the philosophy of Advaita attempt to lead us to that truth. But it should be made clear at the outset that this truth is not ultimately describable.

An intellectual appreciation may be gained but that is not It. Indeed, some modern teachers are at pains to demolish all attempts to rationalize or explain. Instead, they encourage a direct intuitive 'seeing' of 'what is already the case.' This is a misleading instruction and implies a misunderstanding of the terms *aparokṣa* and *anubhava* in the traditional teaching.

The word *parokṣa* means 'indirect or mediate knowledge' – the sort of knowledge we get by perceiving something for ourselves. Thus, say those who speak of 'intuition,' we get only parokṣa knowledge by reading the scriptures or listening to the teacher and that cannot give us enlightenment. They say that we have to take that knowledge, assimilate it and then, sometime later, we may 'intuit' the truth for ourselves – aparokṣa jñāna, 'direct' knowledge. The logic behind this is that the truth or reality, which Advaita calls 'Brahman,' being non-dual, cannot be the object of any means of knowledge (pramāṇa).

Whilst this is true, it does not follow that something else has to happen in order for us to realize the truth. The only pramāṇa for Self-knowledge is shāstra – the scriptures. It is certainly true that simply hearing or reading that 'I am Brahman' is unlikely to bring about enlightenment. It takes time to absorb by reflecting on this. Hence the need for asking questions and further discussing the teaching in order to remove doubts – this is called *manana* (and explains why one should ideally have a teacher). One has continually to review and revisit it before it really becomes intrinsic to one's outlook and nature – this process is called *nididhyāsana*.

The way that modern seekers often think about this, is that hearing the scriptures and having them explained by the teacher (*śravaṇa*) only gives us 'intellectual knowledge.' This is the case, they say, even after asking questions and having our doubts clarified. They claim that we then have to go away and 'experience' this truth for ourselves (*anubhava*). Most believe this happens during the experience of *nirvikalpa samādhi*, the intensely deep meditation in which we lose any sense of a world outside.

If you look up the word 'experience' in a dictionary, you will find that all of the definitions necessitate an 'experiencer' and an 'experienced' thing. Brahman is the non-dual reality. How could Brahman be experienced? Who would be the experiencer?

Furthermore, samādhi is a state of consciousness, albeit one in which one is not in the slightest bit distracted by any external thing. In reality, there is only *turīya* – Consciousness that is the background 'substance' of all apparent 'states.'

Since there is only Brahman, 'we' are already Brahman. The problem is that we do not know this with certainty. Accordingly, nothing that we could *do* will bring this about. This would be 'accomplishing the already accomplished' as the title of Ref. 527 puts it. It is Self-knowledge only that is required, not any action.

These simple (and indisputable for the Advaitin) facts should make the discussion about the 'need to experience Brahman in samādhi' totally redundant.

Incidentally, if someone wants to point out that anubhava does not mean 'experience,' why does everyone keep using that word? What word should they use instead? Words such as 'intuition' still require an 'intuiter' and an 'intuited' thing.

One cannot go away and 'experience' Brahman after hearing about it for the first time. But nor is there some other sort of knowledge to be gained. As Śaṅkara puts it in his commentary (*bhāṣya*) on Bṛhadāraṇyaka Upaniṣad 2.4.5:

> *It should first be heard from a teacher and from the scriptures, then reflected on through reasoning, and then steadfastly meditated upon. Thus only is It realized – when these means, viz. hearing, reflection and meditation, have been gone through.* (Ref. 1)

Two points have to be borne in mind.

Firstly, although the mind cannot 'grasp' or describe reality, it is nevertheless the case that what we call 'enlightenment' occurs in the mind. Once the mind has completely accepted that there is only Brahman, and 'I am That,' there is nothing more to do. Lack of Self-knowledge is the seeker's problem. It cannot be emphasized too strongly that you cannot *do* anything to get enlightenment. You are already 'free' – you just haven't realized it! Accordingly, it just (!) requires someone to convince you of this. Ideally a live teacher who can answer your questions but, failing that, clear and reliable, written or recorded material.

Secondly, even after this enlightenment has occurred, we will still see duality. The world does not disappear; the body will still transmit pain signals to the brain when it is injured. There will be no flashes of light; you will not become permanently, blissfully happy. Some teachers will try to tell you otherwise, and clearly some seekers will be very much attracted by the 'otherwise.' (One can't help wondering if this is the reason some teachers tell them this...)

The Kenopaniṣad explains that the Self cannot be known by the intellect; that it must be understood to be beyond the duality of knower and known. Only the ignorant think that they 'know' Brahman. In fact, it is beyond thought, perception and speech – it is that which *enables* us to think, perceive and speak. Only through understanding this can it be 'known' in any sense.

Brahman cannot be 'known,' in the same way as it cannot be 'experienced.' For knowing, there has to be a 'knower' and a 'known,' which is duality. Nevertheless, there is no other place than the intellect for the 'person' to 'appreciate' the truth of Advaita. This is 'where' enlightenment has to take place. (Yes – actually, we are *not* the 'person,' in reality. But this takes us into much more subtle discussions, which will be touched on in the 'Who Am I?' section later.)

Pramāṇas

This word has already been mentioned 3 times and more will follow later. It is necessary to give a short explanation of what this means and of the six types recognized by Advaita (from Ref. 398).

Enlightenment means 'having Self-knowledge,' so it is important to understand the possible sources of this knowledge. The literal meaning of the word pramāṇa is a 'measure' of any kind but, in this specific context, it refers to 'a means of acquiring certain knowledge.' The various means are as follows:

- **Perception (pratyakṣa)**

This is the principal way in which we garner knowledge – through our senses. Perception gives immediate, valid knowledge providing that the sense organ which is involved is working correctly and there are no mitigating circumstances (e.g., insufficient light can cause us to misperceive something, as in the well-known example of seeing a snake where there is really only a rope).

- **Inference (anumāna)**

The Sanskrit word literally means 'after-knowledge.' It involves reasoning from something that we already know. The classic example is that we see some smoke on a distant hill. We know that when smoke occurs in the kitchen, it always arises from a fire. We therefore infer that there is a fire on the hill.

- **Comparison (upamāna)**

This is the identification of similarity between something new (now perceived) and something already known (in memory). For example, someone owning an Alsatian dog might see a wolf in the wild and gain the new knowledge that the dog is similar to the wolf (and thus may have that species as its ancestor).

• **Postulation (arthāpatti)**
This assumes something to be the case, which is not actually known, but regarding which no other explanation can be conceived. The classic example is concluding that X eats his meals only at night, since it is known that he is thriving, or even getting fat, despite the fact that he is never seen to eat during the daytime.

• **Non-cognition (anupalabdhi)**
This is knowledge of the non-existence of a thing at a location as a result of the failure to perceive it. If we know that X is normally in room Y, and we go into Y and fail to see X, we can conclude that it is non-existent in Y (assuming there are no other constraints, such as the room being dark!).

• **Testimony (śabda)**
This relates to knowledge arising from spoken or written words, especially (in this context) of the qualified guru or scriptures. **Śaṅkara maintains that this is the *only* source for knowledge of reality and hence for gaining mokṣa.**

So 'simple recognition of what is already clear and present,' even if we are able to drop all thoughts and imaginings, only calls into operation the pramāṇa of pratyakṣa. And perception can never give us enlightenment. Some, such as Rodney Stevens, try to deny this:

> *Whenever there is a presence of awareness, that is self-realization. There are also other terms for it, such as the understanding (that you are awareness itself, and not the thoughts, person, and feelings that you appear to be).*
>
> *All that is needed for self-realization is the seeing or recognition that awareness is fully present. There is absolutely nothing to get, attain, reach, or move-toward. Further, this*

understanding is not time-related. Awareness is there for the seeing, at any moment. (Ref. 551)

One can certainly argue that the present moment is the only point in time that can be considered to 'exist' as far as the conventional stream of past-present-future is concerned. But such considerations belong to vyavahāra only – the empirical reality of the world appearance. Absolute reality has nothing to do with time or anything else – it is non-dual!

Being in the present moment is a practice and experience that is relevant to mental preparation – training the mind to be still, dropping thoughts and emotions and simply attending to whatever is happening without comment or judgment. It is in this state that we can best pay attention to a qualified guru explaining the meaning of the Vedantic scriptures. And it is the state we aspire to in the practice of meditation. Once attained, it can lead to the experience of samādhi – another valuable step (although not a necessary one) in the preliminary spiritual practice of the traditional seeker ... but nothing to do with enlightenment. **For enlightenment, we need to gain Self-knowledge.** Anyone doubting this should repeat it mentally every time you hear or read anything that suggests otherwise!

Some General Warnings

Obviously, I cannot say 'never go to satsangs' or 'do not read books by Neo-Advaitins' (I have done both). But ideally, before you do, ensure that you have a good general understanding of Advaita, such that you will be able quickly to realize when a teacher or book is of doubtful value (which may be a euphemism for 'outrageously inaccurate'!). I provide a list of 'Best Books for Beginners' later. When you have read a couple of these, you will be better prepared to venture out into the modern world! The key thing to remember is not blindly to accept anything that contradicts your reason or experience. Śaṅkara points out (Bhagavadgītā Bhāṣya 18.66) that whatever is said in scriptures cannot be held to contradict what is available to basic perception: *"... the validity of the Vedas lies in revealing what is beyond direct perception... Surely, even a hundred Vedic texts cannot become valid if they assert that fire is cold or non-luminous!"* (Ref. 396)

If you encounter anything in a book that sounds unreasonable, ignore it unless it is substantiated by an authoritative quotation. And, if the quotation also sounds preposterous, track down other translations or, ideally, find the original Sanskrit and get someone to give you a literal translation.

You – the Seeker

The aim of this book is to alert you to all the problems that you face when trying to find a reliable and efficacious source for the teaching of Advaita.

BUT ... You ought first of all to ask yourself about your own motives and commitment. Why do you want to do this? What is your present situation and mental outlook? So many of the likely problems that you may encounter in your 'search for the truth' relate to your own psychological makeup, expectations, desires etc. (And some modern teachers take specific advantage of this.)

I am not going to address any of these things in this book – it is not my domain of expertise. If you think (admit?) that there may be such issues, then I recommend that you read a book such as Ref. 590. Note that that book is about the 'spiritual search' in general and is not particularly relevant to Advaita, dealing at length with topics such as Tantra. But the author has vast experience in 'seeking' in general and has qualifications in psychology. She has herself experienced many of the problems that she writes about, and addresses them with authority, providing guidance on how to deal with them.

Non-Advaita Practices

There is a very great danger of picking up books, which look and sound as though they ought to be relevant and worthwhile, but which contain material which has nothing to do with Advaita. If such things are merely mentioned in passing, this is not necessarily a problem. (After all, I am devoting an entire section to it here!) But, if they are given equal billing with genuine topics in Advaita, then they should be given a wide berth. As an example:

> *It is often useful to commence superficial clearing and balancing the chakras before embarking on serious meditation programs which target the system directly. To this end crystals provide a link between the universal spirit energy and earthly manifestation and they are particularly helpful in establishing contact with chakra emotional content.* (Ref. 587)

Initially, unfortunately, someone new to Advaita will not know whether a particular topic is relevant or not. For example, crystals, chakras, kuṇḍalinī yoga, Tantra, Tibetan Yoga, and Shamanism (to mention a few that come to mind) have nothing at all to do with it. Patanjali Yoga, Vipassana or TM meditation, and many more techniques and practices can have value as a means of mental preparation for developing improved attention span, concentration, minimizing distracting thoughts etc. These are desirable, if not actually essential, for a seeker wishing to benefit maximally from attending talks from a traditional teacher. But Patanjali's Yoga, for example, must not be confused with Advaita. Yoga is a dualistic philosophy!

Similarly, any teaching that places emphasis on the way that we function in the world should be suspect. If it aims to increase our confidence, helps us to relate better with others, improves our work productivity etc., then it is not Advaita. I just received an email this morning for example, from an organization ostensibly related to Advaita, advertising a new online course '*Governing Business & Relationships.*' This is not Advaita! It also suggests that maybe lots more money is to be made by marketing to businesses than in merely holding satsangs!

If in doubt, you might try a brief Q&A session with an AI engine on the internet to discover if a topic is relevant. At the time of writing (March 2024), however, these are still not very reliable. The problem at present, presumably, is that they assume that the consensus of expressed opinions on the vast number of websites must be correct. Unfortunately, there are clearly very many teachers and bloggers adding inaccurate material every day! And one of the problems of AI would seem to be that this will be self-propagating.

Satsang

> *Satsang is one of the most powerful tools that the divine uses to forge a path back to the heart of Being.* (Ref. 634)

I have already used this term several times and it is so common that most readers of this book will already be familiar with it. In

Western understanding, a satsang is a gathering of teacher and students in which the teacher will probably give an initial talk on a subject that may or may not have been notified in advance. The seekers will then ask questions which may initially relate to the presented material but probably later to whatever topic is of present interest to the questioner, regardless of whether this is likely to be relevant to others.

It is the usual teaching format in the West today, if not taking place within a traditional organization such as Arsha Vidya or Chinmaya Mission.

If a particular venue is a success, it is likely to be repeated in successive years but, otherwise, there is no continuity of the subject matter.

Many teachers try to imbue it with a mystical aura. For example:

> *What is this beautiful mystery of awareness here right now? How do you know what you are seeing as you read these words? How do you know what you are feeling right now? The inner light or brightness of awareness is shining out of you right now. The ultimate mystery of awake consciousness is here experiencing this life you are living. That is what satsang is ultimately about.* (Ref. 594)

Those organizations that host and promote several teachers at some centralized location (especially in Canada and USA) seem to have a propensity for the word ***'sangha.'*** I don't know where this comes from. One site asks: *"What is Sangha? Sangha is a Sanskrit word meaning 'community'."* But it isn't!

The actual word in Sanskrit is 'satsaṅga' in Romanized form. There is no equivalent letter for 'gh'; the correct letter is simply 'g.' The word satsaṅga means 'intercourse or association with the good' or, in this context, with seekers and teachers of 'sat' – the truth, or what really exists. My first thought was that someone felt that 'sangha' looked (and maybe sounds) more mystical and esoteric. But, on second thoughts, I suspect that the first person to set up such an organization believed it was spelled that way and then later ones simply copied it without knowing any better or bothering to check.

According to the Leela Foundation, *"satsang is sitting with a fully realized teacher who transmits silence and realization."* (Ref. 546) This is two fallacies for the price of one. The topics of 'Transmitting Enlightenment' (not) and 'Teaching through Silence' (not) are dealt with under 'Teaching Advaita' below. Traditionally, a complete scriptural text would be covered at the rate of one or two verses per week until completion.

Unfortunately, very few teachers use it in this simple manner. Satsangs are not:

> *gatherings where busy minds cool down. Through silence, meditation, dialogue, music, mantras and ecstatic dance. In Madhukar's presence you are able to easily relax into silence. Thus you experience a new harmony. His clear guidance shows you how to sustain this balance in your daily life.* (Ref. 592)

According to Jan Koehoorn, its purpose is straightforward:

> *A satsang is a meeting where you can ask questions about your spiritual quest, about your self-examination.* (Ref. 721)

Another example:

> *Satsang is an opportunity to unravel what may stand in the way of us living consciously as our True Nature, to take a good honest look at what we may be running from or holding on to and to ask ourself if we are willing to embrace the totality of life, as it really is.* (Ref. 579)

'Embracing life' is something that the seeker may or may not do, but it has nothing to do with a teacher explaining the non-dual nature of reality! Addressing our psychological issues so as to make us better able to cope with life or live in a more fulfilling way has nothing to do with Advaita or satsang.

Teacher Names

It is best to ignore any book or satsang where the writer/teacher has changed their name to something that sounds as though they are an authority on Advaita. The only time that this is normal and acceptable is when someone belongs to a traditional sampradāya and is finally being authorized by their own guru as a competent teacher. The word 'Saraswatī' after a new name ending in 'ānanda' is an example. This means that the person belongs to one of the 10 orders of monks stretching back to Śaṅkara. But this is an aspect of the tradition, so that future seekers will know to which lineage a teacher belongs. In the case of someone who decides for themself to become a teacher without even having had a qualified guru, this is simply egotistical and misleading, although it does have the unsought for benefit that the seeker can use this so as to realize that to be the case.

Similarly, 'Swami' in front of their announced name is certainly OK, providing that they belong to an organization such as Ramakrishna or Arsha Vidya — see 'Organizations' below. '-ji' appended to their name is suspicious. It is an 'honorific' used traditionally when addressing someone to whom one defers or who is highly respected, or who is older and senior to oneself, or whom one does not know (whether or not they fit into any of those groups). It probably equates to addressing someone as sir or ma'am in the West. But it could certainly be deemed egotistical if the respected person adds this permanently to their own name!

Most teachers set up websites with domains using their own name. It is certainly reasonable that a seeker looking specifically for that teacher will find the site more easily if it is identified by name. However, this very fact calls into question their authenticity. The key aspect of enlightenment is the realization that 'I am Brahman' and not the person with whom I previously identified. Thus, it has to be a fact that an enlightened 'person' is no longer in the slightest bit interested in self-aggrandizement.

It is a fact, for example, that today's academics have problems identifying those texts that were authored by Śaṅkara, because he never put his name to them! They are obliged to use, instead, references to other texts which do have known authorship. The point is simply that enlightenment entails the knowledge that, in reality, there are no others, or even a world, from the perspective of absolute reality. A jñānī teaches seekers for several reasons. He remembers his own plight whilst in ignorance of his true nature, and consequently will have sympathy for them. Teaching acts as nididhyāsana to firm-up on their own Self-knowledge. It will also be perceived as an apparently worthwhile activity to work out their (prārabdha) karma until the body-mind drops.

What a jñānī will have no interest or even thought of doing would be to teach other seekers if he has neither the knowledge nor skills to conduct that teaching.

Some teachers claim to have had an 'enlightenment experience' (whatever that may be) and say that they now want to pass this on to other seekers. But — it cannot be emphasized too strongly — an 'experience' does *not* qualify anyone to teach non-duality to others! **Before visiting any self-proclaimed teacher, you must ensure that the person has actually acquired knowledge from some authoritative source(s) and has the ability to convey this to others.** (That really does need to be emphasized!)

A lot of authors also self-publish their books. So another warning sign may well be the name that they give to their 'publisher.' If this is an 'enlightenment-associated' word, then you would do well to be on your guard.

Organizations

Many teachers have 'founded' organizations with grandiose names that imply that they can save the world if only everyone would come to them and learn about themselves and the world. But, from the present state of the world, little seems to have happened! General guidance, therefore, would be to avoid these.

> *Many large spiritual retreat centers offering classes in everything from conscious divorce to mindful knitting are working with multimillion-dollar budgets.* (Ref. 590 – and this was in 2009!)

The only organizations that you should consider are those that have been established by acknowledged sages, have existed for some significant time, and have grown. There will be more details about these in the 'Advaita Resources' section below.

Effectiveness of Teaching

Another thing to beware of is those teachers/organizations that claim that they will teach you all that you need to become enlightened in just a few sessions. Even ones that offer 'advanced course' over six months or a year, including zoom sessions with the teacher each week, could not realistically do this. But there are even ones that state that they can do this over a weekend!

At the other extreme would be any that require you to pay in advance for some prolonged course of lessons. As noted elsewhere, traditional teaching necessarily takes a long time but the vast majority of modern teachers are not teaching traditional Advaita. (Traditional teachers would, in any case, normally take only 'guru dakṣiṇa' – a nominal, respectful donation on an individual basis.)

Sample Material

Most teacher websites have free sample videos, talks or articles. Since there are so many putative teachers, it is likely that you will simply not have time to watch or listen to whole satsangs for each teacher in order to find one who sounds authentic. I certainly did not. Ideally, therefore, you would just scan a few articles, and maybe actually read one or two in detail if they seem promising. Here, then, is a warning: if a teacher site has *no* free articles, and requires that you buy a book or subscribe to the site if you want an example of their teaching, I suggest that you ignore them and move on! It is not reasonable to expect a seeker to take the promotional material at a site at face value and commit (and probably waste) their time and money.

Bling

If a website is 'loud' with lots of photos and expensively produced advertising; and if it is difficult actually to find some clear statements as to what the 'teacher' actually teaches, then I suggest you should maybe carry on searching. A good teacher will merit that title as a result of what they actually teach, not as a result of having paid lots of money to an agency to produce a fancy website.

Translation

The translation of Sanskrit terms is a major source of confusion for seekers. Ideally, you would have a good understanding of Sanskrit yourself and then look to the context in which a word occurs before you accept a particular translation. If you want an understanding of the usage of a term in Advaita, you have to look for a sampradāya teacher of Advaita and should definitely not rely upon what is said by someone without those qualifications. Modern teachers are likely to distort many aspects in order to provide Western seekers with a version they will find more acceptable (because it fits with what they want to hear).

As an example, I recommend Vivekacūḍāmaṇi, because it is a very clear text summarizing much of Advaita in a way that mostly corresponds with Śaṅkara's teaching (even if it wasn't written by him). There are many versions of this text, some simply giving a translation, others providing pages of commentary on most verses (of which there are around 580. I say 'around' because there are slight differences between versions). I have 11 printed versions of this at the last count, plus another 3 or 4 downloaded. I can only recommend a few of these. Translations cannot always be relied upon, often changing the wording so as to reflect the understanding of the translator. Needless to say, commentaries may diverge even further!

In particular, in respect of this text, I gave a specific example in Ref. 398 of the version almost certainly used as a source by Vivekananda, since it was translated by a friend of his. It explicitly gives an incorrect translation of the original Sanskrit which may have swayed Vivekananda's understanding of Advaita such that he has subsequently misled vast numbers of seekers.

This example relates to the translation of the word 'shastrair' in verse 147 (approximately), which states that bondage cannot be destroyed by weapons.

Two types of weapons are mentioned — astra and śastra. The former are thrown; the latter are used for 'cutting.' Most translations correctly identify this but Vivekananda's friend, Swami Turiyananda, translates it as: *"Neither by weapons, **by any scripture**, by fire, nor by water, can this tree be hewn down…"* (Ref. 399) The word 'shāstra' does indeed normally refer to the scriptures, but in this context that would make no sense at all. Nevertheless, it could well have been significant in giving Vivekananda his attitude of deprecating the value of scripture. He insisted that knowledge from them could never give enlightenment; that one had to 'experience' Brahman for oneself through the practice of samādhi.

You should be aware that Sanskrit words tend to have far more, often quite unrelated, meanings than most English words. It is always necessary to be aware of the context before choosing one of them! It is a perennial problem. If you yourself do not understand Sanskrit, you are at the mercy of the translator. My own understanding is rudimentary, so that I can reassure you that it is *not* a requirement to learn the language. However, before buying and reading any scriptural text, you should try to get advice from someone more knowledgeable. Failing that, you must be very careful and not simply take it for granted that a book claiming to teach Advaita according to Śaṅkara will actually do so.

When it comes to uncommented text, such as a collection of Upaniṣads for example, you need to remember that philosophies other than Advaita also treat them as source material. Dualists are extremely unlikely to translate text in an unambiguously non-dualistic way! In fact, it is not recommended that you *ever* try to read original scriptures which do not have a commentary. They are often ambiguous and sometimes unintelligible. And most are written in the 'god speaking to adherent' style, which is very likely to turn off anyone who rebels against religions. You really need a qualified teacher/writer to explain them. Then it quickly become clear what is being said.

Later on, I will recommend which books I consider to be worthy, based upon my own library.

Few Westerners understand Sanskrit. Accordingly, not only does the text have to be understood and explained, it first has to be translated. If it is being translated into English, the writer has to understand both languages well. But it is even worse than this. There are many concepts in the traditional philosophy that have no direct equivalent in English and, of course, the words were originally directed at a society that differed drastically from our own. Thus it is that the only person really able to communicate the wisdom of the Vedas is someone who can read Sanskrit and speak English fluently; someone who is as familiar with the ancient Hindu concepts and way of life as he is with those of Western society, and who ideally is already enlightened. Needless to say there are not many such people around!

Similar problems apply to someone translating other Indian languages into English. Thus, it is particularly problematic with the talks of Ramana Maharshi and Nisargadatta Maharaj, for example.

Stanley Sobottka (Ref. 205) gave an example relating to the Bhagavad Gītā, which is a practical manual for *Karma Yoga*, describing how we should act in our lives. Chapter II, Verse 47 tells us that we should only concern ourselves with the action itself and not worry about the outcome. We should not do something because we want a particular result, nor should we be attached to inaction. But, says Sobottka, Ramesh Balsekar interprets this to mean that *"there is no free-will and work merely happens spontaneously."* A quite contrary interpretation is provided by Maharishi Mahesh Yogi, who says that *"you have control over action alone, never over its fruits."* And Sobottka also affirms that: *"Any translation will inevitably convey the message that the translator wishes to convey."*

Recorded Talks

In addition to the dangers of introducing misunderstanding as a result of translating a recorded talk into another language, there are many other aspects which are also potential sources of problems.

- Mis-hearing – Written material from either live or recorded talks may be misheard or not heard clearly. The scribe is forced to use prior knowledge and understanding in order to work out what the word must have been.

- Live note-taking – If notes are taken during a talk, there may simply not be sufficient time to record everything that was said. The scribe has to summarize, paraphrase and maybe even invent in order to keep up. If something is not understood, it may be omitted or wrongly recorded. The scribe may not wish to ask for clarification or repetition for many reasons.
- Writing-up – When the notes are written up later, aspects may be missing vital elements; they may be transcribed by someone other than the original scribe; words may be unreadable etc. Again, in this situation, quotations are likely to be invented to fill in the gaps or explain something that, from the notes, was not adequately explained. In such a case, the explanation will be that of the scribe and not that of the teacher.
- Language – If the person doing the writing up also has to translate from a language that is only known in an academic way and not used colloquially from birth, the situation becomes extremely difficult to say the least!

Lineage

The principal book that attempts to explicate the actual philosophy of the Upaniṣads is called the Brahmasūtra. Commentaries have been made by various scholars and their interpretations have not always coincided. In addition to Advaita, two other main branches resulted, one of them dualistic (Dvaita) and the other 'qualified' non-dualism (Viśiṣṭādvaita) but Śaṅkara, in his own commentary (bhāṣya), brilliantly challenges and demolishes all interpretations other than that of Advaita.

In the past hundred years, there has been a growth of interest in Advaita in the West. This has been associated with a number of specific Sages (a Sage is someone who has realized the truth regarding the nature of reality). Ramakrishna (1836–1886) is possibly the teacher most responsible for increasing the popularity of Advaita in recent times, with missions now operating throughout the world. His principal disciple was Swami Vivekananda (1863–1902), who toured the world with the aim of uniting all religions, the underlying truth of all of them being realized in Advaita. It is unfortunate indeed that Vivekananda did not have clear understanding of the traditional teaching and consequently was responsible for propagating some serious misunderstandings. These still cause confusion amongst seekers today. (The nature of these is addressed in depth in my book Ref. 398.)

Amongst seekers in the West, Ramana Maharshi (1880–1950) is perhaps the most famous of all latter-day sages, having influenced so many modern teachers, as well as writers such as Paul Brunton and Somerset Maugham. Nisargadatta Maharaj (~1897–1981), the uneducated servant and tobacconist in Bombay, is also one of the most popular, owing perhaps to the fact that his radical and uncompromising approach appeals to the modern mind. Atmananda Krishna Menon (1883–1959), the originator of the so-called 'Direct Path' approach, was one of the most logical. (His style of teaching has become increasingly popular through his successors, especially Francis Lucille, Greg Goode and Rupert Spira.)

Today, it is principally the disciples of these sages who tour the world giving satsangs and seminars.

Traditionally, the knowledge that gives rise to enlightenment was passed down from teacher (guru) to disciple (śiṣya) through the ages. This is called sampradāya teaching. Of course, it is theoretically possible for this knowledge to arise spontaneously, or in response to some independent event, but habit and our attachment to conventional modes of thinking make this very unlikely. The 'bottom-line' is counter-intuitive and conflicts with the perceived state of affairs. Sampradāya teaching requires that the seeker attend talks given by the guru for many years, so that the scriptures may be unfolded in the traditional manner.

Modern Approaches

There is a relatively new class of teacher, growing in popularity, which denigrates the traditional approach. They insist that there is nothing that can be done to attain this knowledge; that in truth there is no seeker, nothing to be sought. There is no 'self-realization' of a person because there is no person. Reality is already the case – 'this is it,' as the new saying goes. This method of teaching has become known as 'Neo-Advaita,' from the Greek *neos*, meaning 'new.' In fact, the essence of what these adherents say is extremely old, not differing from the final teaching of classical Advaita. The differences lie in their descriptions of the world-appearance and in their style of teaching. As will be discussed later, their approach tends to be of low or negative value for any but the most advanced seeker.

Just so that I cannot be accused of not representing the views of this 'non-teaching,' here is what Tony Parsons, one of its principal proponents, says about it:

> *The Open Secret's apparent communication is illogical, unreasonable, unbelievable, paradoxical, non-prescriptive, non-spiritual and uncompromising. There is no agenda or intention to help or change apparent individuality. Its resonance is shared energetically, not through the exchange of ideas. It is prior to all teachings and yet eternally new. Belief is seen as married to doubt, and experience as a fluctuating personal state. The Open Secret does not recognise anything as being "the truth" nor does it see how something called Traditional Advaita could be anything other than a complex collection of ideas.* (Ref. 659)

Another approach is called Neo-Vedānta, which is quite different from Neo-Advaita. It has its origins in traditional Advaita but has some differences in interpretation. It stems from the somewhat mystical approach of Ramakrishna, but is particularly associated with his disciple — Swami Vivekananda, who is largely responsible for introducing Advaita to the West. More is mentioned about it in the companion book, where the subtleties of the differences will be better appreciated. Therefore, whenever the term 'Neo-Advaita' is used, I refer to the new Western 'this is it' method, and not to Neo-Vedānta. Other sources, especially any of Indian origin, may use these terms interchangeably to refer to the Vivekananda teaching.

The expansion of the internet and its rapid integration into the modern world as the principal reference source has meant that a wealth of information on Advaita is now readily available to everyone. Teachers advertise their services and make available extracts from their books and satsangs. Organizations such as those of Swamis Dayananda and Chinmayananda provide schedules of their meetings. Even the Śaṅkara-inaugurated monasteries (maṭhas) have websites and advertise their programs. Many scriptures are now directly downloadable in both original Sanskrit and transliterated form with many different translations and commentaries. Finally, the most basic and the most abstruse questions that challenge spiritual seekers are discussed on email groups and Facebook by students of all levels.

Examples from all of these sources will be given to illustrate the various approaches. **NB. The reader should note that any given section may quote extracts from several different teaching methods. Although the essential truth is always the same, care must be taken to note the source so as not to confuse them!** I will, however, attempt to ensure that this does not happen. Where quotations are potentially confusing, I will endeavor to clarify.

Talking About Reality

Another major problem is that, intrinsically, it is not possible to describe reality in any sense. As will become clear, who-we-truly-are is the 'ultimate subject'; that which is effectively 'creating' the universe. Obviously, this 'subject' can never be treated objectively – otherwise it would not be the ultimate subject. Therefore, teachers have to approach the truth obliquely, using stories and metaphor, even resorting to half-truths as a step along the way to understanding. But what is half-truth and helpful to one student may appear to be nonsense and distinctly unhelpful to another. It is the perennial problem of the teacher to be able to judge where the student currently is in his or her understanding and lead them onwards from there. This is why a living guru is ideal, so that questions may be asked and answered face to face.

When we read a book or listen to a tape recording of a lecture or dialogue, we are receiving only a particular viewpoint, aimed at a student of a particular level. It may resonate or it may not. The method of expression is crucial. Whilst one person may appreciate logic and intellectual analysis, another may need sympathetic reassurance and practical guidance. Some benefit from the crutch-like support of a personal God, others from the karate-chop of a Zen koan. Ultimately, the truth is one, and everything else that might be said is only at the level of appearance, using a language that is necessarily objective and dualistic. What is ideally needed is a teacher whose words and style resonate with our particular mental conditioning. But being realistic, you are most unlikely to find one who matches your precise personality and intellectual background. If you are lucky enough to have access to someone acknowledged as a good, traditional teacher, you are advised to accept and adapt! Failing that, you are forced into the book-and-internet route, which is very hit and miss (hence the need for *this* book!).

Ignoring Scriptures

It is apparent that many modern teachers are diverging from, or even shunning, the traditional scriptural sources. This is in keeping with the tendency of individuals in modern Western society to want results *now*, to want to hear the bottom line and avoid preparatory material, especially when it may be admitted that that is only provisional anyway. Many students are no longer interested in studying the Upaniṣads, which are often alien to the Western mind, and most of them certainly do not wish to learn any Sanskrit. Thus it is that many of those who now teach are also in this position.

What this means, unfortunately, is that a background understanding of the ultimate claims of Advaita is often completely lacking. Many teachers today seem almost to be providing more of a psychotherapy session through their meetings than a spiritual unfolding of the truth and this does seem to be what many of their students are looking for. But it is not Advaita.

Advaita is about discovering who we essentially are. It is not about establishing the well-being of the person that we initially *think* we are. Therefore, the reader will find nothing in these pages about self-improvement (the Self is already perfect and complete), or about becoming healthier or wealthier (such things relate only to the body or person). The world and our seeming place in it have little relevance to any of these discussions.

What Is Enlightenment?

Enlightenment, the realization that I am eternally free, is the culmination of human evolution. Everything is working against it. The one who pursues it with single-pointed devotion is a salmon swimming upstream in the powerful river of life. (Ref. 416)

The aim of this book is to explain how to go about finding a teacher who can teach Advaita. But the first question you need to answer is 'Why do you want a teacher?' Presumably you will say that you want to be 'enlightened' or to gain 'Self-realization' (don't forget the capital 'S'!). That being the case, you also need to be sure that you know what enlightenment *is* (and that the would-be teacher also knows this!) and how one should go about 'getting' it.

What Is Enlightenment? was the title of a journal published by an organization that was called, at the time, 'Moksha Foundation,' and was initiated by the teacher Andrew Cohen. At the beginning of the first issue, he said:

I have found and continue to find that there is so much confusion, misunderstanding and misinformation as to what Enlightenment actually is and what it really means. That is why I have encouraged my students to start this publication as a vehicle to present our ongoing investigation into this question, and to share our discoveries with those who are also interested in this vast and most subtle subject. (Ref. 539)

This must be one of the peaks of irony, since he was embarking upon a massive exercise of disinformation to propagate considerable confusion about the topic! In an interview on the first page, entitled 'A Passion for Death,' he says:

> *Enlightenment is a condition in which there is a conscious knowing that one has come to the end of becoming. To be fully Enlightened means to come to the end of evolution, the end of any possibility of evolution. Even people who only glimpse what Enlightenment is for a brief period have intimations of the kind of finality that I'm speaking about. It is the element of finality that makes that kind of knowing that I'm speaking about so extraordinary and so difficult to describe to people who haven't tasted it.* (Ref. 539)

This bears little resemblance to the mokṣa described by Advaita. But it was clearly going to be a significant influence in the West to seekers wanting to find out about Non-duality. The journal was published quarterly until August 2008 – 41 issues – and then changed its name to *EnlightenNext (The Magazine for Evolutionaries)* for a further six issues.

The change in title is because his teaching has now evolved even further into what he calls 'Evolutionary Enlightenment,' described as:

> *Evolutionary enlightenment is about the ecstasy that compels us to create the future. And it's not a future that's going to unfold by itself while we go back to sleep. It's a future that we forge the hard way through direct, conscious, intentional engagement with the life-process itself.* (Ref. 540)

It is a tragedy that the truth of our already existing freedom from limitations of any kind should be turned into a striving for some imaginary achievement in the future! As I try to emphasize again and again, enlightenment is only (!) about realizing what is already the case; it is nothing to do with 'evolving' into some superior being with higher consciousness.

Here is Stephen Wingate, from the introduction to his book *The Outrageous Myths of Enlightenment*:

> *What are Self-realization, Awakening, Liberation, and Enlightenment?*
>
> *You are the One Self, Awareness Itself. Stop for a moment right now, and notice this presence of awareness that you are — here and now. Notice that you are spacious, open, awake and free. Notice that these words are arising in this spacious openness that you are. Notice that the activities of the mind — thoughts, emotions, sensations and experiences — all arise naturally and spontaneously in you, this spacious, open presence of awareness.*
>
> *This peaceful, loving, spacious openness is what you are. This spacious openness is the Self, the Liberation, the Awakening, the Enlightenment, the Peace and the Love for which you've been seeking.*
>
> *You have always been, and always will be simply THIS.* (Ref. 502)

This description does not tell us what enlightenment is. 'Simply this' is the modern satsang attempt to tell us what we are — although it has to be said that it does not do this very well! It tells us nothing about how we come to *realize* what we are. 'Enlightenment' is the *realization* of the truth, not the 'substance' of that truth. And, more to the point, being in the present, 'open' to whatever is presented by the senses, totally alert and mentally calm, is NOT who we really are. It is simply an indication that the mental equipment is ready to attend to someone *explaining* who-we-are. 'Peaceful, loving,' and any other good words that you might think of along these lines, relate to the mental attitude. They are descriptions of the mind, not the Self.

Francis Lucille made the following statement on the status of the ego (in a discussion on ajāti vāda):

When we say that the ego doesn't exist, we mean that it doesn't exist by itself as an autonomous entity, that it exists only as an object appearing in consciousness, in atman. This object can never see the consciousness that sees it. The only possible logical inference is that this consciousness sees itself. When this inference becomes actual experience, we call it enlightenment. (Ref. 707)

It is more useful to think of the ego as a 'process' rather than an object. The processes of mind are only possible because of consciousness. The ideas of Consciousness 'seeing,' 'knowing' or 'experiencing' itself are common ones but are misleading. This is still a 'mixing up' of absolute reality with the world appearance. Consciousness does not 'do' anything!

Neo-Advaitins simply tell you that enlightenment is a myth – it is not possible for someone to be enlightened because there is no person in reality. For example:

Enlightenment is really a myth. The problem with non-duality, or the perspective that there is Oneness, is that it is beyond words. So we're doing our best with words to get close to it, but we will never fully describe it with words. It is a myth about enlightenment that there can be a special enlightened person, or guru. There is no person to be enlightened! But there is the realization that there is no separation. There cannot ever be an enlightened person; there is just the realization that there is no separation. (Ref. 573)

Neo-Advaitins frequently use expressions such as 'there is the realization that'; 'it is seen that' and so on. It is never explained where the realization 'occurs,' where the 'seeing' occurs etc. Dispensing with the person also dispenses with seeker and guru and absolves the supposed teacher from doing any teaching. Quite neat, really…

Experience

> *...mystical experiences and experiences of enlightenment take place outside of the mundane realm of consciousness — sometimes they are archetypal experiences and sometimes they come from the nondual reality.* (Ref. 559)

This is nonsense. Mystical experiences have nothing to do with enlightenment. Neither can you 'experience' enlightenment. Enlightenment is Self-knowledge, which is acquired in a normal state of consciousness, albeit an attentive one with a still mind, by listening to a qualified teacher in empirical (i.e., dual) reality.

> *In the winter of 1996-1997 (the actual date remains vague), I was sitting in an ordinary motel room in Palm Springs, California. On this day, meditation went into unfathomable depths, penetrating into and beyond the very core of existence.*
>
> *My thoughts evaporated and my head went from a spherical, physiological casing to an ocean of Divine Light within "seconds" — an ocean still and deeply active. This Light shone from the inside, the outside and from the beyond itself. "I" and "the world" dissolved forever into this immensity of warmly translucent, incandescent Light-Oneness.*
>
> *Simultaneously, I began to feel the palpable manifestation of the Primordial Energy of the universe, the Shakti. It was brilliant, active, and sparking. Shakti had simultaneously been born in that Being of Pure Light.* (Ref. 548)

Sounds fascinating, but it has nothing to do with enlightenment!

Lots of seekers and, indeed, many modern teachers, claim that there are two 'stages' to gaining enlightenment. First one acquires the intellectual understanding by reading books on the subject and attending satsangs. Then, after one appreciates the notion of non-duality and the idea that 'I am That,' one has actually to 'experience' this fact for oneself, probably during samādhi.

But it is not like that. Bob Adamson explains this very clearly:

> *You put the label on it: 'I understand intellectually.' Then we think there is some other way that it needs to be understood. Then we are subtly back in the trap of the mind. Seeing it is seeing it. Two and two is four. Is that intellectual? Or is there a knowing of it? In the seeing of it, nobody can convince you otherwise. The same with this.* (Ref. 9)

Andrew Cohen again, this time in his book *Living Enlightenment,* says that:

> *One who is truly enlightened has directly experienced the ultimate or absolute nature of life itself... That explosive realization liberates the self from the perpetual tyranny of being trapped in a relationship to life that is merely personal.* (Ref. 553)

Most modern teachers seem to think this way. Some scientists are actually endeavoring to investigate and explain this so-called 'experience' in a neurological way. But this is not how it is. Apart from the fact that a non-dual experience is a contradiction in terms, enlightenment means Self-knowledge. And its attainment results from acquiring that knowledge, which one does most effectively by attending to a qualified guru. (I know I have said this before. I will probably say it again. It is the most important thing to be understood when asking yourself whether a teacher is authentic.)

In particular, many teachers speak of an 'Awakening' event, after which everything was different and they subsequently began offering tuition themselves, so that others could 'get it,' too. For example: *"there happened spontaneously a shift in consciousness and a radical new way of viewing life was born."*

Ref. 541 describes what it calls the 'New Age Concept of Enlightenment' and idiomatically labels this as 'Getting off the Wheel.' In addition to the idea of it being the end of an 'evolutionary process,' a 'state,' and the result of practices, it says that: *"On a psychological level, enlightenment is described as a modification, transformation, or alteration of consciousness."*

But, as I pointed out in Ref. 441, *"There is no 'higher Self' that we have to 'reach' — there is only the Self."* And *"Physical manifestations of light, whether 'flashes' or 'blinding' do not signal enlightenment but are a sign that one may need to visit the doctor."*

Whilst it is certainly reasonable that, after gaining knowledge of the difference between the absolute reality and the world-appearance, one's view of what 'matters' and what doesn't is bound to change, there is no physical manifestation of this, and Consciousness remains as it has always been. The only 'shifts' in consciousness are from waking to dreaming and sleep, or states mediated by alcohol or drugs. There are no 'states of higher consciousness,' just as there are no such things as out-of-body experiences or astral travel.

In traditional Advaita, the 'enlightenment event' is triggered by knowledge, transmitted by the teacher or by reading/hearing scriptures. It is the culmination of usually many years of listening to and questioning a qualified teacher. It is a 'catastrophic' event (in the mathematical sense), rather than a gradual one. The 'weight' of accumulated knowledge suddenly tips the scales and the conclusion is incontrovertible.

It is extremely unlikely that such a thing could happen spontaneously, in the absence of such preparation. The lifetime experiences, upbringing and societal influences of virtually everyone are such as to establish firmly in the mind the belief in a personal, independent existence in a real world. To break down these beliefs and bring one to the realization that oneself and the world are not separately real entities but names and forms of a non-dual reality is not an easy process. For the vast majority, it is only after many years of study, following proven techniques of teaching, that such an understanding may arise.

It should also be realized that seeking silence or stillness, as though this were an 'absence of experience,' is another misunderstanding. This is a description of samādhi without using the word. For example:

> *In our desire to awaken, it is natural to seek out experiences which give us a deeper understanding of our true nature. But what is often overlooked in the search is the surrender to stillness; leaving behind all that is known. There is a great restlessness that can be met, and it is possible to stay still and open, not doing anything at all, and discover the sweet peace of your being that is your birthright.* (Ref. 585)

Here, one should not conclude that this is what we should be seeking. The 'sweet peace' is still an experience, and therefore *not* enlightenment.

Presence

Many teachers make statements containing varying degrees of 'obviousness' in the apparent claim that they are saying something profound about the nature of reality. For example:

> *Here's the good news: the truth is really simple. It is not what we think. Really, it is not. The truth of our nature is here, always, no matter what else is going on, no matter what else is happening in your mind, in your life, in your hopes and dreams, in your past and your future, in your relationships or in your therapy. No matter what else is happening in your life, you are here, and it is all happening in you. Sleep comes and goes. Satisfaction comes and goes. Confusion comes and goes.*

> *Clarity comes and goes. Hatred comes and goes. Love comes and goes. You remain. You are never absent. How hard can it be?* (Ref. 503)
>
> *Presence is undeniably here now, requiring no belief, impossible to doubt. We can doubt all our ideas about what this is and what we are, but not the bare actuality of being here, present and aware. This presence is boundless and unencapsulated — there is nowhere it is not. It is radiant and aware, seamless but infinitely varied, ever-changing while never departing from Here-Now.* (Ref. 535)

According to Tony Parsons (all following quotations in this topic are from Ref. 47), Presence is a 'quality' of enlightenment — *"the bridge between the timeless and my illusory sense of separation."*

Tony says that 'presence' is not the same as 'being here now': *"Presence is not to be confused with 'being here now' which is a continuous process of the separate self and has no direct relevance to liberation."*

I have to confess that I don't understand what is being said here. He explains that: *"Presence is a quality of welcoming, open awareness which is dedicated to simply what is."* But that sounds to me like 'being here and now.' I'm fairly sure I will be accused of being stupid or cynical or sarcastic, or maybe all of these. But hey, I have admitted I am a traditionalist when it comes to Advaita.

I think that what he is saying is that 'being here now' is still in duality, with an observer and something that is observed. This is 'simply what is.' He says that: *"At first it is enough to allow dedicated awareness to what is. Letting go of the one who is aware can easily follow."* But it is not clear who it would be who was 'letting go.'

He says that: *"I am presence... So there is no process to learn because I cannot learn or achieve something that I already am."* This sounds like 'I am Brahman.' But he then says: *"Presence can only be allowed and recognized. What I tend to do most of the time is sidestep it or interrupt it."* So we are still in duality, with 'whoever I am' doing things — 'allowing,' 'recognizing' and 'interrupting.' This therefore *cannot* be Brahman. I remain mystified.

And there are plenty of other incomprehensible-on-analysis statements made about this 'topic,' Here is Rupert Spira:

> *It is this transparent, empty Presence that, refracted through the mind, appears as a multiplicity and diversity of names and forms. However, the mind is itself a modulation of that very Presence. In other words, it is pure Awareness itself which, vibrating within itself, takes the shape of mind and, from the illusory point of view of one of the selves contained within that mind, seems to see a multiplicity and diversity of separate objects and selves, each with their own independently existing reality. In other words, the separate self is only a separate self from the illusory point of view of a separate self.* (Ref. 636)

Needless to say, I never use this term! Nor have I ever seen it used in any traditional text.

Being Here Now

> *Just stop! Stop the why, what and how! Accept everything as it is! There is no need to think about it; no need to look for God or philosophical explanations. It is all here and now, if you will simply stop the mind; see and hear without constant rationalization. Whether it is birds singing, kettle boiling, partner nagging; whether it is head aching, tooth buzzing or breeze blowing through the hair and sun dappling the shimmering waves — it is all just as it should be. Nothing affects who you are. All is 'as it is' and 'how it is' is perfect.*

I haven't given a reference for this quotation. Why? Because I just invented it. But there are many, many books available from

Amazon now which have very similar, and equally meaningless, eulogistic styled writings in them. Anyone can write this sort of thing with very little effort, and apparently sell books (almost certainly more than I sell!). But one thing I can tell you – it will not help you to progress to an enlightened understanding of Advaita; not by one iota.

You can identify someone who is using this sort of approach for their 'teaching' by simply parsing their sentences. They may well have a subject, verb and object but, in essence, on analysis, they are merely mystical mumbo-jumbo. The genuine teaching of Advaita will certainly cause you to look at life through a different lens but, when you analyze those sentences, they still make sense and do not contradict reason.

Language should be used in the way that we normally use it – for communication of ideas. Parts of speech should not suddenly be used in contradictory or meaningless ways. For example, "you are the seeing" does not make any sense and you should not be cajoled or deluded into thinking that it does!

If you attend a satsang by someone speaking in such a manner, and if the rest of the audience is attuned to this sort of thing, then it might make you feel good, with a positive outlook, for a short while (quite possibly long enough to buy one of the leader's books before you leave the hall). But it will pass, probably by the next day, and you will have to book another fix soon.

Apologies for the cynicism!

> *The moment you enter the Now with your attention, you realize that life is sacred. There is a sacredness to everything you perceive when you are present... There is an aliveness in you that you can feel with your entire being...*
>
> Eckhart Tolle

It is true that, after a long time (probably years) of regular practice of meditation (for me, this was 2 x 30 minutes every day for probably at least five years), one can begin to experience periods of intense stillness on a fairly regular basis. One is fully awake and able to hear every sound (eyes closed) but nothing disturbs or distracts from the alert yet relaxed peace. It is an intense and unforgettable experience. It is called samādhi and it is an 'experience.' It comes to an end when you stop meditating and you have not gained 'knowledge' of any kind. There will be lots of benefits — general health, ability to concentrate and so on, but no 'enlightenment.'

This practice is an element of what Śaṅkara called sādhana catuṣṭaya sampatti — the four-fold spiritual practices to prepare the mind for studying Advaita.

The value of 'being in the present' is simply that whatever happens to be there gets your full attention, instead of part of your mind being involved in worrying about something in the past or speculating about some future event. Philip Mistlberger gives a good explanation:

> *To witness a wild flower on a hillside — simply to witness it without any mental interpretation at all — is to begin to realize and see its natural form and, at the same time, to begin to realize our own natural state. That is because, if I'm only twenty-five percent present when looking at the flower, then the flower is only going to be twenty-five percent present as well — dull, with hardly any fragrance. However, if I manage to be one hundred percent present when witnessing this flower, then so too is the flower one hundred percent real — vivid, brilliant with wonderful fragrance.* (Ref. 134)

It is because everything is fully 'alive' and our own aware 'capacity' is at full-strength, when we are totally present, that teachers associate this state with the Self, as opposed to the ego. But, of course, the Self is always fully present. It is just that, most of the time, our attention is being partly directed to thoughts and imaginings instead of what is front of us. As a result, what is in front of us seems less vibrant. What many seem to fail to appreciate is that the objects and events in front of us are just as 'real' or 'unreal' as the thoughts in our mind. None of these things are *absolutely* real – they have the same *empirical* reality, which is that they are name and form of Consciousness. This is what we truly are ourselves.

Tony Parsons (again) is someone I always associate with the idea of 'This is IT,' advocating that we should always endeavor to 'be here, now':

> *Firstly, you can't get quickly to where you already are. (laughter) But really take this in. Live with it and try to see deeply what it's really saying. The problem is that you think something has to happen. You are waiting for something to happen. It's actually happening continuously, and you simply don't see it. I don't have anything that you don't have. The difference is that I am no longer looking for anything. This is it, and that's the end of it.* (Ref. 159)

But there are even more extreme examples of this. Bodhi Avasa for example:

> *There is no one right now reading this even if something there is strongly convinced that this is not the case. There is just THIS and it is NOTHING appearing as THIS. This cannot be understood or grasped by the me, but something can resonate there as this is the real nature of what is. In THIS ALL-NESS everything can arise, even the sense that separation is real, and that sense can fall away. There is no need or cause for that to happen. The illusion can remain until death or it can collapse right now.*
>
> *When this is seen (by no-one) it becomes clear that what we were longing for all along has never gone away. There is just everything and nothing. THIS is pure joy, love and freedom.*

The seeing of THIS, the so called awakening, liberation or enlightenment, can or cannot happen. There is no direction or purpose in LIFE. There is no-one there that can do anything about it. Even when an imagined you feels hopeless and helpless there is only hopelessness and helplessness happening. (Ref. 567)

It is obviously a fact that there is *only* the present:

No one can re-live the past, except in memory of past events, nor live in the future, except in expectation of future events. Both memory and expectations occur in the present, and so the present alone exists and is real. Past and future, non-existent, are unreal. (Ref. 101)

So, although 'being in the present' makes us feel more alive, this is all part of the 'illusion.' It can make no difference to who we are. If it makes us think that we are closer to the reality, it is taking us away from the truth. It is knowledge that we must seek, not 'feeling more alive.'

For eternally and always there is only now, one and the same now; the present is the only thing that has no end.
Erwin Schrödinger

The intellectual analysis of the idea of 'being' being the 'reality' can be very persuasive. Here is the introduction to his book *Being* by Nathan Gill:

The bottom line is Being. Being awake or being asleep are actually beside the point.

Usually the idea is that dialogues such as these have the specific purpose of bringing about enlightenment, awakening, liberation — whatever the term used for that which is deemed

> *to be an escape from (or transcendence of) identification as a suffering individual. But our true nature is always Being and doesn't require any enlightenment or awakening. It simply* is *already, whether there's identification or not.*
>
> *In the play of life, whenever there is identification, the story tends to be about improving* what is *in some way. And when that takes the form of the search for awakening, the focus usually falls on getting rid of the sense of individuality, as though it were somehow wrong or unreal.*
>
> *But if there's a sense of individuality and a story about seeking to be rid of it, then precisely* that *is reality. Being has no requirements whatsoever. Nothing needs to be changed or attained in order to* be. *This present appearance is already the perfect expression of Being and cannot be avoided.* (Ref. 479)

This is a very good example of the teaching of Neo-Advaita (which is probably why it was given in full on the back of the book, as well as in its Introduction). It attempts to say how things are in 'reality' (paramārtha in Sanskrit) – ignoring the fact that this is not possible.

It is impossible to describe or talk about absolute reality because it is non-dual. A 'subject' describing an 'object' is a fallacy because there are neither of these. Accordingly, all 'descriptions' are at the level of duality, i.e., in vyavahāra to use the correct Sanskrit term. Therefore, they are bound to fail. The best they can do is to give the reader an insight into what is hinted at.

The second problem is actually a corollary of the first. The seeker is irrevocably a part of the duality. Even if he or she gains enlightenment as a result of what has been said, the world-appearance continues. And the apparent position of the seeker in this world-appearance will also continue. If the seeker has just lost his apparent job and his apparent wife has apparently left him, that apparent situation still continues. So bliss is unlikely to follow the revelation.

It is true that the newly-gained knowledge that it is all an appearance, and that everything is perfect in reality, will mitigate the seeker's previously negative attitude to life. Nevertheless, it is highly unlikely that it will be believed that *"This present appearance is already the perfect expression of Being"*!

Here is an example of how Śaṅkara puts this:

> *Uninterrupted consciousness, utterly free of all conditions, that Brahman am I. Knowing this, how could one be limited by position, tradition or stage of life?* (Ref. 494)

The point is not that enlightenment makes life perfect, but that it brings the realization that who-I-really-am is totally unaffected by the vicissitudes of life. The body-mind of the jñānī is still obliged to live out the remainder of its life from the context of its then current circumstances. If this happened to be in the slums of Mumbai, it is not suddenly going to be relocated to Beverly Hills.

Finally, if you want to be pedantic (something I am often accused of!), you cannot 'be' in the present moment. Sensory input has to be converted by the sense organ to an electrical impulse, transmitted to the brain, converted into a neurotransmitter (or whatever – this is beyond my area of scientific knowledge), and sent to the relevant part of the brain for processing. All of this takes time! By the time that we are 'aware' of whatever appears to be out there 'in the present,' it is all in the past.

Presence-Awareness

The word 'Brahman' comes from a root meaning 'to grow great or strong' and could be thought of as the adjective 'big' turned into a noun – that which could not be greater. We often use the word 'Absolute.' And it seems many authors try to think of other English words with a similar implication. And this is fine, as long as the reader is in no doubt as to what is being said.

What is not acceptable, however, is to give attributes of any kind to the non-dual reality. Thus, for example — a sentence from one of today's emails: *"What we do know about the Endless is that it's incredibly generous and absolutely loving..."*

If we said, 'The Absolute is extremely selfish and hates everything,' the reader would immediately baulk, but 'wouldn't-it-be-good-if-everything-was-like-this' words seem to be totally acceptable. But they are not. It is not acceptable to use ANY adjective!

> *Presence awareness, or unboundedness, which is who we are, is ever present.* James Braha (Ref. 346)

Presence-awareness is another term favored by some teachers to speak of the 'reality,' although it is only a variant on the previous two. It may have been coined by 'Sailor' Bob Adamson — certainly he wrote a book with this title, Ref. 9. But the idea of the 'present moment' being the key to, if not the reality of, enlightenment is an idea promoted by many teachers. Eckhart Tolle's *The Power of Now* is probably the best-known example (Ref. 45). But, even in book titles, there are other examples. Even in my own library, which contains only a few dozen books from modern teachers, are *Embracing the Now* (Ref. 484), *Acceptance of What IS* (Ref. 113), *Right Here, Right Now* (this even has *Present Awareness* in the subtitle) (Ref. 485), *Simply This* (Ref. 367).

John Wheeler addressed this very pragmatically, but not very helpfully. He was asked: *"Is the key just being here and being present? Or is it a knowing of something?"* He answered:

> *John: Are you present? Are you aware? Any doubts about this? Presence and awareness are really two words pointing to the same thing. Your presence is aware. Your awareness is present. It (you) is present and clear and utterly beyond doubt right now. That is it. That is what I am pointing to as your*

real nature. Seeing it, knowing it, or recognizing it is neither sudden nor gradual, because it is always present beyond doubt. Very simple!
Q: Oh! So there is no such thing as becoming present or aware. We are that.
John: Yes. You are already what you are.
Q: So what is the whole idea of the present moment?
John: It is just a concept without much real value... There is no need for awakening. That is also a concept. What is the need for awakening when you are already present and aware? You are that...
Q: Is there no such thing as awakening then?
John: No! If there is awakening, it is just seeing that you do not need any such thing! (Ref. 485)

Needless to say (I hope), this is quite misleading. Note that I do not say 'wrong,' because who-we-really-are *is* already the non-dual Consciousness and we do not need to *do* anything to 'become' it. The problem is that who-we-think-we-are, namely the person who is the 'seeker,' does not know this to be true, in the way that we know that 2 + 2 = 4. Enlightenment, or 'awakening,' is what needs to happen for or to the *person*! It is, in fact, the perennial problem of Neo-Advaitin teaching, namely failing to differentiate reality and appearance, paramārtha and vyavahāra.

It is true that there is only this and it is already the case. If we are talking about Brahman, then it is obviously true (according to Advaita). It is when this is correlated with time and the empirical appearance of a world that things become confused. For example, John Wheeler says that:

The natural state of presence awareness is here now. It is clear and available. It is not an awakening or attainment at all. It is already the case, but has been overlooked. I find the talk of

> *awakening to be very misleading. So, I would say to forget about the steps and processes and just come back to the simple recognition of what is already clear and present.* (Ref. 485)

He uses the term to speak about who we really are, as opposed to the ego that we think we are:

> *Presence-awareness is not a limited person at all. It is the vast, mirror-like, awareness-space in which everything arises. This is you. This is your home.* (Ref. 70)

And 'Sailor' Bob himself says:

> *There is no need to go anywhere or do anything. Presence-awareness is what you are. Just relax into presence-awareness.* (Ref. 346)

The clear implication is that we do not have to do anything to become enlightened. Indeed, it is the 'trying' and the constant 'thinking' that takes us away from the reality of the now. (This, of course, resonates with the modern seeker who has no interest in a lifetime of listening to talks from the scriptures!)

John Wheeler is even clearer in this passage:

> *You do not 'feel' awareness (as if it were an experience), and it does not really come and go, although it may appear that way. Awareness is fully present and absolutely clearly known at all times. Just ask yourself what is knowing thoughts or even the absence of thoughts. When you are not 'feeling awareness' what is knowing that experience? How can that experience even arise unless you are there knowing it?* (Ref. 70)

And this is all true. We are even 'aware' when in deep-sleep, because on awakening we know without any doubt that we did not know anything at that time. But this awareness is still associated with this particular body-mind. Although *I* am aware of my fingers operating the keyboard, you are not. This situation is clearly not non-dual.

Direct Path gives a similar message. Here is Jean Klein:

> *Unthinkable Presence is your real nature in which all appears. Because you identify with your thoughts instead of presence, you feel limited, restricted. In freeing yourself from this restriction you come to live your limitlessness. Then everything that happens in your life will have new meaning.* (Ref. 19)

And the idea is even more 'romanticized' by Francis Lucille. What he says is certainly not wrong but, perhaps unhelpfully, moves the investigation from the intellect to the emotions:

> *At first we try to look at our real nature as if it were an object. Then we understand that this attempt is doomed to failure. Next, we look at it as an absence of object, and at some point we understand that this search, too, is doomed to failure. Finally, we find ourself in a state of not knowing, a state in which the mind has exhausted all of its possibilities and has no further place to go. We reach the understanding that the mind cannot grasp the luminous awareness which enlightens it, and we become still. We have to make acquaintance with this not knowing, to get used to this new dimension, to discover that it is not nothingness. This silent presence is not a mere absence of thoughts. It is alive, it is life itself.* (Ref. 8)

According to Ramesh Balsekar, Nisargadatta pointed to our 'real self' as being prior to the birth of the body:

> *It is this conscious presence that you are, so long as the body is there. Once your body is gone, along with the vital breath,*

> *consciousness also will leave. Only that which was prior to the appearance of this body-cum-consciousness, the Absolute, the ever-present is your true identity. That is what we all really are. That is reality. It is here and now.* (Ref. 7)

The way that (one of the branches of) traditional Advaita explains the 'person' is to say that Consciousness is as if 'reflected' in the intellect. Who-we-really-are is not this reflection. Realizing that this is taking place in all of our experiences is certainly very helpful but it is not enlightenment! In order for Self-realization to occur, we have to go beyond this experience and gain the certain knowledge that everything is Consciousness (Brahman) and I am That, too. There is no experience that could give this knowledge, so that looking, being constantly totally aware or whatever cannot be the answer.

Another recommended practice is that, in every situation that we find ourselves, we see where our attention is directed. It is not at all usual to find ourselves simply attending to what is happening in the present moment; we are not wholly 'here and now.' Nirmala points out:

> *When we look, we discover that most of the time we are in opposition to what is and oriented to what is not... We are constantly evaluating our experience, looking to see what is wrong with it and how it could be improved.* (Ref. 486)

What we should do, says Nirmala, is endeavor to be in the present, by dropping all of the thoughts that 'this is happening to a *me*.'

> *When it's finally okay for the moment to be just the way it is – including the fact that we identify with a me and therefore battle with the moment – then more of our experience can be recognized and included in our awareness. If we are willing*

> *to be present and allow our identification and whatever else is happening, then it's also possible to notice something beyond identification, something beyond our struggle and effort to maintain a me. What that something is, for lack of a better word, is Being.* (Ref. 486)

This certainly sounds reasonable to a seeker but the way that the mind, senses, perception, thought etc. operate cannot bring about enlightenment. The world in which all of this takes place is not real in itself. It is only name and form of the reality. It is certainly true that 'all this is Brahman.' It always has been and always will be, because there is nothing else. But, from the perspective of the seeker, the point is that this fact is not realized. Intellectually, it is thought to be a nice idea but one which does not gel with existing beliefs or present experience.

This is why one of the terms used is 'Self-realization' – realizing the nature of one's Self, which is the nature of everything. Recognizing what is 'already clear and present' may perhaps bring the mind to stillness but it does not entail any Self-knowledge. Knowledge of any kind can only come via a pramāṇa – a 'means of knowledge.' In particular, as Śaṅkara pointed out above, Self-knowledge can only come from shabda pramāṇa – the teaching of a guru or scripture. Perceiving that we are present and aware is excellent if we are attending a traditional class but, in itself, it is never going to give Self-knowledge.

Being Awake

It is certainly possible to use a word like 'Awake' for being enlightened, Then 'waking up' could count as a synonym for becoming enlightened. Joan Tollifson is someone who prefers this way of speaking:

> *Awakening, as I mean it, is being awake NOW to the boundless wholeness in which everything belongs. It has nothing to do*

> *with always feeling blissful, never having any sense of being a person, or behaving only in saintly ways.* (Ref. 608)

The only problem I would have with this is that the words 'awakening' or 'waking up' are used in ordinary contexts, whereas 'being enlightened' or 'enlightenment' tend mainly to be used in a 'spiritual' context (if you will pardon that word). Consequently, there is the danger of confusion.

She does actually go on to say that:

> *I often wish these words like awakening and enlightenment had never been invented because they mostly seem to create a false idea of a goal, the sense that something presently lacking needs to happen in the future or the story that something impressive did happen in the past, or else some kind of identity as either an Awakened One or as someone who "isn't there yet." All of which, as I see it, is missing the point.* (Ref. 608)

And that is a good point always to bear in mind. We are already Brahman, or Consciousness. The problem is not that we need to 'seek' this but that we need to learn it to be already the case. 'Becoming' enlightened is what Śaṅkara calls 'accomplishing the accomplished' (also the title of an excellent book by Anantanand Rambachan – Ref. 527).

What Enlightenment Is Not

There is a booklet by Eric Putkonen called *52 Enlightenment Myths,* listing lots of the misconceptions about enlightenment but not all are without confusion.

Enlightenment is about finding Oneness. *Knowing all is one or having an experience that all is one is not Enlightenment. Who knows? Who had the experience? The little me … the ego. Enlightenment is seeing through the mirage called ego, not just finding Oneness.* (Ref. 571)

This is confusing the need to gain the knowledge that 'I am Brahman' with the mistaken notion that the ego has to be destroyed. This is a pity, because the next myth that is listed is:

Enlightenment means the ego is destroyed. *It is not that there is no ego, as if it was destroyed. It is that the ego no longer fools or causes confusion. Like a mirage. As long as we think there is water there it causes problems, but when we see through the illusion – no problem.* (Ref. 571)

So the actual aspect that is not clear here is 'who is it that gains enlightenment'? Clearly it cannot be Brahman or Consciousness. That is all that there is so there is never any condition of being 'unenlightened.' It is the person, the seeker, who is enlightened. Strictly speaking, it is the mind of the person that gains the Self-knowledge that we call 'enlightenment.'

In my book *Enlightenment: The Path Through the Jungle* (Ref. 441), published a couple of years before Eric's list, I had sections entitled 'What enlightenment is not' (I only got to 48 'myths') and 'What enlightenment is.' Since understanding this is critical to the entire business of enlightenment and its teaching, I provide a summary below, adapted from Ref. 398.

It has nothing to do with 'merging with Brahman,' or 'becoming one with' or 'returning to' God. It is not a 'higher' or 'altered state,' 'higher Self,' 'transcendental,' an 'expansion of consciousness' or an 'evolutionary step.' It has nothing to do with the heart or other mystical ideas. It is not about 'experiencing the Self'; it is not about 'experience' at all. It is not about 'becoming' free or being 'liberated' – one is *always* free. It is not about fulfilling or ending desires or ambitions, or about providing meaning and purpose.

One is not, subsequently, permanently blissful. It is not about destroying or expanding the mind or dissolving the ego. One does not acquire any special 'powers'; and gaining enlightenment is not associated with any special experiences. Enlightenment cannot be transmitted, whether by laying-on of hands or by paying lots of money to someone on the internet. And enlightenment does not have physical accompaniments, such as 'flashes' of light. Also, Brahman is not 'attained'; it is *knowledge* of Brahman that is attained.

Enlightenment does not result in any change to who we really are. So, for example, the following is *not* true:

> *Enlightenment permanently alters the functioning of your brain. For some it happens instantaneously, but for most a spiritual path is followed until this physiological breakthrough happens.* (Ref. 577)

The reality remains as it has always been; what changes on enlightenment is our *understanding* of all of this.

There are no 'degrees' of enlightenment. Someone may have just begun the notional 'path' of seeking or may be on the brink of enlightenment, but enlightenment itself is binary — one either is or is not enlightened.

Similarly, there are no 'levels' of enlightenment. For example, the following is not remotely true, according to Advaita:

> *There are levels of realization that transcend self-realization. The culmination of self-realization is the initial realization of THE SUPREME knowing, recognizing, and delighting in THE SUPREME.*
>
> *Realization beyond self-realization includes no-self-realization and apex God-realization, apex I-realization, and apex Source-realization.*
>
> *Enlightenment and turiya also transcend, and include, self-realization.* (Ref. 581)

Finally, although I would hope it is not really necessary for me to say it, enlightenment (or 'awakening' if you really must) has nothing to do with other-worldly gobbledygook. For example:

So at the beginning of 2021 I started receiving divine energy transmissions. This is when another directs light energy into your physical system. These particular transmissions were — like water in a basement — designed to get to all the nooks and crannies that language can't get to. And to dissolve the belief in separation at the root. This was measured using an energetic scale (akin to that of David Hawkins), ultimately reaching 1000 in September 2021. And full awakening. (Ref. 574)

What Enlightenment Is

Again, the following is a brief summary from Ref. 398, based upon Ref. 441.

A person becomes enlightened when self-ignorance is removed in the mind. The jīva then realizes that he/she is the Ātman: I am not a *'part'* of Brahman; I *am* Brahman and always have been 'free.' After enlightenment, it is known that there never was a 'person'; but this seeming person still functions in the world, knowing it to be mithyā — simply name and form of Brahman. The illusion of separateness is seen through, but the illusion continues (like the sun 'rising' in the morning). We are freed from self-ignorance and delusion and no longer seek fulfillment 'outside.' Enlightenment is the end of identification with body, mind and intellect; it is the recognition that we are the non-dual Ātman-Brahman.

Enlightenment is equated to 'liberation.' 'Mokṣa' means 'liberation' or 'emancipation'; 'release from worldly existence.' And scripturally it is usually used in the sense of 'no more saṃsāra' — the recurrent cycle of birth and death. But, given the ultimate illusoriness of those concepts, it is better thought of as release from ignorance. We are no more taken-in by the world and the thralldom to the ups and downs of life. We finally realize how things really are — namely that there is only the unlimited

Brahman. It is not in any sense 'becoming' something other. We have always been Brahman; we just did not realize it before.

Śaṅkara, in his bhāṣya on the Bṛhadāraṇyaka Upaniṣad (3.3.1), refutes the suggestion that liberation might be brought about by some action:

> *No, for knowledge dispels ignorance. Because knowledge removes the obstruction of ignorance, liberation is metaphorically said to be the effect of knowledge; but work cannot dispel ignorance, And we cannot imagine any other obstruction to liberation but ignorance that can be removed by work, for it is eternal and identical with the self of the aspirant.* (Ref. 1)

Enlightenment cannot involve any physical 'change.' Since we are already Brahman, any change would mean a change in Brahman which is not possible. It is simply a reconfiguration of the way in which we 'see' the world — a mental reorientation. This might well result in a dramatic change in outlook and behavior (or it might not), but we are not the mind. It could even indirectly result in changes to the body; e.g., a dissolute lifestyle would almost certainly cease and improved physical health would probably then follow. But we are not the body.

Knowledge versus Belief

We need to be clear about what is meant by 'Self-knowledge.' It is not simply believing that reality is non-dual, in the way that we might believe that most of the universe is made of dark matter. Science has numerous examples of beliefs being overturned as its tools become more sophisticated. At an individual level, our most firmly-held beliefs are often simply the things that we were told by our parents when we were very young and did not question. In regard to those aspects that fall within the realm of experience, these beliefs may be modified or even dropped in later life but such things as religious beliefs may simply never be questioned.

I mention Osho and his jokes several times later but here is another observation I made in Ref. 384 regarding beliefs (the joke is from Ref. 83):

> *Ultimately, it could be said that "we believe whatever we want to believe", as the Greek statesman, Demosthenes said. The rebel mystic Osho has a good joke to illustrate this: A man was driving home from work one night in the pouring rain when he passed a young woman struggling with some shopping. He stopped and offered her a lift. When they got to her house, she invited him in for a coffee. One thing led to another and eventually, they ended up in bed making love. Much later, he got up to return home realizing that his wife was going to be demanding a good explanation. By the time he arrived home he had worked out what to do and he took a piece of chalk from the glove compartment and put it behind his ear. As soon as he entered the house, his wife loudly demanded to know where he had been all of this time.*
>
> *"Well, darling," he began, "I stopped to give this girl a lift home. She invited me in for coffee and then we went to bed for a couple of hours."*
>
> *"I've never heard so much rubbish," his wife replied. "I know perfectly well what you've been up to. You've been out with the boys playing pool again; I can see that chalk behind your ear!"*

Possibly the definition most frequently encountered for knowledge is that it is 'justified true belief.' The phrase originated with the Greek philosopher Plato, and Chittaranjan Naik explained:

> *When Socrates spoke those words, he was merely trying to distinguish between knowledge and true belief. Considering that*

> *the results would be the same were a person to hold true belief or possess knowledge about a thing, Socrates asks: then why is it that knowledge should be so highly valued whereas true belief should not? Socrates' answer to the question is that it is because knowledge is stable (it stays put) whereas true belief is like an untethered stallion that is liable to run away from the person holding such a belief. Hence, says Socrates, it is not sufficient to merely have true belief but one must employ reasoning to justify the belief so that it does not escape from a person like an unrestrained stallion galloping in all directions.* (Ref. 578)

And this idea fits well with my understanding of Śaṅkara. As is stated below, in the section 'You Also Need Scriptures,' Śaṅkara accepts that scriptures are the only source of knowledge about Advaita (and you need a guru to explain them). But, in addition to both of these, reason must never be dropped in any of this. We apply reason to all that we read and hear. This was pointed out above, right at the very beginning of 'Some General Warnings.'

Who Is It Who Is Enlightened?

This is a question that seekers may not even ask. After all, it is not a sensible question, is it? But, once we start thinking about it, we may become increasingly unsure.

Bodhi Avasa gives the radical-sounding, Neo-Advaitin position:

> *The whole concept of something, some event, called enlightenment exists in this idea that there is SOMEONE present to get enlightened. A someone that is no more than an assumption of the mind. Enlightenment therefore does not exist as there is none for whom it can exist. That therefore leaves only THIS, what is, appearance manifesting in Nothingness. Already this is always the case. It is the case right now. There is only enlightenment.* (Ref. 685)

Jean Klein, on the other hand, makes a similar, but more restrained and reasonable-sounding statement:

> *Liberation does not concern the person, for liberation is freedom from the person.* (Ref. 19)

This may seem both clever and confusing. After all, it is not the Self that is liberated! And that is the crux of the matter. In reality (pāramārthika), there is no person. Therefore, *in reality*, the statement has to be true. But all of this – life, person, world, Advaita, enlightenment – is taking place in empirical reality (vyavahāra). In empirical reality, there *is* a seeker, who is following the teaching of Advaita in order to gain enlightenment and be liberated.

Here is another example, from Randall Friend:

> *The unmistakable truth about enlightenment is that there is no one there. There is no one who gets it, no one who could become it, no one who could ever reach it, find it, stumble upon it, realize it, attain it. There is no one there to be bathed in the light of God…*
>
> *That very freedom, that liberation, that peace, that love that was being sought, was already attained, always there. It was seemingly hidden but completely in full view, always.*
>
> *The search was clearly and unmistakably over, not because all the answers were found or figured out but because the seeker, the person, was seen to be false, a fiction, non-existent.* (Ref. 628)

The idea that enlightenment is 'freedom from the person' is just a clever play on words. It is certainly true that enlightenment entails the realization that there are no persons in (pāramārthika) reality but it is nevertheless *the person who realizes this*!

In order to understand this explanation, which may seem convoluted or even unintelligible, it is necessary to explain another concept used in Advaita (the Vivaraṇa branch) – namely cidābhāsa.

In order to understand this concept fully, it is necessary to explain much more first – an investigation into the nature of waking, dreaming and deep-sleep states is usually carried out. The confusions and explanations of these other aspects will be given in the companion to this book – *Mining for the Truth*. For the time being, consider the following metaphor, taken from Ref. 478:

> *Suppose that we have a dark, shuttered room. It is so dark that we are unable to find anything inside it. We are only able to open the door and, although there is bright sunlight outside, this does not penetrate far enough to illumine the interior. There is no electricity and I do not have a torch. I do, however, have a mirror. By positioning myself in the doorway, I can hold the mirror at such an angle that the sunlight reflects in the mirror and illumines the contents of the room. Although the mirror is itself inert, having no light of its own, it becomes a source of light by virtue of reflecting the light from the sun, which does have its own light. This, of course, is also how we get the moonlight by which we can see during the night, when there is a moon in a cloudless sky. The light of the moon is simply the reflected light of the sun.*
>
> *The parallel can now be made with our own inert equipment and Consciousness. Brahman is the equivalent of the sun, the only true 'source' of Consciousness. Brahman 'illumines' the instrument of the mind, which itself is not a source of Consciousness. But, by virtue of this illumination, the mind is able to reflect the Consciousness via the senses into the 'room' of the world and become aware of the objects therein and interact with them (including the body-mind itself).*

Ridiculous though it might initially seem, our body and mind are inert. Consciousness is not the emergent phenomenon of a complex brain, as science would have you believe. Although there is only Consciousness in reality, there is certainly the appearance of many conscious entities, of which I am just one. Who exactly am I, then?

Who Am I?

> *When we stop and ask 'Who am I?', what we find is nothing. We find only Presence, Awareness, Consciousness, which is aware of the thoughts, feelings, sensations, and experiences of the individual that we assume we are. This Awareness, this noticing of everything, is who we really are!* (Ref. 484)

No, it isn't!! The non-dual reality is not 'aware' of anything; does not *do* anything. And, assuming that we are provisionally accepting that reality is non-dual, what would this 'everything' be that is being noticed? If I find that Awareness is noticing the skepticism in this mind, do you also find this? Do you find a keyboard typing this sentence in front of your eyes? Of course not. If you pick up almost any modern book purporting to be about Advaita, you will be almost guaranteed to find (lots of) statements that simply do not stand up to common-sense reasoning. Traditional Advaita certainly makes statements that challenge everyday experience and may well initially seem to be outrageous. But the teaching proceeds step by step, with more sophisticated explanations superseding earlier ones; and the final conclusions are always consistent and reasonable.

Here is a typical Neo-Advaitin 'description' of enlightenment:

> *So in liberation it's seen that there is no person, and phenomena – feelings and thoughts, visual stimuli, tactile stimuli, aural stimuli – simply arise. That's what I mean by 'this.' There is the seeing of this, the seeing of whatever phenomena present themselves. In liberation it is seen that these phenomena*

> *simply arise in awareness without a person mediating them.* (Ref. 487)

The practice of rephrasing a sentence so as to omit the pronoun 'I' is a very common one amongst Neo-Advaitins. Instead of 'I see,' we say, 'it is seen'; instead of 'I went into town,' we say, 'this body went into town.' I referred to it in *Back to the Truth*:

> *As an example of misunderstanding of the teaching, some years ago, in some satsang circles, it was not uncommon to encounter people habitually referring to their bodies and minds as totally 'other' than themselves. "The body is experiencing aches" may not seem too strange but "the desire to visit the bathroom was observed" is positively arcane. This mode of expression became known as the 'Lucknow Syndrome,' in honor of the location in India where Sri Poonja used to hold his meetings.* (Ref. 467)

In fact, I just encountered an extreme example of this on the internet: *"the unit benefits from Awakeness recognizing itself"*! (Ref. 554) It is an immediate indicator of non-traditional pseudo-teaching.

Here, one is bound to ask: who is it who sees these phenomena arising? Only 'I see them' makes any sense at all — 'I' the author and not the 'I' of all his readers. As soon as one ventures into this sort of discussion, one has to be incredibly careful about the language used if it is not to be either misleading or confusing, even if it actually makes some sort of Advaitic 'sense.'

The question 'Who am I?' would seem to be simple, and to have a straightforward answer. Anyone with some background reading in Advaita will know that I am not the body-mind, not the 'doer,' not the father-mother-son-daughter etc. And, although I am probably not yet convinced, I will probably say that in reality I am Consciousness, Brahman, Absolute etc. But, even if I believe it, I will still carry on answering to my name, making statements such as 'I want,' 'I am going,' 'I disagree' and so on. Clearly, the situation is not so simple after all.

To begin with, it depends upon the context of what is being said. For example, am I endeavoring to speak about our experience in the empirical world, or am I trying to talk about how things are in the non-dual reality? Obviously, I cannot actually do the latter anyway; there is no such thing as someone speaking in a non-dual reality!

I looked at this problem in Volume 1 of *Confusions* (Ref. 398) under a number of headings and I posted the material to my website. You can read all of the related material at Ref. 488. The series begins:

> *Who are we speaking of when we use the words 'I' and 'you' in writing and speech?*
> *Since we are Advaitins, there are actually three possibilities:*
>
> > *'I' could mean Atman/Brahman, if used from the 'as if' pāramārthika viewpoint;*
> > *'I' could mean the reflected Consciousness (cidābhāsa);*
> > *'I' could mean the usually understood 'named person'.* (Ref. 398)

In reality, who I am is Brahman — *aham brahmāsmi* the scriptures tell us. But Brahman is not walking around in this world — the body is matter, controlled by a mind that is subtle matter 'animated' by Brahman in some way. We associate the 'person' with this body-mind but 'inert' things do not act or think. This is why we have to use a metaphor such as cidābhāsa.

The mind is not 'conscious' in itself, it is inert. But when Consciousness is 'reflected' by the mind, the mind appears to 'manifest' consciousness. Accordingly, when I am speaking or acting as a person in the world, 'I' is effectively a 'mixture' of the non-dual Consciousness and this particular, inert body-mind. But a teacher or writer of Advaita has to convey details of both the reality and the appearance in such a way that the seeker is not simply confused. We have to be very careful when speaking or writing that the listener knows exactly what we are talking about. For example, statements such as...

> *His (Ramana's) teachings are pointing our attention back within ourself to see ourself as we actually are, namely pure existence-awareness (sat-cit).* (Ref. 471)

... leave me very unsure whether what is being said is actually meaningful in an Advaitin sense.

As already noted elsewhere, many teachers talk about 'getting rid of' the ego but, analyzing in the above manner shows that it really makes no sense:

> *Even now, if you entirely eradicate the personal ego based on the multifarious nature of the non-Self, you will experience an intense and limitless awakening, as your true nature, the supreme Self, shines out.* (Ref. 470)

Who will 'eradicate' the ego? Who will 'experience' an awakening? From where will the 'Self' shine out, and to whom? All statements such as this are mixing up the absolutely real (pāramārthika Self) with the empirically real (vyāvahārika self); the non-dual reality with the normally experienced duality of the apparent world; the real Brahman with the mithyā person. Consequently, the above sentence makes no sense at all. Since the reader of it at the time probably assumes that it should (the author is respected), confusion results. Either that or, if the reader does not examine it too closely, it is thought to make sense and the reader learns nothing at all.

Any teaching of Advaita, if it is to help rather than confuse the seeker, has to be very clear. We have to be totally sure that we *understand* what is being said, irrespective of whether or not we believe and accept it. Otherwise, it serves no useful purpose. There are many seekers around today who are reliant upon secondary (or tertiary or worse) written sources for their understanding of the teaching. And I am sure that many persist earnestly for years, believing that what they are being told is true and will lead eventually to enlightenment. Many others no doubt give up when they find they are no nearer to reaching any conclusion.

As an addendum to this section, I received an extract from the new book of satsangs from Ganga Maa today. (This is the name taken by a new teacher in the 'tradition' of Ramana Maharshi.) A sentence from this is: *"The 'I' thought is the thinker. It might try to escape by distracting you with thoughts, but if you hold onto it without being distracted, it will disappear."* (Ref. 762) I responded to the sender as follows:

> *But who is the 'you' who is being distracted by thoughts? Who is the 'you' who "holds onto it without being distracted"? Can a thought 'escape'? Can a thought decide to 'escape by distracting you'? By generating more thoughts?*
> *(Traditional) Advaita is never contradictory to reason!*

I await the response with interest!

What Do We Do to Gain Enlightenment?

You Cannot Do Anything

The Open Secret is not saying "there is nothing you can do about enlightenment", that would imply that there is an individual who cannot do something. So there is no one to choose to self-enquire or sit and watch television all day, EXCEPTING IN THE DREAM. That is what is meant by the statement "there is no-one" — it means that there is no separative individual except in the dream of individuality which is illusory.

Tony Parsons (Ref. 658)

This is the core message of the Neo-Advaitin. They are saying that, in reality, there is only Brahman (although they would never use this word!); there are no 'people.' Consequently, there are no seekers, enlightened or unenlightened. What they do not go on to say is that neither can there be any teachers, so what are they talking about?! They will, of course, admit that to be so also if asked, and claim that it is all an illusion or dream.

And this is actually no different from the message of Gauḍapāda. His clear statement in his kārikā on the Māṇḍūkya Upanishad (3.48) is:

No jīva is born. This (jīva) has no cause. This (Brahman) is the absolute truth in which nothing is born. This duality consisting of the subject and the object is nothing but the (apparent) motion of consciousness. Consciousness is ever free from objects. Therefore (it is) said to be relationless. (Ref. 747)

This is the final teaching of Advaita, called ajāti vāda — no creation.

But it is not much help for a seeker who has every reason for believing him or herself to be a real person wanting to discover the truth and escape saṃsāra. Such a person requires a teacher who can bring them to the complete realization of this truth. Simply stating it as a fact is a waste of breath.

The Path

The Upanishads are replete with short phrases (called mahāvākyas — 'great statements') that tell you that you are already 'That.' "Consciousness is Brahman," "That thou art," "This Self is Brahman," and "I am Brahman" are the well-known ones. So any spiritual pursuit is aimed at realizing this truth. There is nothing that you can 'do' to attain enlightenment. James Swartz:

> *The idea that enlightenment can be gained through action — the experiential notion of enlightenment — does not work, because it is contrary to the irrefutable non-dual nature of reality. It is based on the appearance of things, not on the reality of things. And appearances are not permanent, so an enlightenment that I may gain through action will not last.* (Ref. 447)

Generic 'spirituality' almost invariably claims that there is a path, or choice of paths, to enlightenment. And the teacher or writer usually claims that they know this from their own experience and can show you how to follow it. There are many books that purportedly document (one or more of) these paths, e.g., *The Journey to Enlightenment* (Ref. 587) and *Liberation IS: The End of the Spiritual Path* (Ref. 589). And yet we also have a book such as *No Path To Enlightenment* (Ref. 588). What should we believe?

Even, apparently, within Advaita itself, some people will tell you that there are various paths you can follow, according to your particular personality and temperament. Active people have Karma Yoga; the religiously-inclined have Bhakti Yoga; the intellectuals have Jñāna Yoga. Others who are 'more' (or is it 'less'?) knowledgeable, may even talk about Raja Yoga, or even Kuṇḍalinī Yoga. (These last two have nothing to do with Advaita.) The fact is that, although some of these may be valuable as mental preparation, the only means of attaining enlightenment or Self-realization is to gain knowledge of this. Jñāna Yoga means gaining Self-knowledge through śravaṇa and manana as described below.

Attend a Satsang Meeting

Some teachers would have you believe that, in order to become enlightened, you just have to attend one of their meetings and follow instructions. For example, one website offers 'Awakening Sessions' and states that:

> *First, you come to see through undeniable evidence, exactly what you are not. Once that's accomplished we bring our attention toward what you really are. Not everyone wakes up, but very nearly everyone does.*

I suppose that there is no room for complaint here. 'Awakening' is not defined and the statement could simply mean that most people fall asleep but usually do re-awaken by the end of the session. (I also could not find out how much these sessions cost – one has actually to book one in order to find out.)

It is not surprising that speed is of the essence these days. Modern seekers don't want to sit around for years learning this stuff, they want to realize the truth now and they can then get on with their lives. (I do sarcasm as well as cynicism!)

For example:

> *In this Virtual Conference Center, our vision to bring some of the world's foremost spiritual teachers and pointers of our time*

> *together in one place over a weekend so that what may have taken years to accomplish on your own can be understood and accomplished in a three-day immersion.* (Ref. 566)

Here is another. It will take just one weekend and only cost £230:

> *In just a weekend (for just £230), the 'Dissolving the Ego' course will "show you how to recognise the Self and how to move beyond any limitations and live in constant peace. It is based on Helen's own direct experience of the fastest and easiest way to go peacefully beyond the egoic sense of self. You will learn how to find your true Self and live from that place of peace. You will also learn how to go beyond all duality and causality to find total freedom."* (Ref. 575)

[Note that, when I last looked, the 'Dissolving the Ego' course had been incorporated into the 'Dissolving the Ego Graduate Program (GP)' – a 'monthly subscription plan' for between £10 and £100 per month. It wasn't clear precisely what the determining criteria were. So perhaps, it wasn't taking just one weekend after all…]

It is a fallacy, however, that all that is needed for enlightenment is a single trigger to 'snap' us out of our belief that the life-experience we are living is the actual reality. Nathan Gill gave a very good metaphor for this in Ref. 25. He has a questioner suggest that there is a similarity to watching a movie in the cinema. You are totally involved in the movie and then someone nearby unwraps a sweet, creating a loud crackling noise. Your attention is entirely distracted. Nathan's comment is:

> *That's right, exactly. That's all that's happening today. You have gone into the cinema and someone is constantly crackling sweet wrappers!*

The questioner then asks how we can remember to unwrap the sweets and crackle the paper and Nathan gives a typical Neo-Advaitin reply:

> *'You' can't remember. 'You' is the mesmerization that disappears when the wrapper crackles.*

It is a 'half-true,' 'half-false,' but mainly confusing statement, no doubt intended to 'wake us up.' We can sort of see what is being said but it is unlikely to have a lasting impact. It is indeed difficult to understand 'who' we actually are but it needs patient and repeated explanation rather than a casual, and probably irritating 'kick.' Look back at 'Who am I?' in the previous section for an attempt to give a taste of this.

Practice

As already noted, many think that 'intellectual understanding' has to be 'converted' into a 'direct experience' through some sort of practice, before we can become enlightened.

An interesting possibility to explain this is that it arose from the distinctions made by Sāṅkhya and Yoga philosophies prior to Śaṅkara. Ref. 542 states that:

> *Franklin Edgerton (Ref. 543) had shown that Sāṅkhya and Yoga in the early Indian history did not stand for any philosophical or metaphysical system, but for two distinct ways of conceptualizing salvation, Sāṅkhya a standing for the soteriological scheme which understands liberation as a result just of knowing a truth, knowing how things are, whereas yoga referring to the pursuit of liberation by some form of action or practice that is ultimately non-intellectual.*

It is also possible that this idea has been propagated via the disciples of Ramana Maharshi. For example, Ing Jiri Vacek had a long article entitled "The Path To Self-Knowledge," in one of the *Mountain Path* journals. At the very end of the article, he says:

> *Now go and practice. This is the way, not barren and endless intellectual reasoning. Only direct experience can help us, not mere intellectual knowledge, which, without practice, is utterly worthless.* (Ref. 544)

Katie Davis, on the other hand, is one of those who claims that practice of any kind takes us away from who we really are:

> *Practicing is ego's strategy of postponement. It is a moving away from who you are. Why do you need to practice to be who you already are? A mountain doesn't practice to be a mountain for the future. A mountain is a mountain now. By practicing, you conceal the infinite treasure for which you are searching. Even searching is too much doing. There is no seeker. This is the same delusion. You do not need to search for inherent Being.* (Ref. 584)

Michael James is one of the modern-day proponents of Ramana Maharshi. He is the principal 'presenter' and 'answerer of questions' at the UK Ramana Maharshi Foundation. He also maintains the position that the intellectual understanding needs to be followed up by 'practice':

> *… those who claim to be followers of advaita, fail to recognise the practical implications of vēdānta, and therefore mistake the mere study and exposition of vēdānta texts to be the actual practice of vēdānta.* (Ref. 471)

But you can only 'practice' in the sense of the Pūrvamīmāṃsā philosophers, the ones who believe that it is the early, ritualistic parts of the Vedas that are important and that the end parts (Veda-anta) are merely supporting intellectual rationalization.

But Advaita is not something to be practiced; it is knowledge to be assimilated! Michael goes on to say:

> *Since advaita means 'non-twoness' (a-dvi-tā), the correct practice of advaita cannot be any practice that entails more than one thing.* (Ref. 471)

But he does not explain how there can be any 'practice' at all, if it is not dualistic. Chamber's Dictionary defines the word as *"The process of doing something or carrying something out. The performance of an act."*

David Godman believed that the idea that 'practice' was needed, stemmed from the fact that many of Ramana's adherents were unable to assimilate the teaching directly. He says:

> *Most of his followers found this high-level approach a little too theoretical — they were so immersed in the self-limiting ideas that Sri Ramana was encouraging them to drop that they felt that the truth about consciousness would only be revealed to them if they underwent a long period of spiritual practice. To satisfy such people Sri Ramana prescribed an innovative method of self-attention which he called self-enquiry. He recommended this technique so often and so vigorously that it was regarded by many people as the most distinctive motif in his teachings.* (Ref. 17)

It is clear from some of his dialogues that Ramana did *not* believe that practice was a sine qua non for all seekers; it was only relevant for those who were 'not ready'; i.e., who had done insufficient sādhana catuṣṭaya sampatti to prepare the mind for śravaṇa.

> *Q: How can I attain Self-realization?*
> *A: Realization is nothing to be gained afresh; it is already there. All that is necessary is to get rid of the thought 'I have*

> *not realized' ... There is no reaching the Self. If Self were to be reached, it would mean that the Self is not here and now and that it is yet to be obtained. What is got afresh will also be lost. So it will be impermanent. What is not permanent is not worth striving for. So I say the Self is not reached. You are the Self, you are already that. The fact is, you are ignorant of your blissful state. Ignorance supervenes and draws a veil over the pure Self which is bliss. Attempts are directed only to remove this veil of ignorance which is merely wrong knowledge.* (Ref. 17)

Practice of any sort can only prepare the mind for undertaking Self-enquiry. It cannot itself give enlightenment. Practice can never bring about jñāna! We are already the Self – we just haven't realized it! Michael James again:

> *The knowledge that can be gained from books or spoken words is only conceptual knowledge, and since such knowledge is known only by ego, it exists only in the realm of avidyā, and hence it cannot eradicate ego, whose very nature is avidyā.* (Ref. 471)

This has the clear implication that śravaṇa-manana does not in itself give enlightenment; one needs to 'do something' so that we turn the purely intellectual knowledge into mokṣa. This is contrary to Śaṅkara's teaching. It is Self-knowledge alone that gives enlightenment. Practice involves 'doing' and this is rejected by Śaṅkara as a means to enlightenment, as is any combination (samuccaya) of knowledge and action.

John Wheeler is very clear that no practice is needed:

> *Your true nature is here and now, not in the future. And you do not need to practice to be what you are. Even talk of awakening and liberation is a diversion from the immediacy of what is being pointed to. Once the mind gets hold of the notions of awakening or liberation, there is invariably an attempt to turn this into*

> *some kind of goal, which the individual hopes to attain. This is the very opposite of what is being pointed out.* (Ref. 70)

Ignoring the last sentence, what is said here is not wrong. We are already Consciousness; we do not need to do anything to 'become' it. But the point that is missed, and the one which is the totally crucial point, is that we do not initially *know* this to be so. We have to learn about it in such a way that we are completely convinced. Simply being told it is not going to work!

James Braha asks 'Sailor' Bob: *"So, there's really no need to do all those purification techniques, meditation and yoga and all?"* and Bob replies:

> *No, no need whatsoever. Of course, if it happens, there's nothing wrong with it. But all they will produce are experiences. They come and they go.* (Ref. 346)

Again, this misses the point completely. The 'purification techniques' are not intended to be an end in themselves. Yes – they are 'only' experiences and cannot in themselves give enlightenment. But their purpose is to prepare the mind for the actual teaching via scriptures and guru. It is that which will bring enlightenment. Without the initial practice, the mind will almost certainly just throw up its usual barrier of objections and disbelief, effectively providing an obstruction to any clarifying teaching that might otherwise get through.

Only someone who is able to still the mind and senses, and exercise discrimination and directed attention will be able to acquire the Self-knowledge that equates to mokṣa.

As an example from the scriptures, the Kaṭha Upaniṣad (2.24) says that:

> *But he who has not turned away from bad conduct, whose senses are not subdued, whose mind is not concentrated, whose*

> *mind is not pacified, can never obtain this ātma by knowledge.* (Ref. 156)

Self-enquiry (ātmā vicāra)

The 'investigation into the nature of the Self,' is carried out by the iteration of śravaṇa-manana under the guidance of a qualified teacher. This simply means listening to the talks with a suitably prepared mind and then asking questions afterwards to clear any doubts. Śaṅkara points out that śruti (the Upaniṣads) is the *only* source of knowledge about the Self. Ātmā vicāra is not *"the simple practice of being keenly self-attentive"* as Ref. 471 would have it. Doing that will certainly help to prepare the mind for carrying out the investigation but it is never, in itself, going to bring about enlightenment.

> *All his teachings are therefore centred around and focused on this simple but deep practice of self investigation and self-surrender.* (Ref. 471)

I have said before that I do not think that Ramana ever intended that his instruction to carry out ātmā vicāra meant simply some practical exercise. He was perfectly well aware of Śaṅkara's statements to the effect that only knowledge could remove ignorance and I have always understood that, by vicāra, he meant the traditional scriptural inquiry, since śruti is the *only* source of this knowledge.

Śaṅkara says that *"the Upaniṣads reject the claim that there can be anything apart from Vedic knowledge of the unity of the Self that can bring about liberation"* (Brahmasūtra Bhāṣya 2.1.3, Ref. 34) and *"Other things are cognized by the ordinary means independent of scriptural evidence; but the truth of the Self cannot thus be known by any other means of knowledge but that."* (Bṛhadāraṇyaka Upaniṣad Bhāṣya, 4.4.20)

Destroy the Mind

Freedom is when the mind is cremated: absolute destruction of the mind is Freedom. Then mind is no-mind... Ego subsides Here and Now in Being-Bliss-Awareness. (Ref. 15)

One of the favorite ideas in modern Advaita books is that, since it is the mind that is the cause of all our problems, what we must do in order to gain enlightenment is 'destroy' the mind. The notion comes from the Sanskrit term manonāśa, which Monier-Williams (the principal recognized Sanskrit-English dictionary) translates as 'loss of mind,' although the word nāśa is given as 'loss, disappearance, destruction, annihilation, ruin, death' – which does seem fairly unambiguous!

Ramana Maharshi is apparently one of the main sources for this idea. (I use the word 'apparent' because one is bound always to have some doubt about whether a given statement truly represents Ramana's beliefs, since so much of his purported teaching comes from translations by others. See the discussion on 'Translation' and 'Recording' above.)

Therefore, since we can be aware of ourself as we actually are only by attending to ourself so keenly that we thereby cease to be aware of anything else whatsoever, self investigation is the only means by which we can eradicate ego, annihilate the mind and thereby permanently free ourself from all problems and all forms of suffering. (Ref. 471)

Unless by one means or another
Mind dies out and certitude
From true self-recognition comes,
The knowledge which mere learning brings
Is like the horse's horn unreal. (Ref. 455)

The ego is an aspect of the mind. Just as we continue to exhibit personal preferences after gaining Self-knowledge, we also continue to be able to think, reason and discriminate. Indeed, as we know from the example of past sages (including Ramana), those who are no longer so distracted and diverted by desires and fears etc. are able to use their buddhi *better* than those who are still swayed by egotistical motives. The history of the teaching and teachers of Advaita demonstrates clearly that the mind cannot (and need not) be eliminated on gaining mokṣa. Manonāśa does not mean that the mind is destroyed. If it were, a jñānī would no longer be able to function in the world and we would never have had any enlightened teachers (including Ramana!).

'Eradicating ego,' 'annihilating mind,' 'freeing ourself from all problems and all form of suffering' — what would be left? Without an ego or mind, there would presumably still be a body-shell, with no mind to process sense data or to think or speak. 'Vegetative state' springs to mind! Wouldn't suicide be easier? This is certainly not the means of gaining mokṣa that is described by scriptures. Traditional teaching tells us that saṃsāra continues until such time as we gain the knowledge (in our mind!) that we are actually Brahman. Where else could this be known, other than in the mind?

Yet Sadhu Om is quite unequivocal on the matter, and links destruction of the mind with the attainment of 'bliss':

> *The second kind of absorption is 'mano-nasa', that is, destruction of the mind; in this kind of absorption the mind dies, and under no circumstances will it revive. Since it is dead, it can no longer give rise to misery. Therefore, the happiness obtained through the second kind of absorption, the destruction of the mind, is eternal. It is the supreme bliss.* (Ref. 472)

Annamalai Swami also emphasizes that the words of the teaching are of no value:

> *Don't be interested in the words that the mind is serving up for you. It is putting them there to tempt you into a stream of thoughts that will take you away from the Self. You have to ignore them all and focus on the light that is shining within you.* (Ref. 243)

And he says that, after realizing the Self,

> *you won't have to worry about anything any more. In fact you won't be able to, because the mind that previously did the worrying, the choosing and the discriminating will no longer be there. In that state you won't need it and you won't miss it.* (Ref. 243)

Sadhu Om confirms: *"permanent destruction of the mind is permanent destruction of misery."* (Ref. 472)

So – vegetative state is what we are looking for: no mind, no problems!

It cannot be emphasized enough: You are already Brahman and happen to be functioning through a mithyā mind which enables this to be appreciated. There is nothing else 'within' you; certainly no 'light.' If you see lights within you, a visit to the optician or neurologist is called for. It is the words that trigger understanding and ultimately enlightenment. The mind is your servant, not your enemy! Look after it and nourish it with the authentic teaching of Advaita.

Destroy the Ego

Another possible reason for wrong ideas here relates to the function of ahaṃkāra – making the mental identification 'I am this,' 'I am that.' The ajñānī makes the mistake of thinking that he/she is a person rather than the ātman; attaching attributes to 'I am' and thinking that these are defining characteristics. Ahaṃkāra says 'I am' but associates it with some mithyā element of creation.

What happens on enlightenment is simply that I no longer make this mistake in my mind. When I think 'I am,' I do not attach any attribute. I know that, although the body has certain physical aspects and the mind contains particular thoughts and emotions, I am not any of these things. That is, that particular aspect of the ahaṃkāra function no longer takes place. (Obviously I still answer to my body's given name and will say 'I like X; dislike Y' and so on but these no longer involve identification.)

Also, by concentrating on ego, the implication is that the memory, thinking and discriminative elements of the mind are not a problem; it is the 'controlling function' that has to be removed. Presumably the other aspects would simply become redundant, in the same way that a car ceases to be a source of pollution and accidents if there is no one to drive it.

> *Bhagavan* (i.e., Ramana) *is an expert doctor who has precisely diagnosed the root cause of all our problems, namely ego…* (Ref. 471)

But this is not the 'root cause' of all our problems. The 'root cause' is lack of Self-knowledge. When, following the gaining of Self-knowledge from śravaṇa manana with a qualified teacher, we are enlightened, the ego does not 'disappear' or get 'destroyed.' We continue to function in the world but those traits which we associate with egotistical people will be considerably attenuated.

> *in order to see ourself and everything else as the one infinite and indivisible brahman that we actually are, we need to permanently cease rising as ego.* (Ref. 471)

> *Ego's destruction by strong self-enquiry*
> *Is what is known as Self-attainment.* (Ref. 455)

Having an ego does not necessarily mean that we do not have Self-knowledge. A jñānī is simply no longer influenced adversely by egotistical thoughts – desires and fears are mostly under control because it is now known that 'I am not this body-mind.' I use the word 'mostly' if we are speaking about someone who has recently gained Self-knowledge. Once this becomes totally and irrevocably accepted, that 'person' has become a jīvanmukta or jñāna niṣṭhā. But the ego is still not 'destroyed' – that will not happen until the body and mind cease at death, which takes place on exhaustion of the prārabdha karma.

Michael James describes the 'practice' that leads to enlightenment:

> *That is, when we as ego attend to ourself so keenly that we thereby cease to be aware of anything else at all, we will cease to be ego, whose very nature is to be always aware of things other than itself, and will remain as we actually are, namely just as pure awareness, whose nature is to never be aware of anything other than itself.* (Ref. 471)

We are always what we are, namely Brahman. The point is that Consciousness is 'as if' functioning through this apparent body-mind. One function of this mind is ego – ahaṃkāra. The other functions are 'thinking' (manas), intellectual discrimination (buddhi), and memory (citta). The precise nature of these is not relevant. The point is that there is a 'subtle' aspect to the jīva, as well as the gross body, and this aspect which we call 'mind' or antaḥkaraṇa has various functions. There is no *entity* called 'ego' to 'rise,' 'fall' or be 'destroyed.'

Accordingly, we are never an ego and the 'nature of this ego' is not *"to rise, stand and flourish by attending to things other than itself,"* nor can it *"subside and dissolve back into its source (namely sat-cit) by attending to itself alone."* This reification of a function is analogous to the way in which the reification of 'ignorance' has led to a thousand years of confusion in Advaita, as I have analyzed and described in Volume 2 of *Confusions in Advaita* (still to be published at the time of writing; hence no reference). The ego cannot 'attend to itself' and 'dissolve into its source,' thereby bringing about enlightenment. It cannot be emphasized enough that Self-realization (and 'liberation') can only come about by gaining Self-knowledge. Scriptures and Śaṅkara make this abundantly clear.

Some modern teachers also recognize this clearly. Felipe Oliveira says:

> *... there is no such thing as the death of the ego in relation to enlightenment. That is an invention based on some ideal of enlightenment, not based on actual enlightenment. It is fantasy spurred by the desire to eliminate what we do not like or what causes us trouble.* (Ref. 572)

When we realize that we are Brahman and the entire universe is mithyā, then we appreciate that there is nothing that we desire or fear – we are already perfect and complete. It is *then* that the ego function is necessarily diminished, since no purpose would be served apart from maintaining basic operation of the body-mind until its death.

A further objection relating to the ego is the repeated assertion that the ego 'rises.' For example, *"In sleep we do not rise as ego, and hence nothing else seems to exist."* This is an unnecessary complication, presumably used to support the later contention of enlightenment being the dissolution of the ego. The sleep state is simply the state in which we are not aware of anything because the senses and mind are at rest and effectively not functioning. If there is a loud noise or someone repeatedly calls our name, we will wake up, so they are not completely inactive. Ego, being an aspect of mind, obviously does not function either. In both waking and dream states, the mind is active, along with an ego-function. Things 'seeming to exist' has nothing to do with ego per se. Certainly, what we desire and fear is likely to influence our dreams (at least), so that we could say that ego is a factor. But actions take place in waking which may not involve the ego at all – e.g., an automatic response to help others in an emergency, with no thought for oneself.

We haven't 'risen as ego.' Ego is an intrinsic element of mind. It is true that 'ahaṃkāra' is the 'process' by which we identify who-we-really-are with the body, mind, etc. and we need to acquire the knowledge that this is a mistake in order to realize our true nature. But this is all perfectly natural and there is no need (or possibility) to destroy either ego or mind. It 'dies' naturally when the prārabdha karma of a jñānī comes to an end.

Ramana was not the only teacher to speak of the need for the ego to die. Here is Atmananda Krishna Menon:

> *True life begins when the ego dies and consciousness dawns.* (Note 895, Ref. 13)

But here it seems more clearly related to the belief that 'I am the body-mind.' This mistaken notion has to be replaced by the realization that 'I am Brahman.' In note 887, the questioner asks: *"Is it right to hate the ego?"* and Atmananda answers:

> *Yes. Because the ego is something which does not exist. So you hate the non-existent because you want to be the existent Reality. The best way to annihilate the ego is not to think frequently of annihilating it. This will thereby only strengthen the ego. You need only to ignore the ego at every turn, and the ego will die a natural death.* (Ref. 13)

Attenuated Ego

It is certainly true that enlightenment brings the realization that who-I-really-am is not the body-mind (or ego)! This means that, although the susceptibility to physical, and even mental, pains continue for the jīva, it is known that 'I' am not in pain – the pain 'belongs to' the body-mind. This means that there is an end to 'suffering,' in the understanding that it is not 'my' pain.

Similarly, such things as the knowledge that this body has an associated name are not suddenly destroyed. If someone calls the name of an enlightened jīva, they will respond just as they did before. Personality traits will not be affected (although, since there is no longer any 'identification' with them, the responses may change). Outwardly, it is quite possible that others will not notice any difference.

Wayne Liquorman uses some highly original metaphors in his material and the way that he talks about this aspect is particularly useful. He points out that a very significant change occurs in the human mind at the age of around two-and-a-half:

> *A profound shift occurs in which we change from spontaneous, free-flowing beings, to creatures in which everything is about 'Me!' and 'Mine!' and how to get what 'I' want and think 'I' need. It is the moment that the false sense of personal authorship (FSA) starts. It is the false sense that 'I', as this body-mind organism, am the source of making things happen. It is this false sense of authorship that creates suffering, because the new perception is that 'I' am in control of things.* (Ref. 457)

His effective definition of enlightenment, then, is that it is the dissolution of FSA. This is almost the same as the death of the ego but not quite. He continues:

> *... after Enlightenment, the human organism is no longer suffering. There is Total Acceptance within the organism. There is Total Acceptance because it is 'understood' that What Is, Is. There is no longer a separate claiming 'me' to become involved with What Is, claiming it as 'mine'.* (Ref. 457)

All of this must, of course, be understood in the context of the discussion above on 'Who is enlightened?' And 'Who am I?'. And, lest it be forgotten, there is far more to enlightenment than this. "All this, verily is Brahman," and "Thou art That," say the scriptures!

Neti, Neti

One of the classical teachings of traditional Advaita is this one from the Bṛhadāraṇyaka Upanishad. It means simply 'Not this, not this' and the idea is that we apply it to whatever it is that we think we are – not the body, not the mind, not the intellect. We are the 'Consciousness' that is 'behind' these appearances, or is their essential 'substance.' And not only traditional teachers point to this. Here is 'Sailor' Bob Adamson:

> *The whole conditioning is to look outside yourself – not realizing you're complete already. We're conditioned that the more we gather, or learn or experience, the more whole or complete we will be. That's what the search is – a search out there, away from reality. We're That from the very start, so there's nothing we have to search for. All we have to do is see what is false. And then the false drops off. You're always one without a second.* (Ref. 346)

There are in fact three traditional messages in this: Neti, neti; tat tvam asi (you are That); pūrṇamadaḥ, pūrṇamidam... ('perfect prayer,' also from Bṛhadāraṇyaka). But all of this really needs explaining carefully, step by step. It is simply not possible to hear this sort of thing once and expect everything suddenly to be clear and totally accepted.

Stop Thoughts

> *The only way to end this vicious cycle of seeking and to experience a true and lasting sense of completeness is to*

> *transcend the mind by totally letting go of all thoughts and surrendering fully into the present moment.* (Ref. 586)

Some teachers convey the message that simply stopping all thoughts and attending solely to the present moment is what it is all about; that if we can do this, we will attain all that we have been looking for. This, of course, is nonsense. 'Stopping thoughts' is undoubtedly a remarkable experience. But it is *only* an experience and has nothing at all to do with enlightenment. Its value lies in training the mind to be able to fall still and give attention where it is required. I would also say that it is impossible for any seeker to acquire the ability to do this over the course of a few satsangs! (I mentioned my own experiences in 'Being Here Now' above.)

We are already and always the Self. Thoughts, whether they assert or reject this fact, do not obscure the truth. Meditation is a mechanism for stilling the mind and effectively 'stopping' the thoughts, and it is valuable practice. It is valuable because it enables us to listen to a qualified teacher explaining Advaita without our minds either losing attention or constantly throwing up objections and questions while the teacher is speaking. But, in itself, it cannot bring enlightenment because the thoughts are not preventing it.

Swami Dayananda points out the anvaya-vyatireka logic which illustrates this. This is the Nyāya logic of 'invariable concomitance.' (Don't worry about understanding any of that!) The example used is that of the rope and snake. Thoughts do not cover Ātma, just as waves do not cover water. He explains:

> *Elimination of thoughts is not knowledge; it is not self-discovery. Thoughts do not cover Ātma. Thoughts come, I am. Thoughts go, I am. Compare this with: snake is, rope is; snake is not, rope is. So there is the mistake of equating thoughts with 'I'. If I do not know who I am, this original mistake is never corrected by removing the thoughts. Vedanta does not*

> *accept thoughts as the cause for sorrow. The mistake of taking thoughts to be Ātma is the cause of sorrow. This is entirely different from what modern Vedanta and Yoga say.* (Ref. 523)

What 'covers' Ātma is ignorance and, to remove that, we require Self-knowledge. It also needs to be appreciated that this is another likely source of confusion. 'Ignorance' is not a real thing either! All that it means is 'lack of knowledge.' It now becomes obvious that it must be removed by 'bringing in' Self-knowledge to eliminate that 'lack.' (Note that this is disputed by some traditional teachers of Advaita. It is a complex topic and I devoted most of the second volume of *Confusions* to it (Ref. 476). Nevertheless, it makes everything much simpler, and does not cause any problems, if you think about it in this way.)

Knowledge

> *There is nothing you need to do to become what you are, but there is something you need to recognize in order to stop being what you are not.* (Mooji, Ref. 401)

The first volume of my book *Confusions in Advaita Vedanta* dealt at considerable length with the topics of 'Knowledge, Experience and Enlightenment.' The evidence is overwhelming that the only way to enlightenment (as defined in an Advaitic sense) is to gain Self-knowledge, ideally from the scriptures as explained by a qualified teacher.

Consequently, any 'teacher' who claims to be enlightened as a result of some 'experience,' and who promises to explain how you can have this experience yourself and thus gain enlightenment too, is a con artist – steer clear! Variations on this theme apply equally. In order to 'qualify,' a would-be-teacher must have studied Advaita for many years, ideally with a sampradāya teacher. (This is someone in a formal lineage stretching back for many generations, possibly even to Śaṅkara. They will have learned all of the techniques, metaphors, stories etc. that have been proven to work in leading a seeker to a final realization of Non-Duality.)

It is certainly possible for someone to learn about all of this without studying with a sampradāya teacher but a seeker should be very suspicious! Perhaps the simplest way to approach the problem is to look at the teaching schedule. If a teacher travels around the country/world giving 2-hour 'satsang' sessions in each location, where they only answer questions, and they never give long courses (months and years) of tuition to regular students at a regular venue, they cannot be teaching Advaita.

The reason why enlightenment can have nothing to do with experience is simple. If it is true that reality is non-dual, then it must be *already* non-dual. It has always been, is, and always will be non-dual. There is no separate world; there are no separate people (in reality). 'You' cannot experience *anything,* because there is no other thing to experience. Consequently experience, or action of any kind, can have nothing to do with gaining enlightenment. Clearly the problem is that you do not currently know any of this. You have to acquire this knowledge.

Everything that we know and experience is in what Advaita calls 'empirical reality' or vyavahāra. We cannot directly know or experience the true reality, because it is non-dual. The best that we can do is to appreciate all of this intellectually – and that is enlightenment.

If you are really alert, you will now ask a question: Isn't 'acquiring knowledge' an action, too? And the answer, of course, is 'yes.' The entirety of being ignorant, becoming a seeker, acquiring knowledge, and becoming enlightened is an empirical appearance only. The metaphor of a cinema screen is sometimes used. There appear to be actions of all imaginable categories going on, good and bad, exciting and boring, but in reality there is only the screen itself with images being displayed on it. Within the context of the empirical life-appearance, you have to acquire Self-knowledge in order to realize the truth of You, Consciousness, being the reality behind it. You, the person, are just another character in the movie. (As with most metaphors, don't try to take this one too far! They are used to provide you with the initial insight, and provoke you to look further than the simple appearance.)

Knowing the Self

This is a commonly used phrase, equated with being enlightened, but do all those who use it mean the same thing? And do they all agree what is required to reach the state of being able to say truthfully that they now 'know the Self'?

Its popularity probably stems from Ramana Maharshi. David Godman (Ref. 17) quotes from Ref. 278 (my bolding):

> *... innumerable methods under different denominations, such as yoga, bhakti, karma, each again with many modifications, are being taught with great skill and in intricate detail only to entice the seekers and confuse their minds. So also are the religions and sects and dogmas...*
>
> *Objects perceived by the senses are spoken of as immediate knowledge [pratyakṣa]. Can anything be as direct as the Self — always experienced without the aid of the senses? Sense-perceptions can only be indirect knowledge, and not direct knowledge. Only one's own awareness is direct knowledge, and that is the common experience of one and all.* ***No aids are needed to know one's own Self.***

Tom Das, a modern adherent of Ramana, is even clearer:

> *Everyone has self-knowledge. Self knowledge is the Self. They are one and the same. Sri Ramana Maharshi says in Talks, no 280:*

> *'There is no moment when the Self is not nor when the Self is not realised.' and*
> *'Even now you are Self-realised.'* (Ref. 557)

Again, there is the implication that we don't have to devote lots of effort to the 'search for enlightenment.' It is just a case of dropping it all and being in the present, seeing what is there without the overlay of egotistical desire. But, whether it was simply a case of mis-translation, or misunderstanding on the part of whoever recorded the talk, this cannot be what is meant. Yes, we are already the Self. You might even say that the Self realizes this, except for the fact that the Self does not 'do' anything since there is *only* the Self! But, unless we have acquired this knowledge from somewhere and it has been realized to be true, we cannot claim that we are 'Self-realized'!

Here is an example from one of today's emails, referring to a teacher who is actually Direct Path but apparently influenced by Ramana's *Who am I?*:

> *What he teaches is the mantra/question, "Who is this 'me' that gets triggered?" Every time we experience an emotional reaction — worry, self-doubt, anxiety, guilt, shame, resentment, anger, depression, or loneliness — we affirm the mantra and look within to see if we can find the "me."*
>
> *Eventually, it becomes obvious that the "me" cannot be found, other than a "story," a belief, a memory that comes-and-goes in the spacious awareness or presence we are.*
>
> *Then we can turn our attention on the world around us and share this vital message of peace, love, and joy that we have awakened to!* (Ref. 750)

It cannot be emphasized enough that enlightenment is not an experience and has nothing to do with what is apparently happening in the world around us or how we feel about that.

It is about the certain knowledge that the world is mithyā and there is really only Brahman.

Śravaṇa, Manana, and Nididhyāsana

I have mentioned these several times already but have no qualms about doing so again. Traditional Advaita makes it very clear that there is only one way to gain enlightenment. That is by listening to a teacher explaining the message of the scriptures. Śravaṇa literally means 'the act of hearing' or 'acquiring knowledge by hearing' but, in the context of the scriptures, it means 'that which is heard.' It is the pramāṇa of śabda or testimony – the authority of the scriptures, as explained by a qualified guru.

Having heard the teacher explain what the scriptures tell us, it is almost certain that some things will require further explanation. There are many Upaniṣads and the same messages are given time and again. The Gītā and the Brahmasūtras also present the same teaching so if one source does not resonate, there is a good chance that one of the others will. There are also various metaphors available to convey the same essential message. Traditional teachers have a wealth of proven methods available to them. Answering our doubts, need for clarification or expansion, is the aim of manana. The literal meaning is 'thinking, reflection' and it is certainly possible that thinking over what has been heard may make it clear. But it is almost certain that a qualified teacher will be able to do this for you more easily.

This process is all that is needed in order, eventually, to gain enlightenment, when all has been explained to your satisfaction.

But a clear distinction has to be made at this point. Many seekers believe that, on gaining enlightenment, all of the problems of life (and death) will disappear. Although their job, home, family etc. will obviously continue as before, they think that there will now be no further concerns, about present or future. After all, they argue, they will now know for certain that they (and everything else) are Brahman.

But it is not quite like this. The reason is that habitual modes of thought and behavior tend to continue! Gaining enlightenment means obtaining Self-knowledge and 'converts' the seeker into a jñānī, someone with knowledge or wisdom. Complete loss of worries and fears, total satisfaction with whatever might be one's present situation in life — these are the 'fruits' of that knowledge, jñāna phalam. Gaining the fruits 'converts' the jñānī into a jīvanmukta — one who is 'liberated while living.'

In order to effect this conversion, the jñānī has to do nididhyāsana. This simply means 'going over' or repeatedly revising what has been understood from śravaṇa-manana until it is fully assimilated and one starts to 'live' from that knowledge, rather than from the habit.

This is not the meaning that is usually given to this stage by modern teachers. They tend to favor such things as samādhi. When the listening and doubt-removal have been completed, they say that this 'intellectual knowledge' has to be converted into a direct experience by deep meditation. As already explained, this is nonsense.

If the jñānī fails to become a jīvanmukta in this lifetime, 'full liberation' is obtained when the body dies. There is no rebirth for the jñānī because the karma from previous lives, which is not maturing in this lifetime, is 'burnt' on Self-realization and no more is acquired thereafter. So, once the current (prārabdha) karma is used up, that is it. (This is the traditional explanation incorporating the concepts of karma and reincarnation.)

Teaching Advaita

Teaching in General

The 'truth' of Advaita is that there is only Brahman. 'Everything' is Brahman. 'You' are Brahman. And, pedantically, that is all you can really say. But of course, simply telling someone that is unlikely to enlighten them! Accordingly, there are 'prakriyās' (ways of explaining things, stories, techniques etc.) to help seekers move their understanding in the right direction. Traditional Advaita has many of these, proven over several thousand years to be helpful in explaining things. For example, karma and reincarnation are fundamental to these. The jīva is 'trapped' in saṃsāra – the eternal round of birth and death – until Self-knowledge dawns and saṃsāra is ended. But this is only a prakriyā. In reality, there is only Brahman. There has never been any creation and no one has ever been born, let alone re-born.

Most modern teachers try to bypass all of the gradual traditional methods and endeavor to leap to such final pronouncements as the one above. But, to my mind at least, they are not very successful. The 'bottom line' of Advaita is so radical that very few can accept it without lots of preparation. If you want to get there, you are far safer, and more likely to 'reach the destination,' if you follow the proven techniques. They may be slow and ponderous ... but they work!

> *Let anyone believe and follow whatever spiritual philosophy and practices that they want to believe, because what they believe and follow is what is best suited to them at their present level of spiritual growth.* (Ref. 471)

One cannot really argue with this sentiment. Śaṅkara acknowledges the value of the Karmakāṇḍa (the early and major part of the Vedas, with its guidance on dharma and its many rituals). This helps prepare the minds of those whose prior knowledge and mental ability are insufficiently developed to be able to take on board the teaching of Advaita. And Sureśvara (one of Śaṅkara's direct disciples) says that whatever paths we follow, we must eventually arrive at the teaching of Non-Duality.

This attitude is an aspect of the belief in karma and reincarnation. Any progress in this life will be carried over by the subtle body into the next life. If we choose to relegate that idea to the status of an immature belief (because we read elsewhere that there has never been any 'creation'), then we conclude that it must be rather important not to waste time following unhelpful beliefs!

The worry is that a seeker whose mind has been sufficiently prepared is then presented with confusing notions that do not allow that understanding to progress. Traditional Advaita with a qualified sampradāya teacher has been proven for over 1500 years to succeed. Newly developed ideas and techniques have no such pedigree. Seekers must beware!

Teachers utilize such prakriyās in order to help the seeker understand what is being taught. But they are never intended to be taken literally. The pañca kośa prakriyā is a good example. This says that our 'true Self,' the ātman, is 'covered over' by five sheaths, like the sheath, worn on a belt, that protects a dagger. The first sheath is 'made of food' — the gross body that we 'inhabit.' But this prakriyā does not literally mean that the ātman is covered over by various layers. It is simply used to explain that, initially, the seeker identifies with the body; later he or she will identify with the mind, etc.

The likelihood of this prakriyā being misunderstood is heightened by the fact that many teachers (not just modern ones!) talk of 'going within' in order to 'find the Self.' The seeker should always try to remember the there is *only* the Self (which is therefore 'everything' and 'everywhere'). These metaphors are never meant to be taken literally. The idea is simply that one should realize that thinking that we are the body, mind or the intellect, or anything else, must be a mistake. Once we have discarded all these notions, the one that is left – the 'I' that is none of those things – is who I really am. And realizing this is what is called 'Self-realization,' or 'enlightenment.'

The explanations given above are in accordance with Śaṅkara and prasthāna traya; they are not *my* claims! It is what the teaching of Advaita tells us. We cannot simply choose to claim something quite different, inventing different meanings for the commonly used terms – and still call this 'Advaita.' It becomes a different philosophy, which may still be efficacious for some seekers but it no longer has the backing of 5000 years of proven teaching.

Also, you can be certain that someone who has not themselves spent significant time *learning* the teaching methods, scriptures and prakriyās of Advaita is not going to be *teaching* Advaita! To understand Advaita sufficiently to be able to do so requires many years of study, not merely reading one or two books and attending an occasional satsang by someone else claiming to be teaching Advaita!

Psychological Issues

Mariana Caplan talks a lot about these, e.g. in Ref. 568. The personal examples described there took place in the early 1990s, but seem to echo the time of the hippies, when the 'in thing' was to 'drop out' and travel to India to find a guru or, for the less adventurous, join a commune in the backwaters somewhere.

The commune environments are presumably intended to mimic the ashrams in ancient India when earnest seekers gave up their materialistic lives and sought a way out of saṃsāra. But it seems that now, it is more of an opportunity for the powerful and unscrupulous to gather a band of devoted slaves to serve their every need in the belief that enlightenment will eventually be dispensed. Those impacted are at the age of disaffection with the world and wish to escape it, rather than face the seemingly impossible task of striving to improve it.

With such close proximity between teacher and student, sharing all of life's ups and downs, even if not actually sharing a bed, it seems inevitable that personal issues would conflict with spiritual seeking and cause confusion at the very least. Ref. 568 addresses all of these things. But, to be very clear, I will not be considering any teaching that involves communes or any sort of long-term 'living together' of teacher and seeker. It is true that 'personal considerations' may sometimes obscure or otherwise impede the transfer of knowledge, but such things are not relevant to the issues being considered here.

Also, 'communes' must not be confused with 'organizations' that have multiple locations. These will be mentioned briefly later. Chambers Dictionary defines a commune as: *"A group of people living together, sharing possessions, income, etc, for the benefit of the group as a whole."* An organization, as I am using the term, provides scheduled talks, meetings, tasks, worship or whatever, on an occasional basis. People attend periodically or regularly, but only for a short time for each event after which they return home. (The exception is that those who are studying to become teachers themselves probably do stay for a significant time. Swami Dayananda's courses, for example, lasted for three years with full residence at the ashram.)

It is unlikely that a seeker at an organization will have anything more than a simple student-teacher relationship with the guru. They will ask questions after a talk and receive answers, and that will probably be all. It is possible that a teacher may offer advice on 'personal problems' but 'psychological' aspects of a 'relationship' between them simply do not enter into the equation.

Adhyāropa-apavāda

Advaita uses the method of teaching referred to by this Sanskrit term. All it means is that you give a simple explanation first and reserve the more subtle explanations until the student is better versed in the basics. But this has the inevitable repercussion that some of what is initially presented in the way of explanation may turn out to be wrong! Adhyāropa means 'wrong attribution' and effectively means that what is being taught *now* is not actually how things really are; it is an explanation to satisfy the listener for the time being. When the seeker's understanding has matured, the teacher will give a better explanation. This is called 'apavāda,' which means taking back, or contradicting, what was said before.

If this style of teaching is not followed, giving a sophisticated explanation first may cause rejection of the entire philosophy. If you encounter differential equations before you have learned basic algebra, not only will you not understand them, you may even think they are meaningless squiggles. This is, of course, an extreme analogy. There is nothing complicated about Advaita. Indeed, the final teaching could not be simpler – who-you-really-are is the non-dual reality. But the seeker new to Advaita could not possibly be expected to accept that at first hearing.

'False' Teaching

You probably already know that the ultimate message of Advaita is that there is only Consciousness (or Brahman, or non-dual reality, or the 'Absolute'...). This means that anything that we can perceive or conceive is Consciousness. Or, as Advaita usually puts it: it is name and form of Brahman. We (who are Brahman) perceive a form in the non-dual reality and effectively 'single this out' and give it a name, as though it were a separate entity. It is in this way that we try to make sense of and describe the appearance of the universe.

When it comes to talking about the teaching of Advaita, the same applies. Whatever we say cannot be the truth about Brahman. We can say nothing at all about it that is ultimately true because that would be to objectify it and render the reality dualistic (i.e., with us as the subject).

Accordingly, no teaching can be 'true' or – another way of putting it – all teaching is provisional. The value of any teaching is measured by its effectiveness in producing the result of Self-realization in the one who hears it. If a seeker is enlightened as a result of a particular way of teaching, then that teaching was valid for that seeker. No teaching can really be called 'false.' This should be remembered as I criticize specific quotations throughout this book. I am criticizing because they are likely to mislead and confuse, especially if combined with material from other sources. Ideally, you should find, and stay, with a particular teacher/writer whose style and content has proven successful with others. This, indeed, is why Śaṅkara is considered to be the perfect teacher. He established monasteries in India specifically to propagate his methods from teacher to disciple in perpetuity.

Unfortunately, even these are not infallible. Over the centuries, there have appeared teachers who sought to 'improve' upon Śaṅkara; to explain or further rationalize what Śaṅkara 'really' meant. When two different interpretations appeared, there ensued arguments about who was 'right' and later commentators then indulged in arguments about the differing interpretations. Thus we find today that writers can make claims about the 'correct' teaching which even contradict each other. Academic Advaita is a potential minefield!

But many modern teachers have chosen to ignore the tradition completely, claiming 'direct' knowledge from their own 'experience.' Here is the most hazardous territory of all and why I described the search for the truth as being like a 'path through the jungle' in my book on looking for enlightenment. (Ref. 441)

Many modern teachers clearly know and understand very little about Advaita. The impression one gets from some of the books claiming to be about enlightenment is that the writers had some brief exposure to the ideas, realized that there was a market for books and talks, and launched themselves on a possibly lucrative career!

Another suggestion as to why there are so many 'false gurus' was made by Swami Muktananda (Siddha Yoga, not Advaita):

> *Why do false gurus exist? It is our own fault. We choose our gurus just as we choose our politicians. The false guru market is growing because the false disciple market is growing. Because of his blind selfishness, a false guru drowns people, and because of his blind selfishness and wrong understanding, a false disciple gets trapped. A true disciple would never be trapped by a false guru. False disciples want a guru from whom they can attain something cheaply and easily. They want a guru who can give them instant samādhi. They do not want a guru who follows discipline and self-control; they want one who will participate in their own licentious lives. They want a guru who is just like they are.* (Ref. 609, quoted in Ref. 568)

Traditional Teaching

This is generally accepted as being the teaching that was 'systematized' by Śaṅkara around the eight century CE, through his commentaries on the principal Upanishads, the Bhagavad Gita and the Brahmasutras, together with his own writing. The background, method and conclusion of this has already been explained.

Direct Path

This is the teaching that mainly stems from Atmananda Krishna Menon (1883–1959) – see the section on 'Teachers' below. As such, it is relatively recent and cannot be classed as 'traditional.' I had a long discussion with someone, comparing the two approaches — see Ref. 749. The essential idea behind it is that, by directly observing our perceptions and actions in the moment that they occur, we can dissociate ourselves from any sense of subject-object 'participation' and realize ourselves as unlimited 'knowledge-awareness.'

I indicated my own experience at one point as follows:

> *I spent quite a few years primarily with Direct Path teachings — Krishna Menon, Francis Lucille, Ananda Wood and Greg Goode. I thought this was the best. It was not until I started reading more strictly traditional styles however (Chinmayananda, Dayananda) and especially listening to Paramarthananda, that it all started to become clear. What more can I say? Traditional has 2000+ years of honing of prakriyās and answering questions. Direct Path has 100. Sampradāya teaching is very well proven to work; Direct Path is haphazard to say the least. I suggest that the perceived benefits of Direct Path — short duration, do it yourself, part time, carry on with normal life etc. — are what really appeals to the modern seeker. Traditional requires commitment over many years; regular attendance of talks, sādhanas to purify the mind etc. And you have to REALLY want enlightenment. 'Normal life' gradually subsides into the background!* (Ref. 570)

And that remains my position.

Neo-Advaita

The 'non-teaching' of Neo-Advaita seems to have originated in the twentieth century. In particular, it must have been brought about by the satsang-style of teaching, which comprised seekers who were unwilling to devote the time and effort required for correct, traditional teaching, and teachers who were prepared to accommodate them by holding simple question and answer sessions rather than insisting that the topics be taught properly in the time-honored manner of sampradāya.

Neo-Advaitin teachers frequently and candidly announce that they are not teachers, since they have nothing to teach!

> *I have no teaching, for how can you put silence, love, freedom into a teaching? It is a living experience. It's more like an intimate sharing that comes from my heart. I'm just an ordinary man who has found the eternal self, which resides in everyone. I'm just a friend, and only in friendliness and love can this flower of truth be given. By being open and receptive, you can catch this fragrance and rediscover your true nature.* (Ref. 547)

Sri Poonja explains that 'paths' and 'practice' are actually anathema to discovering the truth:

> *On three accounts searching and practice are foolishness and misleading and are only the clever mind postponing Freedom … a searcher reinforces the concept of an individual sufferer that is separate from Freedom, and that self is something 'other' than That Here and Now…*
>
> *Practice takes ego which reinforces subject-object relationships and all practice is through body mind and senses which reinforces body mind identification…*
>
> *Direct practice is Now itself, just Being itself, not waiting for the next moment or the next thought or the next life to accomplish something…*
>
> *Prescribed sadhana requires and reinforces ego to become something special when really we are One.* (Ref. 15)

Neo-Advaita appears to offer the easy path – easy because there is no path! They deride all of the 'intellectual nonsense' of traditional teaching. There is nothing to do because 'This is It' already. It is just a matter of dropping all of the mistaken notions, such as that 'I am bound and want to get liberation.'

Here is Richard Sylvester:

> *Many teachers of non-duality suggest that there is someone who can do something to heal their sense of separation; in other words that there is a person who is able to discover that they are not a person. The absurdity of this idea is often camouflaged by highly complex and subtle thinking.*
>
> *Teachings about non-duality frequently present the seductive idea that liberation can be realized through an evolutionary spiritual path. This has no actual connection with non-duality but it can offer us a convincing, although meaningless, story about it.*
>
> *A way of searching may lead to a person being more comfortable. That is fine but it is all that you get — a person who is more comfortable in their prison. If you are in prison, it is better to be comfortable but that doesn't get the person out of the prison they perceive themselves to be in.*
>
> *Nothing will get the person out of their prison because the person is the prison. When the person drops away, it is seen that there never was a prison in the first place.*
>
> *Then it is seen that 'I' and 'you' are the light in which everything arises.* (Ref. 495)

It is clear that he has understood the 'bottom-line' message of Advaita. The problem is that the multiple-step path to that understanding has been discarded. It is as though you are being asked to climb onto the roof of a building, but the rungs of the ladder have been removed. The key to realizing this is the wording of those last two sentences — "it is seen." It should trigger the question: "By whom?" He actually falls into the same trap as those he derides in his opening sentence *"a person who is able to discover that they are not a person."* The only difference is that now, apparently, the person sees that the person has dropped away!

Tony Parsons takes this message even further (Tony is the acknowledged guru of Richard). Recognizing that 'it is seen' is likely to trigger that doubt. He extends it to 'it is seen by no-one'!

> *There is no person that becomes enlightened. No-one awakens. Awakening is the absence of the illusion of individuality. Already there is only awakeness, oneness, timeless being, radical aliveness. When the dream seeker is no more it is seen (by no-one) that there is nothing to seek and no-one to become liberated.* (Ref. 496)

The Neo-Advaitin teaching has now been around for maybe 20 years so the demand for it is clearly not abating. Here is an example from 2024:

> *The Meetings point to the unknowable, singular, undivided nature of "what is" already — home. By being already, searching for home is a hopeless endeavor. There is no real separation, "what is" is freedom — for no-one. Consequently, the Simply This message has nothing for the individual. There is nothing to become, to get, to know or to understand, the message offers only loss. The loss of the need of seeking.* (Ref. 582)

As soon as you start to think about it, there is no avoiding the discussion of 'Who am I?' that was raised earlier.

Accepting What Is

There are quite a few 'teachers' today whose promotional blurbs speak of non-duality but, when you begin to look at the lower-level content of talks and 'live sessions,' it is all about making life more bearable. It is about accepting whatever is happening now, however much you wish it were different, and stopping the search for something 'better.' As an email in my inbox this morning puts it:

> *The exhaustion is really your dearest and most trustworthy friend, for it contains within itself an invitation to deep rest, and the end of seeking... Every meditation and contemplation is designed to help you deepen your acceptance of what is and bring a sense of rest and slowness into every moment of your life.* (Ref. 751)

Attend zoom sessions several times per month (indefinitely, at $400 per annum) and you will learn how to cope with life.

> *Everything is perfect right now. Feel it. Don't think about it. Feel it.*
>
> Robert Adams, quoted in another email received this morning.

None of these quotations is exactly 'wrong' but what are they saying that is actually useful? Or which lead you to a greater understanding of who-you-really-are? I am sure that, after a while, one could produce these 'inspiring' exhortations without effort, different every time and yet exactly the same... and equally valueless.

Jeff Foster expresses the starting-point problem of the seeker very well:

> *Put very simply, we seek purity, perfection, and completeness outside of this present experience because we see our present experience as broken, as incomplete, as imperfect, as not whole in some way.* (Ref. 453)

That is effectively the starting point of his book *The Deepest Acceptance: Radical Awakening in Ordinary Life*, and the end point is that:

> *It's about awakening to the completeness and deep acceptance of* this *moment, as it is. It's about seeing that* these *waves are already deeply accepted, here and now. Tomorrow's integration is not my job. The story of yesterday's awakening is irrelevant. Here and now is where all life is. And there is* only *here and now.* (Ref. 453)

It cannot be denied that the acceptance of whatever situation we are in, along with the dropping of any desire for it to be different, frustration that we 'allowed' it to happen, concerns about our ability to cope, and so on, will lead to a much easier life. Without a multitude of thoughts vying for attention, we will be able to act appropriately and move on to the next situation without accompanying self-congratulation or rebuke.

Consequently, teaching all of the related material, practical and psychological, training the mind to approach problems with attention and stillness, will undoubtedly lead to more positive outcomes. Our attitude to life and ability to 'succeed' in our endeavors will all improve.

But none of this has anything to do with Advaita. It is the 'Being Here Now' mistake that was described earlier.

Need for References

As explained, the teaching derives from the Upaniṣads, Brahmasūtras and Bhagavad Gītā and their principal explicator Ādi Śaṅkara. When a writer states, for example, that 'Śaṅkara said this,' it is essential that a precise reference is given to where it was said so that readers can check for themselves. This is not because readers intrinsically distrust what they read (usually the opposite is the case – if it is written in a book, it must be true!), but because they may wish to see the context in which the quotation occurred. Readers *should* be mistrustful if sources are *not* given.

Ideally, when scriptural quotations are given, both the source (scripture and verse) and the particular translation (actual book reference, translator, publisher) should be given. Check the length of the Bibliography to help to gain some insight into the extent of the writer's background research. It is revealing to note that most books by modern teachers do not even *have* a Bibliography! Everything is as they say *because* they are saying it. (And at the same time, they are telling us that, in order to become enlightened, we have to get rid of the ego!)

It often turns out that a 'Śaṅkara text' being quoted from is not even thought to have been written by Śaṅkara by modern academic consensus. Another frequent problem is that a word-by-word translation of the original Sanskrit will show that he said no such thing! The statement is rather a 'translation' chosen to correspond with the particular idea currently being expounded by the writer.

It should be noted, incidentally, that I am not accusing any such writers of lying or being deliberately misleading. I am sure that, in most cases, they genuinely believe that they are paraphrasing what Śaṅkara 'actually meant.' But I prefer to rely upon what Śaṅkara actually *said*! He obviously had a command of the Sanskrit language that was infinitely greater than any modern academic or monk, so that the word he chose was the word he meant to use! The danger here is that he may have chosen it to fit in with metrical requirements or he may have been being intentionally flippant or sarcastic, for example. In such cases, we may have to rely upon the judgment of the Sanskrit academics. It is because of problems such as these that one has to be constantly alert when reading books on Advaita.

Whenever a fairly knowledgeable reader finds a 'translation' conflicts with their own prior understanding, they should, if possible, seek out a literal translation. Naturally, a novice seeker is most unlikely to be able to do this easily. Hence the need to use only trusted sources as arbiters of meaning. Unfortunately, my own Sanskrit knowledge is fairly limited. Fortunately, my email associates, amassed over the past 25+ years, include several relative experts in Sanskrit, whom I was able to consult for the examples given in my *Confusions* books.

Explanation of the Word *Mithyā*

We cannot say anything at all about Brahman because Brahman is non-dual and thus has no attributes of any sort. Attributes are adjectives – big, colored, frightening etc. And adjectives describe nouns. We often mix up adjectives and nouns without realizing it. The example used by Swami Dayananda in Ref. 112 is a wooden table. It seems obvious that 'table' is the noun and 'wooden' is the adjective. But this is a mistake. The actual substance of the table is wood. This was originally in the form of a tree but it was chopped down and sawn into pieces that were then assembled into the form of a table. A carpenter could disassemble it and make it into a chair instead.

Accurately speaking, therefore, it is wrong to call it a wooden table. We should really call it 'tabley wood'! The Sanskrit word we use for the table is 'mithyā' and it is one of the most important words in Advaita; yet one rarely, if ever, used by satsang teachers. It means that the thing we are talking about is not a 'substance' in its own right. A more well-known example is gold ring, bangle and chain. Gold is the actual substance and it can be melted down and formed into any of these types of jewelry. But, regardless of in which form it happens to be, it is always only gold.

Although the table is mithyā, the wood is not actually 'real' (satyam) either. The wood is a complex of lignin, proteins and other organic chemicals. And each of these chemicals is made up of atoms of carbon, nitrogen, hydrogen, sulfur, etc. The atoms are made of protons, neutrons, and electrons, which in turn are made of...

Each of these 'states' can be thought of as an attribute of some more fundamental substance. If what is apparently a substantive is realized to be an attribute, then it requires a more fundamental substantive. Advaita tells us that every apparent substantive is like this. Everything is ultimately name and form of Brahman, which itself is not an attribute.

Something made from a more fundamental substance can be called a 'product.' A product has attributes and can therefore be described. In his commentary on Taittirīya Upaniṣad (2.7), Śaṅkara says that:

> *Only attributes in a product can be clearly described. And that which has a well-defined attribute is a product. And Brahman is not a product, as Brahman itself is the cause of all the products. Therefore Brahman cannot be described.* (Ref. 466)

The reason for all of the above explanations is simply that, because Brahman cannot be described, if a seeker asks the guru to do this, the latter is unable to answer. And that brings us on to the idea of 'teaching' through silence.

Teaching 'Through Silence'

Since we cannot say anything definite about Brahman, we need stories in the scriptures like that of the teacher Bhadva.

Śaṅkara explains in his Brahmasūtra commentary 3.2.17 that the Vedas tell us Brahman has no distinguishing features (Bṛhadāraṇyaka Upaniṣad 2.3.6: neti, neti – not this, not this). He quotes an example from the Vedas. Note that he does not give a reference. It is thought by some to be from an Upanishad that is no longer available (there are known to be many that have been lost in history). This passage is translated:

> *Also, this idea is conveyed by the śruti text which relates how Bhadva, being questioned about Brahman by Baṣkali, explained It to him by silence. When Baṣkali approached Bhadva with the request, "Please teach me Brahman, Sir," the latter was silent. When the request was repeated a second and a third time, he said, "I am teaching you indeed: but you do not understand. Silent is that Self."* (Ref. 483)

The idea of silence being equated with 'reality' comes from the use of the word 'OM' as a means of meditation in the Māṇḍūkya Upaniṣad. The Sanskrit word 'OM' is actually spelt with the (Sanskrit) letters A, U and M. In speaking, the vowels A and U combine to give the sound O. In the Upaniṣad, A is equated with the waking state, U with the dream state and M with the deep-sleep state. None of these states is real in itself, their reality derives from Consciousness which, in this context, is called turīya. And turīya is symbolized by the silence that follows each chant of the word OM. (My book at Ref. 379 is a commentary on this Upaniṣad and the verses (kārikās) written on it by Gauḍapāda. The specific commentary on the Upaniṣad itself is contained in an Appendix and this may be read in its entirety at Ref. 493.)

The 'original' teacher of Advaita is said to have been the god Ṣīva, appearing in human form as the teacher Dakṣiṇāmūrti. The latter is traditionally said to have taught through silence but reason tells us this cannot have been the case. Dakṣiṇāmūrti is associated with a hand-sign called the cin mudrā (which means 'sign of Consciousness'). It is made when the first finger of the hand is bent to touch the tip of the thumb, forming a circle separate from the remaining three fingers. The full symbolism of this is explained in an appendix to Ref. 493 (and the sign itself forms the cover-image of the book). But the point of explaining all this is that, *once all of the progressive teaching has been given,* this symbol will remind the seeker of the fact that she is not the waker, dreamer or deep-sleeper but the one reality – and it does this without the teacher needing to speak a word. Clearly, before one has been taught this, it will not mean very much at all!

And maybe this symbolism is used by modern teachers who hold 'silent retreats' at which participants abstain from speaking. Such a retreat setting may lead to a sense of peace and relaxation, but whether anything is actually learned from the enforced silence is questionable.

The idea of teaching through silence is often linked with Ramana Maharshi, who says, for example:

> *Does preaching consist in mounting a platform and haranguing to the people around? Preaching is simple communication of knowledge. It may be done in Silence too… Again how does speech arise? There is abstract knowledge (unmanifest). From it there rises the ego which gives rise to thoughts and words successively. So then: Abstract Knowledge → Ego → Thoughts → Words.*
>
> *Words are therefore the great grandson of the original source. If words can produce an effect, how much more powerful should the preaching through silence be? Judge for yourself.* (Talk 285, Ref. 49)

It has to be remembered, however, that, notwithstanding Ramana's unquestioned abilities and achievements, he was not a sampradāya teacher and some of the things that he says are not in accord with traditional teaching as per Śaṅkara. He cannot therefore be quoted to substantiate the idea of teaching through silence.

The simple fact is that enlightenment equates to Self-knowledge and a teacher has to use words to convey this knowledge. A teacher *might* respond to a question with silence only in the specific instance where any answer might mislead. In Ref. 112, Swami Dayananda says:

Knowledge cannot take place without a pramāṇa, a valid means of knowledge. There is no other way. A medium of communication is necessary and you must have the discipline, the saṃskāra of that language, because the communication is in the form of words. The means of knowledge is in the form of words. And that alone culminates into knowledge.

It is said, Lord Dakṣiṇāmūrti conveyed by silence. He taught by mudrā, a sign made by position of fingers. Mudrā here stands for language. In reality, He taught through words. If He was silent, all our Upaniṣads would have been in the form of blank pages! In fact silence is good for two reasons: either it is inconvenient to answer and therefore you do not answer or sometimes whichever way you answer is a problem, and so you do not answer. You become mauni, silent.

[Note that a 'muni' is a sage who has taken the vow of silence.]

This is another example where common sense tells you that the literal interpretation cannot be correct. A teacher cannot 'explain' something to a seeker without speaking. Even if he possessed the supernatural power (siddhi) of telepathy, the seeker would not! (Obviously, I would deny that such things exist in any case.)

And this is a general point that should always be borne in mind. If you are an intelligent adult, with years of education and experience behind you, and something that you are told by a 'teacher' is contrary to what your own reason and experience tells you, then your faith in that teacher needs to be very high before you consider accepting it as true.

Ācārya Sadananda provides a good, simple summary of this topic:

Silence is bliss only when the mind understands what needs to be understood. Otherwise, silence is only the bliss of ignorance. (Ref. 638)

Transmitting Enlightenment

Transmission most commonly seems to occur in some degree of contact with a being who has Realized this actuality. This may be through explanations/teaching, or through more direct perception of the example of this actuality being embodied. It is unimportant how it seems to occur, only that it does, for entry into the conscious practice of this Yoga. (Ref. 624)

It seems to be a very common misunderstanding that this is possible and there are quite a few teachers who claim to be able to do it.

Dolano is apparently one of those who can:

Dolano, a modern day twenty-first century Zen Master and friend who transmits the liberation of the mind like no one else. (Ref. 569)

Also, I would have thought that Zen masters follow Zen and not Advaita, although her site claims that her teachers were Osho, Ramana, Poonja and Gangaji.

This Supernatural Spiritual Condition continued without pause or interruption for about one year. Upanishadic-style Unity Consciousness, the Self, revealed in all its glory was felt, seen and understood as existing within and without. I lived in Brahman Consciousness — the Self expanded out in all directions to infinity. There was nowhere to ascend, descend or expand outside the Self. Unassailable Unity prevailed...

During this time, I became conscious of my ability to instigate Self-Realization in others. (Ref. 548)

Sri Poonja is another teacher of whom it was claimed that he could 'transmit' enlightenment even, apparently, without any effort at all on his own part:

> *Someone like Papaji who was living 100 per cent in higher consciousness — everything he did was enlightened ... he'd be reading the newspaper, watching the cricket, chewing his pan and people would be sitting next to him and getting enlightened, having total satsang, total darshan with Papaji.* (Ref. 78)

And it seems that he could pass this supernatural ability on to others:

> *Ramana, who was named after Papaji's teacher Ramana Maharshi, has merged with the consciousness of his teacher and now has the ability to "transmit" this awareness and grace from his Guru.* (Ref. 532)

I was surprised to see that Isaac Shapiro is another. Poonja was his teacher, also, so maybe he is the source of this erroneous notion:

> *Isaac is an invitation to live as awareness. Resting in presence with him, allows a direct seeing/knowing for yourself. In some traditions this is called transmission...* (Ref. 576)

Back in 2002, I found this on a website:

> *Enlightenment happens by transmission. Books are bondage. It is time to stop reading, and start receiving. Transmission is a mysterious thing that may never be explained. My research in this area continues, and at some point may be documented, but for now the only useful work is that of creating enlightenment, rather than writing about it.*

I just did a quick search on Google and discovered that, in 2023, this 'teacher' is still advertising 'Enlightenment Transmission' and organizing meetings, over 20 years later. I cannot imagine how much money has changed hands and how many sincere seekers have been involved and subsequently disappointed! Of course, enlightenment is not something that is recognized in any legal forum…

As I pointed out in Ref. 441:

> *Some satsang teachers encourage the idea that enlightenment can be transmitted from guru to disciple (i.e. by simply being in their presence). This fits in with the 'nothing to do' idea and also makes people keep coming back in the hope that the effect might be cumulative … like radiation.*

James Swartz was highly critical of the whole notion:

> *Some schools of Neo-Advaita subscribe to the notion that enlightenment can be transmitted in some subtle experiential way via the physical proximity of a master. Traditional Advaita disagrees with this view for the reason that ignorance is deeply entrenched in the aspirant's thinking and that it is only by deep reflection on the teachings that the ultimate assimilation of the knowledge is achieved. This assimilation is often called 'full' or 'complete' enlightenment. The 'transmission' fantasy fits nicely into the Neo-Advaitic conception of easy enlightenment as it does away with the need for serious sādhana. One need do nothing more than sit in the presence of a master and presto-chango!... one wakes up for good. If this were true, however, the tens of thousands who sit at the feet of enlightened masters everywhere would be enlightened.* (Ref. 349)

Vivekacūḍāmaṇi says that:

> *There are sons and others to discharge the debts of the father. However there is no one other than oneself to free one from one's own bondage.* (53)

Who but one's own self, even after the lapse of hundreds of millions of years, could destroy the bonds of ignorance, desire, action, and so on? (57)
(Ref. 383)

If knowledge could be transmitted by merely being in the presence of the teacher, we could dispense with schools and universities altogether!

Incidentally, although it is not Advaita, there is an organization that offers 'Self-realization (LOC 1000)' transmission over the internet. RASA Transmission International offer Skype or Zoom sessions via their teachers Ramaji and Ananda. Ramaji's credentials are impressive:

Ramaji was asked by the Higher Power to become a spiritual teacher in Spring, 2011. He refused because he did not want to become just another non-duality sage "trying to talk the ego to death." The Higher Power agreed to provide a powerful new way for seekers to awaken immediately. A few months later Ramaji was doing a simple spiritual prayer to heal a loved one. A huge ball of radiant white light came down. The RASA Transmission for spiritual awakening and enlightenment was born. (Ref. 552)

In case you are wondering, RASA™ stands for 'Ramaji Advaita Shaktipat Attunement.' This is explained:

"Advaita" means oneness or unity. "Shaktipat" is the direct spiritual download of this oneness or unity consciousness (LOC 1000). During the RASA, Ramaji or Ananda Devi open your Crown chakra. They then bring the Divine Light down from above your head. This Light enters the top of your head and turns your brain into Light. This Divine Light quickly and easily reprograms your brain for effortless stabilization in enlightenment.

And, instead, we choose to spend years studying books and listening to gurus. We must be mad! See Ref. 125 if you want to read more. Apparently the book also awards 'LOC scores' to many current teachers!

You Do Not Need a Guru

This is all Self, speaking to Self. No GURU is required to direct you to who you already are. (Ref. 549)

... a playful piece about finding the true spiritual teacher, the true guru, the true answers, inside of our own hearts:

I used to be a spiritual teacher.

I had to quit when I realised there was no such thing.

Or rather, everything is a spiritual teacher.
The cat. The carpet. A chair.
A tree. A mountain.
My dad with dementia.

Heartache. Joy.
My own. Yours.
The man sleeping on the pavement.
The breathtaking night sky.

It's all a teacher.
It's all a guru. (Ref. 555)

Most Neo-Advaitins will tell you that no teacher is needed for you to be what you already are ('here and now'). The fact that they will charge you more than a nominal fee to attend a satsang, in order to be told this, is beside the point. Many (most?) satsang teachers today point to this 'being in the present moment' as what matters. Being 'enlightened' is simply being present *all the time*! To be fair, one assumes that they do not mean simply being physically present, but being mentally alert with attention directed to what is 'here and now.' Traditional Advaita tells us that this is simply the prerequisite to learning about Advaita from a guru.

People who maintain that a guru is not required in order to gain enlightenment usually cite Ramana Maharshi as proof. It is accepted by all that he was enlightened and yet it was also known by those around him that he never attended classes from a sampradāya teacher. This, they say, is proof that a formal teacher is not required. Those defending traditional views usually say that he must have attained sādhana catuṣṭaya sampatti and undergone the usual process of śravaṇa-manana in a previous incarnation.

Mariana Caplan, in her book *Do You Need a Guru*, calls it 'The Ramana Maharshi Argument.' She says:

> *I have heard it well over a hundred times throughout my travels in India and work in the West. To say that we can do it because Ramana Maharshi did it is like saying we can become the President of the United States because George Bush did it. Of course it is* conceivable, *for there are no essentially greater or lesser human beings on the planet. But how realistic is it?* (Ref. 558)

Maybe this analogy is not quite so obvious these days, but you get the point! She gives another quotation from Robert Ennis to make the point very clear:

> *The chances of someone awakening without a teacher are like the chances of getting pregnant without a partner. The spiritual teacher is the partner that is necessary for spiritual birth. Not too many immaculate conceptions happen.* (Ref. 558)

Krishna Menon relates it to the ego. He says that the ego *"takes leave of you,"* and you *"visualize the truth at once"* when you listen to the spoken word of the guru, but it *"lingers on in the form of the word"* when you read the material yourself. (Ref. 13, No. 1015)

My own view is that this is putting things too strongly. Listening to talks or reading books can be an effective śravaṇa, if one is in the right frame of mind. And many traditional teachers would concede that this could be sufficient. The problem is that they have to be the *right* books — the ones that speak 'your' language and are pitched at 'your' current level of understanding. But it is very difficult to fulfil these criteria. Who would know what 'your current level of understanding' is? *You* probably wouldn't for a start! Then you run into problems of translation and use of language; using just the right metaphors to resonate with you, and so on.

You Do Need a Guru

The biggest problem with books or recorded talks is that the author or speaker is not present to answer your questions, doubts, and requests for clarification. This is the stage of manana, and most traditional teachers would agree that this stage is necessary for most seekers. If you are unable to fulfil this requirement, the only alternative is to listen to more talks or read more books, ideally by a different (but still trustworthy) teacher, who will couch the teaching in a slightly different language, thereby *effectively* giving you the manana stage.

It is important to put the concept into context and not give in to outlandish ideas, even if those ideas seem to be accepted in classical traditions. Ref. 561 gives a useful metaphor but presents it as though it is literally true. He (V. Krishnamurthy, known as 'ProfVK,' was a senior moderator in the Advaitin discussion group) likens the guru to a dream character who appears in the dream and tells you, the dreamer, that you are dreaming, so that you can wake up. He says that the jīvanmukta (someone who is not only enlightened but who has assimilated and integrated the knowledge completely, so that his or her life outlook is transformed) is someone:

> *...who is in that absolute state of awareness all the time but he can also descend to our level of the ordinary mundane worldly waking state. He therefore prods us, with all the powers that he has, to wake up from this dreamworld of ours, which we think is real.*

There is no 'absolute state of awareness.' The jñānī (realized man) is someone who has Self-knowledge — in the normal waking state. Accordingly, there is no 'descending' involved; simply communication, preferably at the level of understanding of the seeker, which is a skill that ideal teachers have. The jñānī has no 'special powers.' If he succeeds in passing on his Self-knowledge (by teaching, probably over a number of years), then we will realize that this world is mithyā. But there is no 'waking up' involved, other than metaphorically, and the world will not disappear as a result!

Śaṅkara states that a seeker needs a guru in a number of his commentaries. For example, *"Only when learnt from an accomplished Master, Self-knowledge will be fruitful"* (Chāndogya Upaniṣad 4.9.3); *"One who has a teacher understands"* (Chāndogya Upaniṣad 6.14.2) (Ref. 563). In Muṇḍaka Upaniṣad 1.2.12 commentary, he says explicitly that *"even if the brāhmaṇa himself is well versed in other śāstras he should go [to] a guru only to gain brahma jñānam, and not try to understand it independently by himself."* (Ref. 386) [A 'brāhmaṇa' was one of the four traditional Hindu castes, studying the Vedas.]

The Yoga Vāsiṣṭha is a well-known scripture that may well pre-date Śaṅkara, although he does not refer to it. It might be popular because of its many stories and elaborate dream sequences, although its philosophy is that of Yoga rather than

Advaita (the clue possibly being in the title). It is stated in this that the guru cannot actually give Self-knowledge to the seeker, only facilitate it.

> *Self-knowledge or knowledge of truth is not had by resorting to a guru (preceptor) nor by study of scripture, nor by good works: it is attained only by means of enquiry, inspired by the company of wise and holy men. One's inner light alone is the means, naught else.* (Ref. 38)

There is even a story to convey this. A miser loses a coin in the forest and spends days searching for it, thinking of all the things he might do with it to gain more. In the end, he finds a precious stone instead and returns home happy. The miserliness and searching were the cause of finding the stone, even though he wasn't looking for that. Similarly, says Vāsiṣṭha, the guru does not give the seeker Self-knowledge but his instruction enables the seeker to find the Self.

I would disagree with this explanation in the way that it is represented by the story. What happens is that the guru explains what is told by the scriptures and answers doubts about it. The seeker then realizes that it is in fact true. He is not discovering something different from what he has been told by the guru. This is an example of what was explained under 'The Truth' in the section on 'The Content' above. And it carries another warning — when you have doubts about what you are told by a modern teacher, you cannot simply go to any scripture to see if it confirms what you have been told. The scripture (or at least its modern translator or commentator) may also be wrong!

Michael James devotes several paragraphs in his book on *Ramana's Forty Verses* to explaining the correct mechanism for learning Advaita but says that "*this is a very crude and superficial understanding both of the meaning of the term guru and of the real role of guru."* He claims that the established (over the past couple of thousand years) procedure laid down by the scriptures and elucidated by Śaṅkara is an invalid one and that his understanding of Ramana's teaching is a *"much deeper and more refined understanding about the real nature and role of guru."* I'm afraid that I cannot believe that Ramana himself ever claimed this and it cannot be true.

If it is written anywhere that he really did say that *"guru is not a person but the eternal reality that always exists and shines in our heart as our own being, 'I am,'"* I suggest that this was a mistranslation or misunderstanding. The respect and reverence that a seeker may hold for a teacher may indeed prompt acknowledgement of that teacher's absolute nature, which is also our own nature. But, from a vyāvahārika perspective, there is still a guru-jīva imparting knowledge to a seeker-jīva. The seeker is lacking the knowledge that would precipitate enlightenment until the teacher has conveyed it.

Mark McCloskey warns:

> *Do not follow anyone who says that he or she has the answer, the whole truth. The truth is not contained in any person, religion or ideology. The truth is freedom itself, and it is within you already. Perhaps the teachers, gurus, priests, rabbis, lamas and others in the world may have a glimmer of truth to share (and this is a very, very small minority of them) and if they are sincere and are compassionate, you will resonate with them.* (Ref. 550)

Swami Paramarthananda gave a brilliant short lecture summarizing the need for a guru. This is available for download (Ref. 556). Any specialized worldly knowledge requires considerable study before we can begin to understand. How much more then must be the case regarding an appreciation of reality itself. There will always be room for doubt and error when a finite mind attempts to grasp the infinite. We may easily overlook some aspect, or be misled by others, when our knowledge is limited. We need the understanding of those who have gone before to ease this endeavor. He says:

> *Therefore, Guru is important, Shastram is very important, Teaching is very very important and Learning is very very very important. And if these come together, a person will get Self Knowledge and Liberation.* (Ref. 556)

Finding a Guru

> *When the blind lead the blind, none of the followers can see that the leader himself carries a white cane.*
> David Carse (Ref. 313)

Clearly, once you have accepted that you should ideally have a guru, you want to ensure that you find someone who both knows the truth and is able to convey this to others. Unfortunately, this is easier said than done. James Swartz gives some mature and informed advice:

> *Seekers should view all teachers, gurus, meditation masters and their teachings unsentimentally. Claims of spiritual attainment should be taken with a grain of salt. The more a teacher self-promotes, the longer the beard, the more extravagant the name, the slower the speech, the more grandiose the claims of special powers, the more your suspicions should be aroused. Suspending your critical faculties, though passing for devotion in certain circles, is dangerous. Enlightenment does not need advertisement. When you have assimilated life's lessons and sincerely long for liberation, the self will manifest a respectable purified teacher.* (Ref. 416)

Not sure I agree with the last sentence, even though it is said in one of the scriptures, but the rest is worth taking to heart!

If you ask yourself the question: which came first, the seeker or the guru, you will realize that the answer has to be 'the seeker.' If a could-be teacher is worthy of that role, then obviously he or she must already be qualified. Being qualified, they know that they are Brahman and therefore already perfect and complete. They do not want anything, so they are certainly not looking for would-be disciples! They are simply 'inhabiting,' as it were, this body-mind form until it fulfils its prārabdha karma and 'dies.' Despite, all this, their ability to perform the role of teacher should already have been established by previous seekers.

On those grounds alone, one might argue that any 'teacher' who is advertising their services cannot be fully qualified. But, if they do not live in India, it is unlikely that they would be able to survive by begging, so being paid sufficient monies to pay for basic accommodation and food is not unreasonable. However, it does seem that most Western teachers hosting satsang meetings request considerably more than this! Perhaps, if someone requested only a small payment, potential followers would conclude that they couldn't be any good...

You might well think that the most popular teacher is the one you should follow. For this, you should look who has sold the most books or has the most followers on Facebook, or whatever social media is currently in vogue. Hopefully, however, you do *not* think like this! You have to realize that the people who make a teacher popular are mostly not yet enlightened and are swayed by charisma and ability to speak in an authoritative and entertaining manner. Osho, for example had a massive repertoire of amusing jokes and stories and we know how popular he was!

Jed McKenna commented: *"Popularity among the soundly asleep may not be the best criterion by which to judge a method for waking up."* (Ref. 562) He claims that you *do* need a guru because, although what is said in any given book *may* be true, you will not be sure until you yourself are enlightened (by which time you will have no need for the book). And there is no real arguing with that.

Exercising common sense is usually all that is needed. Avoid teachers who appear to head 'cults'; who exhibit arrogance rather than humility; who answer questions in such a way as to entertain the audience rather than allay your concerns and help your understanding to progress. Watch and speak to those who follow that teacher in order to gauge their attitudes and purpose. Do not commit time and effort until you are convinced.

The Vivekacūḍāmaṇi (around verse 34) indicates the characteristics that one should look for in a guru:

> *The guru is well-versed in the Vedas; he is sinless; he is not smitten by desire; he is a knower of Brahman; he is super-eminent; withdrawing himself into Brahman, he is ever at peace; he is like a smoldering fire unfed by fuel.* (Ref. 564)

The qualities that should be cultivated by the seeker are given by Kṛṣṇa in the Bhagavad Gītā 13.7–11:

> *Humility, absence of ostentation, non-injury, patience, uprightness, adoration of the preceptor, purity, steadfastness and self-control. Indifference to the objects of the sense, absence of egotism, the awareness of the evil of birth, death, old age, sickness and pain. Non-attachment, absence of excessive clinging to son, wife, home and the like and a constant equal-mindedness to all desirable and undesirable happenings. Unswerving devotion directed to Me (God) with whole-hearted discipline, resort to solitary places and dislike to a crowd of people. Constant contemplation on the knowledge pertaining to the Self and insight into the knowledge of Reality.* (Ref. 565)

It is lists such as this that make one appreciate the statements in the scriptures to the effect that enlightenment is very rare amongst men! But one should also note that these qualities are to be 'cultivated' and that it is not necessarily expected that a seeker will already have them! One might also deduce that the teacher must have had (and still have) them in order to have become enlightened him or herself!

One certain fact is that anyone who is enlightened will have a seriously attenuated ego. Consequently, if someone is presenting themselves as a teacher, and claiming to be enlightened, yet also exhibiting egotistical behavior, you may confidently shun their services! Note that even the most enlightened teacher will still *have* an ego. Without one, they would be unable to function in the world! But it should not advertise itself!

Francis Lucille expresses simply the nature of a guru:

> *A real teacher doesn't take himself for a teacher, he doesn't claim to be different from his student, he doesn't try to manipulate him. He leaves him with a feeling of enhanced freedom, of increased autonomy. He is not a father or mother figure, nor does he try to convert the student. His behavior is a perfect example of devotion to the truth and of extreme humility.* (Ref. 8)

A genuine teacher is never going to ridicule or humiliate you. He knows that he is Brahman; he knows that you are Brahman; there is no 'need' for him to teach at all. Therefore, any true teacher, by the very fact of playing the role of teacher, must be compassionate.

> *Therefore, having properly approached a teacher who is an ocean of compassion and the best among the knowers of Brahman, inquiry into the truth of oneself is to be done by one who wants to know the truth.*
>
> Vivekacūḍāmaṇi 15 (Ref. 58)

Dead Gurus

Many seekers will identify Ramana Maharshi or Nisargadatta as their guru. What they really mean is that they have been inspired by a book that they have read (which will be a translation of talks, or question and answer dialogues). The problem with dead gurus is similar to that of trying to gain enlightenment from reading books – they are unable to answer your questions in order to clear your doubts. In fact, it is really the *same* problem, because you have to read books in order to learn what they said. And you are then into the other problems already identified under 'General Warnings' above. What is true, however, is that a dead guru is preferable to a false guru! Śaṅkara is the best dead guru of all because, not only was he the effective source of most of the explanations but also he has been studied and 'explained' by some of the most astute Advaitins that have lived over the past 1200 years. So, although he can no longer answer your questions, it is likely that one of his commentators will have done so!

Crazy Mystics

Some seekers who are totally new to the genre may have picked up the idea that they have to go out into the world (almost certainly India) and track down a guru who will accept them as a disciple. They imagine that this is a one-to-one relationship, in which they will 'serve' the guru, possibly for years, and the guru will in exchange 'bestow grace' and transmit enlightenment to them. It will be hard, and entail many sacrifices, but the rewards are infinite. (Sarcasm showing again, I'm afraid!)

Needless to say, perhaps, such a path would be extremely risky. A seeker would have to be very, very sure of the merits of the guru. Not least that they were actually qualified to teach but also that their morals and behavior were beyond reproach. 'Taking advantage' in such a situation would be far too easy for the guru. It seems very likely that a teacher who only took one or two students for years at a time would be unlikely to be very experienced in this role! The "perils and rewards" of this mode of seeking are described at length in Ref. 568, for those who are interested.

Note that I am not saying that this 'path' does not exist. It clearly has in the past and maybe still does to some extent. But this book only addresses the options available to the seeker in Advaita, because that is the only one with which I am familiar. I would earnestly advise anyone considering the 'Crazy Wisdom' route to think again, and again, and again ... until the idea is dropped!

You Also Need Scriptures

Śaṅkara is very clear about the need for both a guru *and* the scriptures:

> *'It is to be realized through the mind alone, (following the instruction of the teacher)' (Bṛhadāraṇyaka Upaniṣad 4.4.19). The mind that is purified by the instructions of the scriptures and the teacher, control of the body and organs, etc. becomes the instrument for realizing the Self.* (Ref. 396)

That quotation is from his Bhagavad Gītā commentary 2.21 but William Cenkner says that:

> *In the Gītā bhāṣya, he [i.e. Śaṅkara] says that the Self is seen when one is equipped with teachings of the scripture and the teacher. In commentaries on the Upaniṣads he consistently links the two, observing that the mind "is purified by the teacher and the scripture" and "those alone who follow both scripture and teachers transcend ignorance."* (Ref. 560)

And, in a footnote, he lists numerous places where Śaṅkara makes statements such as those.

Clearly, if all that was needed in order to gain enlightenment was to use the pramāṇas of perception and inference, the seeker would not need the help of either a guru or scriptures. He could do it all himself, or maybe with some help from science, since those are the sources of knowledge that it uses. In fact, the pramāṇa of śabda, testimony, is the one that matters. This relates to knowledge arising from spoken or written words, especially (in this context) of the qualified guru or scriptures. **Śaṅkara maintains that this is the *only* source for knowledge of reality and hence for gaining mokṣa.**

Consequently, it could be argued that any teacher who attempts to enlighten seekers without any reference to, or use of, the knowledge and prakriyās contained in the scriptures is doomed to fail. Whilst it is theoretically possible for someone to possess this knowledge and those skills without ever having utilized scriptures to derive them, they would then be teaching purely on their own cognizance. And why should a seeker accept that?

Traditional teaching requires one to attend talks unfolding scriptural texts regularly for many years. Gradually one comes to appreciate the truth about what is being explained and finally full realization can dawn. Even then, one is most likely to have to revisit that teaching until it is incontrovertible and one 'becomes' a jīvanmukta. Reading just a 'few relevant texts' and meditating on the Self is not going to replace this extensive teaching and give us Self-knowledge.

Saṃpradāya

The word literally means 'bestower' or 'presenter.' It refers to the long-established tradition whereby a teacher passed on all of his knowledge, as well as the means of presenting this to a seeker, to his disciple(s), who usually lived with him at an āshrama, which the dictionary defines as 'a hermitage; the abode of ascetics.'

The Upaniṣads used to be transmitted by word of mouth prior to any written record. Hence the fact that they were called 'śruti,' meaning 'that which is heard.' They were learned by heart and chanted as a form of ritual practice to ensure that they were correctly passed down from guru to disciple. When it came to texts such as the Brahmasūtra, an additional ploy was to make the sūtras as short as possible. This had the benefit of making them easier to remember but the disadvantage of making them more difficult to understand. Hence the need for a teacher who fully understands them because they were completely explained by his guru (and the chain of teachers stretching back into history).

The other ploy used by those teachers writing down their knowledge for posterity was to write in verse form. Words following one of the widely recognized metrical formats were obviously going to be easier to remember than long prose explanations. Unfortunately, this did mean that a writer would often have to choose a word that fitted the meter, even if it was not ideal from an explanatory point of view. This was not a problem as long as the sampradāya continued, because each successive teacher would have learned the explanation (and better words) from his teacher. Of course, as soon as the sampradāya is broken, and a teacher has to provide his or her own explanation of a verse that is now not so clear ... the Chinese whispers begin!

Thus, it is easily seen that, if your prospective teacher belongs to a recognized sampradāya, you can be fairly sure that their teaching will be reliable. This is because it will be the same teaching that has been proven to be reliable for hundreds, if not thousands of years. It will not be based upon the 'revelatory, earth-shattering experience I had when taking LSD for the first time,' nor upon the three or four books I happened to read based upon something someone once told me on Twitter.

Advaita Resources

General Points

Note that I have not put these into an appendix, as I did in *Back to the Truth,* since the information could be considered to be the main part of the book. I have tried to include representative quotations from each teacher so that the reader may assess their 'relevance' from the perspective of Advaita, based upon the information and warnings that have been provided elsewhere in the book. (Note that some quotations may have appeared earlier in the context of the discussions.)

In particular, I am neither recommending, nor condemning, particular teachers. If a seeker finds their teaching to be helpful, then clearly I am in no position to deny that. What I do indicate, however, is whether or not what they say appears to be in accord with Advaita. Also, I confess, I do occasionally put a '?' or '!' after an entry [in square brackets]. The reason should be apparent but, in general, it would suggest that I either do not understand what a quotation means or do not believe it!

Obviously, I have not read everything presented at each website, or read the published books of all teachers. I will probably be accused of picking unrepresentative quotations — and this may well be true. However, the quotation *was there,* and I provide the reference so that you can check (or read more). Seekers looking at these sites are also likely to come across them. It is incumbent upon those who advertise themselves as teachers of Advaita to ensure that what they teach makes sense in the context of Advaita.

Before perusing this list, it is important that I first of all list a number of general observations and warnings that the reader should bear in mind.

Social Media

Some teacher/writers have now moved to social media sites and I confess that I still maintain my absence from these fora on the grounds of the increasingly negative aspects*. Accordingly, I am unable to report on any material that is *only* available there. Also, I noted that some Facebook sites were 'by invitation only.' Maybe the reason for this is to prevent disruption by people who only want to ridicule the teaching. But, if the teaching is authentic, reading should be open to anyone. I can't help cynically wondering if some sort of 'subscription' is involved.

(* I recommend Ref. 752 as an enjoyable dystopian SF book to read, which does a '1984 style' warning of how social media might develop. There is also a film based on this, although films never seem as good as the book, if you have read that first.)

Old versus New Websites

Many sites, to which I provided links from my own site over 15 years ago, are still available but have not had any new posts for over 5–10+ years. It almost seems as though there was a peak of interest around 2010, in the same way that TM and meditation had a surge of interest around 1970 with hippies and Maharishi Mahesh Yogi. Now there are just a few key figures apparently still very active. Are these the ones who proved to be the best teachers, or are they the ones who are most charismatic, the best at marketing or simply unable to make any money elsewhere?

This is not (just) cynicism! When a new seeker looks around to find a teacher, he or she is almost certainly going to rely on Google and will therefore find the most popular websites, which are also likely to be the ones which are the most attractively presented. Once a seeker attends a satsang, speaking to other attendees will elicit details about which teachers were found to be the most 'impressive.' (They probably want to know about the quality of teaching but maybe the answers that they get are based more upon the appeal of the teacher.)

Looking through currently active websites, blogs, conferences etc., it certainly appears that the past 10–15 years has seen a deterioration in the quality of material available to seekers. In the last decade of the twentieth century and the first decade of the 21st, it seemed as though there was much striving to 'import' (and 'impart') the wisdom of the Indian teaching of Vedanta and 'translate' to a Western mindset. Of course, this is how I saw it at the time, since I was a part of it.

But interest now seems to have declined. Discussions seem more restricted to those who were never affected by the rise of Neo-Advaita and the surge in interest in the West. One cannot help thinking that many of the teachers who sprang up were attracted by the 'fame and fortune' aspect rather than an unselfish wish to transmit their assumed knowledge. The demise of some is no doubt the result of the discovery that they did not have much of value to teach after all. (Note that one cannot automatically *assume* that this is the case. One example was John Wheeler, who now has no presence on the internet. But I know from my own discussions with him, and from his published books, that he was both knowledgeable and sincere.)

One might think that a good indicator of the authenticity of a teacher may be how long a website has been active (providing that it is still active). If a teacher was giving satsangs 10 years ago and is still doing so, then it suggests that what they are saying has value. Of course, this attitude would penalize those who have just started teaching – but then maybe this is as it should be. Any teacher should be obliged to prove his or her worth over a reasonable period of time. Nevertheless, my own finding is that one cannot rely upon this. I suggest that an entertaining and charismatic speaker can trump a knowledgeable one and soon put them out of business! And there certainly seem to be some teachers around who are still very successfully *not* teaching Advaita.

The opportunity for discussing teachers with other satsang attendees has obviously diminished. Many sessions are now conducted one-on-one by Skype etc. Zoom sessions with numerous people are also not conducive to informal conversations amongst seekers. But I suppose that the ubiquity of the various social media sites ensures that word *does* get around, probably much faster than it used to do! But perhaps, knowing that their comments are likely to be read by many others (including the teachers themselves), what someone says may be either less revealing or more sensational than was actually merited.

And, of course, all that I have said above should be tempered (or magnified) by the fact, already admitted, that I have no personal presence on Facebook, Twitter, Instagram, or whatever forum or name is in vogue by the time you read this! (The one exception to this is 500px, where I post my photos. But no discussion ever takes place there! And, despite the fact that all my photos are watermarked 'Advaita Vision,' I have still to receive a single enquiry!)

General Warnings

There are quite a few of these. When searching the internet to look for a teacher or organization, or looking for a good book in a 'spiritual' bookstore, it is important to be aware of these pitfalls, which may well be deliberately positioned to catch you out!

The teachers listed below are the ones that I found to have what appear to be active listings on the internet, although I have also mentioned those who may have been significant, when I listed them in *Back to the Truth*. They are mostly satsang teachers and/or ones offering one-to-one consultations via telephone or Skype etc.

It should not be concluded that those teachers whose names are familiar, who have sold lots of books or who have professional websites are the ones to follow. As Mariana Caplan points out:

> *If we closely examine many of today's most popular teachers, we will find that in many cases their popularity is less a function of their realization, and more a result of highly effective strategic marketing.* (Ref. 568)

As noted above, I almost called this book 'Self-seeking in Modern Advaita.' This play on words highlights two important points:

- a perennial problem regarding many modern teachers.
- the danger of insufficient clarity and unambiguity in the words that we use.

If you search on the internet for spiritual, or non-dual teachers, you will find many who seem to be taking advantage of the fact that most seekers are really looking to 'improve' their lives; to be happy, be less affected by the usual upsets, personal and worldly. Consequently, such teachers advertise themselves as people able to provide these seekers with the answers for which they are looking. As a result, if you are looking for modern satsang teachers who are actually teaching Advaita, you are quite likely to be disappointed by them.

Having spent considerable time, attempting to generate a list of all current 'non-duality' teachers, I estimate that far less than 10% of those you will find actually teach Advaita. Maybe another 10% teach non-duality from some other source, but the majority do seem simply to be 'self-seeking,' aiming to make as much money from the gullible seeker as they can, without giving much at all in return.

Éric Baret claims that Advaita is too difficult for ordinary people anyway, who should rather study Tantra:

> *Jean Klein had two teachings — he was teaching advaita vedanta for the very bright people, and tantra for the very stupid ones. So, advaita is an elitist teaching which is only proper for people with the highest level of mental discrimination, who are immensely purified. That means, who have no link with emotional life.* (Ref. 570)

There is some truth in this. Traditional Advaita does acknowledge the value of bhakti yoga and karma yoga for those who are not mentally prepared for listening to the teaching. And it is certainly true that only jñāna yoga can give the Self-knowledge which equates to enlightenment. But all of this is not the subject matter of this book.

Therapists

My perusal of the internet was primarily to try to discover the currently active 'Western Advaita Teachers.' It was not to criticize or condemn any 'Spiritual Teachers' or 'Therapists.' It may well be that some of these are extremely good at helping those with 'life problems' who wish to live a 'happier life' — I have no way of knowing (although some sites do contain what are claimed to be personal commendation from those who have been treated). But, if such a one makes statements implying that they are teaching Advaita when they are not, then genuine seekers should be aware of this so that they can avoid misleading information and maybe nugatory expenditure! And — as I keep repeating in different ways — **improving the quality of your life has nothing to do with Non-duality!**

Even teachers who are apparently aiming actually to teach some principles of Advaita seem to recognize that most people who attend satsangs will be doing so in order to address personal 'life' problems. Mooji says:

> *If the world, as it is ordinarily perceived and experienced inside the human mind and ego, was indeed real, then one would be pressed to declare: 'Oh my God, we are really in deep shit.' Luckily for us the shit is only inside our heads and can be easily flushed out by satsang.* (Ref. 401)

Many teachers seem to have begun their careers in an inauspicious way, whether in prison, alcoholism or taking drugs (or a combination of these). It is interesting to note that the state of Oregon is now actually licensing the use of psilocybin for treatment of psychological issues:

> *The Oregon Health Authority announced last week* (May '23) *that it has issued the first license for a psilocybin treatment center, opening access to the promising mental health therapy to adult patients across the state. The psilocybin service center license was issued to EPIC Healing Eugene under the regulatory framework created by Measure 109, a 2020 ballot measure to legalize psilocybin therapy that passed with nearly 56% of the vote.* (Ref. 538)

The intention is that such treatment will not need to be prescribed by a doctor. Anyone will be able to undergo a session, providing that they have a 'preparatory session with a licensed facilitator' and that the drug is taken at a licensed 'service center.'

It does not take much imagination or cynicism to predict that this will eventually be linked with 'non-dualism' and promoted as promising or even guaranteeing an 'enlightenment experience'! Hopefully, anyone tempted to do that will read this book first.

Standard of Website Material

I have to say that, although I might have anticipated it, I was extremely disappointed with the general 'standard' of the material that I found. Scarcely any 'teachers' gave any indication that what they were teaching was Advaita. Even the word 'Advaita' was hardly used by anyone. Instead, 'non-duality' seemed to be favored, although the context in which this word appeared was often clearly *not* non-dual.

This means that someone who openly claims themselves as being 'awakened,' in order to promote their 'teacher' status on their website for example, is probably more interested in 'selling tickets' than in helping a seeker to gain Self-knowledge. A genuine teacher may actually need some financial support for basic necessities but will never solicit money to enable a luxurious lifestyle.

I also got the impression several times that some who now promote themselves as teachers have very little background. One admitted only attending a 3 or 4-day residential twice (and not even completing the first one). But apparently that was sufficient to 'tip the balance' and this person now 'teaches' others. It cannot be emphasized enough that, even if a person could be enlightened after such a short exposure to the teaching, that would not qualify them to teach.

Timothy Conway scathingly exposes how giving satsangs does not mean the teacher is actually qualified to do so:

> *The truth is that 'giving satsang' in the way many people do it today is the easiest thing in the world! Once one has learned some of the Absolute-truth rap (easily available after reading just a few books or articles), a certain basic peacefulness and ease in social settings, and, last but not least, the dialectical questioning 'maneuvers' (e.g., "Who is asking the question?" "Who wants enlightenment?" "Have you traced that thought/feeling back to its source?" "What would you be if you gave up that belief?" etc. etc.) one could 'give satsang' easily, endlessly, while half-asleep. It all flows out quite effortlessly from the conditioning one sets up in the mind.* (Ref. 522)

In addition to being enlightened, one has to be familiar with the entirety of the traditional teaching, with all of its metaphors and intermediate steps, in order to be able to pass on this understanding to less able seekers.

It was noted above that many 'teachers' admit to varying degrees of dissolute youth. There is at least one who was an alcoholic, in prison and in an asylum, now charging lots of money for the knowledge which was presumably gained as a result. I suppose the idea is that such a lifestyle brings you down to the bottom, at which point you really start questioning what it is all about and how you should try to recover a life. I can see that this could be seen as a positive point. It is certainly true that one does not acquire mumukṣutva (the desire for enlightenment, overriding all other desires) until one has become really dissatisfied with life! Of course, this should not be seen as a reason to take such a path!

> *The greatest enemy of knowledge is not ignorance; it is the illusion of knowledge.*
> Stephen Hawking

Cynical it may be, but my impression was that many people are taking advantage of the ignorance of would-be seekers who are dissatisfied with their lives and the state of the world and are looking for a 'point-of-view' that will enable them to inculcate a more optimistic outlook. That is, many 'seekers' would not even call themselves that. They know nothing about Advaita or any other non-dual approach so will be unable to spot an equivalent lack in a supposed teacher.

Magazines

In the topic 'What Is Enlightenment?' above, I referred to the magazine of that name which was published quarterly from 1992 to 2008. One presumes that it was not running at a loss!

And that prompts another warning: beware of magazines; *any* magazines, whether relating to 'spirituality,' 'mysticism,' 'yoga,' etc., if they purport to explain to you about non-duality or enlightenment. Magazines have to make a profit if they are to survive. So people have to buy them. Consequently, they are going to tell readers what they *want* to hear, not what they *need* to hear! (More cynicism of course, but am I wrong?)

Books

I don't know about you but, when I am buying products on Amazon, I always look at the number and quality of reviews. If lots of people, who appear genuine, give 5* reviews and make positive statements, then I am usually persuaded to buy it in preference to other, similar products. After all, I usually have nothing else to go on.

I also use this technique when buying fiction books (although I usually scan through all the Kindle books that are on special offer before beginning the review analysis). Doing this has enabled me to discover some excellent authors that I would otherwise probably not have found.

When it comes to Advaita books, such a method is usually not possible. So few people buy books on Advaita that there are virtually no reviews at all, except maybe one or two from the author's friends! 'Spiritual' books in general are not so constrained, because lots of people who don't know anything about non-duality, but know that they would like to improve their lives, buy them. So, you might think that following this procedure before choosing a spiritual book would be a good idea.

Unfortunately, I now know that some publishers are asking those authors who send out newsletters, or who have mailing lists of correspondents, specifically to ask these recipients to read advance material from forthcoming books and to post reviews! Not only this, but they even ask that these reviews should be posted within a specific time frame. That, of course, makes it likely that the book will be pushed into the 'Best Seller' list (maybe even before the printed book becomes generally available)!

Accordingly, it is becoming increasingly likely that any search will be strongly pointed to a book whose value is debatable. Certainly, you can no longer rely upon reported 'popularity.' There is no indication that bad reviews will be filtered out (maybe that will come next, aided by AI?) but it means you need to be even more vigilant in reading reviews to convince yourself that a good review is genuine and not 'incentivized' by whatever means!

Organizations

I realized during the process of searching for current teachers that some of these may promote themselves by establishing an 'organization' with a suitably 'enlightened' sounding name. One assumes they think that this will bestow an aura of greater authenticity, or enable them to reach new seekers more easily than would a 'normal' sounding surname, even if it has a 'Swami' in front of it or a '-ji' following it. Again, I don't wish to single out any specific example, but those looking to find a teacher should be aware of such potential ploys.

Another point worth noting is that an organization may decide to pitch some of their talks, not to the individual seeker searching for truth, but to commercial organizations wanting to motivate their management (and thereby, one presumes, to increase their profitability). They may justify this on the grounds that they are widening their audience and intending to act as a trigger for potential seekers, rather than simply a 'school' for those already committed. But I cannot help feeling that this is a corruption of the pure principles of sampradaya teaching.

I already gave an example of this at the beginning of the book. Another I have just come across is the book *Ancient Wisdom for Modern Management* (Ref. 639). This was published nearly 20 years ago and is from the publishing arm of Sri Sharada Peetham at Sringeri.

A much more recent example is that the Chinmaya Mission has begun a new Home Study Course, called 'Make It Happen':

> *Make It Happen™ is filled with powerful ideas, eternal principles and self-empowerment exercises specifically designed to guide one through the unfoldment of one's inner personality. This dynamic programme takes one on a journey of self-discovery, helping to unravel the question of life's true calling and providing one with highly effective tools to Make It Happen™. Committing to the Course will result in a powerful change in one's life and will help discover success in the outside world as well as fulfilment within.* (Ref. 640)

Not to be left out, it seems that Arsha Vidya may even be venturing into this territory. The emailed notification received April '24 announced:

> *Talk on 'FREEDOM IN ACTION' by Brahmacāri Pratyagātma Chaitanya* [who studied with Swami Dayananda]. *We all can be more relaxed while pursuing our goals-within the ever changing dynamics of people, situations, and means. Being relaxed might involve some clarity regarding our ends, and about maintaining some passion within the changing means. We will see what is that clarity you can gain. And what is that passion you can keep up-to be more relaxed throughout the journey.* (Ref. 757)

Although not really clear what this talk will be about, it certainly seems to be more about life and its challenges than about seeking enlightenment.

Language

Many of today's teachers seem to use some of the language of Advaita but lack any clear indication that they understand Advaita. Favorites are words such as 'awakening,' 'silence,' 'heart,' 'attention,' 'spiritual,' 'love' and, of course, 'non-dual.' It is almost as though they are aiming somewhere between the 'religious-oriented' help that a local church might give and a psychotherapist, which no one would want to admit to needing. But it seems unlikely that any actually have the skills of either of those practitioners and are simply relying upon their own similar experiences.

Many give an impression that they may have opened a book on Advaita and picked out some key phrases. They then put these together in a mystical, new-agey manner in a sentence that is structurally correct but entirely meaningless.

Beware, for example, of any site or book that uses the word ***'love'*** liberally. This is a word that is rarely encountered in any Advaita teaching. Teachers who give prominence to considerations such as 'suffering,' and how to 'improve' your life in any way, are unlikely to be speaking about Advaita. Rather they are addressing the factors that will have brought you to look in this direction and concentrating on those. This is not how Advaita operates. The teaching is not at all interested in your particular human condition; it is to bring you to the realization that all of that is irrelevant. All of it is mithyā.

Language is always a problem. I am almost exclusively including sites in English, as I am not proficient in any other language. I have used Google to translate a few German and Dutch sites.

I have written about the problems surrounding translation (of those teachers who spoke in other languages) and I have mentioned the problem of some Sanskrit terms used in Advaita having no simple English equivalent (e.g., mithyā discussed above). There is another problem with some writers. They attempt to circumvent or avoid these problems by writing in poetry (or by using just a few words and splitting each sentence over several lines in a seemingly arbitrary way so that it appears to be poetry). However, I have to say that I see it as avoiding the effort to use logical, well-written English properly to explain an idea. I freely confess that I am not a poetry-lover but it often seems that material purporting to be poetry is no such thing.

This creates its own problems. Principally, to my mind, it leaves it up to the reader how to understand what has been written. Maybe it forces them to think more deeply about what has been written and thereby come to an understanding of a concept which cannot adequately be described. At least, that may be the intention of the writer.

The (buzz)word ***'Presence'*** has been discussed above. It also appears that the word ***'non-dual'*** is being used in a way that ignores its literal meaning and instead uses it simply as an emotionally positive word, engendering happiness rather than misery. The subtitle of Ref. 506, for example, is *A Nondual & Loving Approach for Healing Violence Inside & Out*, and one of the website reviews states: *"The path to Love has never been more clear: read; absorb; transform; freedom."*

Ref. 507 offers *"Mindful-Nondual Therapy is a holistic approach to healing and awakening that integrates mindful and nondual principles with cognitive therapy."* However effectively a therapist might treat a patient, one thing that the treatment cannot be is 'nondual'!

Another example is Ref. 534. This is apparently a huge organization, which claims connection with Osho (which I do not contest). It lists dozens of 'facilitators' who specialize in one or more of: OSHO Active Meditations, OSHO Meditative Therapies, OSHO Mystic Rose, OSHO No-Mind, OSHO Awareness Intensive, OSHO Born Again, OSHO Therapist Training, OSHO Breath Training, OSHO Pulsation Training, OSHO Core Integration Training for Work with Deep Spinal

Tissue, Advanced Kinesiology, OSHO Tibetan Pulsing Healing, Hypnosis, yoga, meditation, dance therapy, sound healing, Kundalini Yoga, Chakra Dance etc. etc. There is even OSHO Reminding Yourself of the Forgotten Language of Talking to Your BodyMind! (I kid you not!) The practitioner of this last art is called Turiya, so you know you are in safe hands.

I wouldn't dream of suggesting that this is all nonsense. After all, the home page of the site explains that it is all *"Based on Osho's profound insights into the human condition, and his scientifically developed methodologies and meditative techniques."* But clearly it has nothing to do with Advaita.

Call me pedantic (many have), but I continue to be so to avoid the confusion that may otherwise ensue! Another example I often quote is kārikā, which refers to a 'concise statement in verse' and is usually associated with the extensive and very important commentary written on the Māṇḍūkya Upaniṣad by Gauḍapāda. There is also a word 'karika,' which means an 'elephant' and a word 'kāraka,' which relates to actions and instrumental causes. So it *is* important to be accurate!

Maybe the most frequently encountered word in the entire spectrum of such teaching is ***'spiritual.'*** At the beginning of this book, I pointed out that it was advisable first of all to ask yourself whether you had any psychological issues that should be addressed before embarking on any path of 'seeking.' And I referenced the book by Mariana Caplan (Ref. 590) as being excellent for clarifying all such issues.

She has vast experience of the various 'paths,' having sampled many herself and met, or even interviewed, many well-known teachers, all with her ongoing background of a PhD in Psychology. She may be the most knowledgeable person about different methodologies – Yoga, Tantra, Zen, Shamanism etc. – without, however, having specialized in any one.

In particular, that book is of no value for finding out about Advaita and, it has to be said that it does not seem to correlate in any way with the aim of Advaita, namely to gain Self-knowledge. Instead, it speaks at length about 'spiritual' things.

What does this word even mean? Ref. 590 uses the term frequently. In general, many of the usages simply refer to the 'path' of a seeker. Thus there are: *spiritual possibilities and potential; spiritual life and fulfillment; spiritual standpoint; spiritual development and maturity,* leading to *spiritual illumination, spiritual emergence* and *spiritual wisdom.* Also, a term such as *'spiritually transmitted disease'* is a useful way of explaining the misdirection of groups that turn into cults. And *'spiritual shopping'* and *'spiritualized ego'* are self-explanatory.

Naturally, there are *spiritual teachers* or *practitioners of spirituality* and perhaps even a *spiritual community.* But the word often seems to be a 'catch-all' adjective to refer to ethereal, intangible and not-really-explicable, 'good' stuff, as opposed to boring and bad 'material' stuff. And there is clearly the potential for the good things to turn bad, when people don't follow the rules. Then you can get *spiritual bypassing* and *spiritual scandals.* But what about *psychospiritual transformation; spiritual psychology; spiritual codependency; spiritual awareness?*

There are some 'explanations.' For example: *"Spirituality ... helps us discover the nature of mind itself — what Hindu and Buddhist traditions refer to as nonduality." And "As we engage a process of physio-psycho-spiritual integration, we become increasingly sensitive to more subtle levels of energy, both within ourselves and in the world that surrounds us."*

But I would have to use a somewhat pejorative term to talk about 'explanations' of this type: 'psychobabble.' In fact, so does the Chambers Dictionary, as I just discovered. It defines this word as *"Needless, meaningless or mindless use of jargon generally, eg by those involved in some of the modern spiritual and therapeutic movements or organizations."*

Incidentally, Chambers defines 'spiritual' as:

1. *Of, of the nature of, relating to, spirit, a spirit, spirits, the mind, the higher faculties, the soul*
2. *Highly refined in thought and feeling, habitually or naturally looking to things of the spirit*
3. *Incorporeal*
4. *Ecclesiastical, religious*
5. *Witty, clever, as a Gallicism*

I guess the first definition is the one mostly intended, although the word on its own still does not provide any explanation – what is the 'soul' or the 'higher faculties'? Clearly there is no inkling here of 'I am Brahman'!

Also, even the word 'non-dual' finds itself in some incongruous sentences. How about *'embodied non-duality,' 'non-dual psychology,'* and of course *'non-dual spirituality'*?

Simply, when searching for worthwhile teachers and writers, you must be ruthless in only selecting those who use unambiguous and reasonable language that is actually comprehensible – even when they are talking about 'spiritual' matters, and especially when talking about 'non-duality'!

Typical Example

Self-realization is the final understanding that who you really are is the awareness that is here in this very moment. You don't have to do anything because there is nothing that you could do to bring it about – it is already here! It is not something you can 'practice'; not something you can 'learn'. No one can 'explain' it to you or 'give' it to you. Simply stop 'trying' and 'doing'! Stop 'looking,' whether in books or on the internet. You don't have to 'look' anywhere; just recognize that it is you yourself, here and now, ever and always.

Listen to me repeat this sort of thing for an hour or two, hand over $150 and come back again next month.

This is not a quotation from any of the teachers listed below. But in my search through contemporary websites, I did come across many similar expressions. Rather than reproducing any of them here, and risking indignation from seekers or teachers, I wrote one myself. You can write one, too, just as good! The point is that this sort of communication, irrespective of its truth or falsehood, does nothing to convey Self-knowledge and hence cannot give a seeker enlightenment. It is far cheaper to buy a good book (like this one!!).

Teachers

Before I jump into the actual list that I compiled from my searches, I need to make some more general points and also introduce the major 'historical' teachers, since these are the ones that today's teachers will usually refer to as their inspiration or effective 'guru.'

Traditional Teachers

I have almost completely excluded traditional teachers from this list. I define a 'traditional teacher' as one who:

a. Belongs to a recognized sampradāya.
b. Knows all of the main scriptures in depth and can quote key passages from memory.
c. Knows the metaphors, analogies and stories that have been used successfully in the past to convey understanding.
d. Knows Sanskrit – can speak, write and translate literally into English.
e. Teaches groups of seekers, covering a particular scripture with weekly talks for as long as it takes.
f. Is unquestionably accepted as fully enlightened.
g. Has the essential qualities of a good teacher – speaks clearly; has a good command of language; has interpersonal skills; is an interesting and amusing speaker etc.
h. Does not demand any money for seeker's attendance. Such teachers are almost invariably saṃnyāsins, who have renounced all material possessions and rely upon others (typically an ashram) to supply their basic needs. Those who are not associated with such an organization will only accept donations given in the spirit of devotion (this is called dakṣiṇa, which was originally the 'fee'

given to the priest who officiated over a ritual that he had been asked to perform).

Therefore, I do not cover organizations such as Arsha Vidya, Chinmayananda, Ramakrishna/Vivekananda. There are one or two exceptions to this where I have included a teacher who is well-known via other routes, such as regular videos on YouTube or contribution to blogs or discussion groups.

The reasons for exclusion are partly because the list would become far too large, and I would also be extremely likely to omit some because I do not know about them. But also, the point is that this is the route a seeker *should* take if at all possible, since it is almost guaranteed that the source will be reliable. The only reason such a source might fail is on point g above.

If you read in the Upaniṣads about someone 'approaching a guru,' the attitude of humility will always be pointed out. The would-be disciple approaches 'with sticks in hand.' This refers to the wood used for a sacrificial fire and is a symbol of the would-be disciple's preparedness to serve the teacher. If accepted, he would in fact act as a servant for some time before the guru would begin to pass on his knowledge.

The 'Classic' Modern Teachers

Many seekers think that traditional Advaita as taught by the 'original' teachers such as Śaṅkara and Sureśvara is inaccessible, requiring too much reference to the ancient Upaniṣads and the Bhagavad Gītā, to mention the better known texts. Looking at commentaries that rely on these shows that one has to be familiar with many 'weird' Sanskrit terms. Some of the books even have totally incomprehensible, original Sanskrit script (Devanāgarī) in them! It is not really surprising, then, that many turn to the famous, relatively modern teachers such as Ramana Maharshi, Nisargadatta Maharaj and Atmananda Krishna Menon. Even these are not entirely 'approachable' to the Western mind so that those teachers who claim to be disciples of the above are the ones who gain the most attention. After all, one can actually attend talks given by them and ask questions. Failing that, one can probably see some of their talks on YouTube.

Relatively well-known of such disciples are:

- **Ramana** – Pamela Wilson, Ganga, Catherine Ingram, Isaac Shapiro, Mooji, Michael James
- **Nisargadatta** – Wayne Liquorman, 'Sailor' Bob Adamson, James Braha
- **Krishna Menon** – Francis Lucille, Greg Goode, Rupert Spira

(Apologies that only a few are shown. See the 'Teacher' references at my website for much more information (Ref. 753). These are quite detailed, albeit somewhat out of date.)

I do not include the essentially traditional lineages of Ramakrishna and Vivekananda there because they maintain a relatively formal teaching methodology through their monastic organizations. Nor have I included Osho who, irrespective of the various accusations against him, used Zen, Christian and other teachings as well as Advaita.

Ramana Maharshi

This section is quite long because there are many related references attributed to the teaching of Ramana in this book, from a number of different sources. And there is a danger that the reader might conclude from the examples that I give that my opinion of him is not good. This would not be true. In fact, I created and maintained a website for the UK Ramana Maharshi organization for many years. I have read and highly recommended a number of books written by others about his teaching. What has happened is that, in recent years, especially as a result of writing the books about *Confusions in Advaita Vedanta,* I have come to realize that his disciples are relating ideas that are likely to cause confusion in seekers who study them. And I have no way of establishing whether or not they truly reflect Ramana's understanding. Accordingly, my criticisms should mostly be construed as being a criticism of the writers' translation and/or commentary, rather than a direct criticism of Ramana.

I have commented in several of my books that, as a one-to-one teacher, in person, Ramana was clearly an excellent teacher. He had the ability to perceive the nature of the questioner's concerns and provide an appropriate response. However, these responses were most unlikely always to be appropriate for all seekers, who would inevitably have different problems and different prior understanding of the teaching. We know that the style of teaching of Advaita is one of providing simple explanations first, then later taking those back and giving more sophisticated ones (adhyāropa-apavāda).

Most of the material that we have regarding Ramana has been translated, often by a seeker who attended talks given by him, and are transcribed from memory of what was thought to be understood at the time. Accordingly, there are multiple opportunities for misrepresentation! It is hardly surprising that some of the things we read appear to be at odds with a traditional understanding of Advaita!

The other problem here is that I have no knowledge of Tamil. Accordingly, if I were to attempt to review and comment upon the main text, I would have no means of checking what Ramana *actually* said. Hence, I would be unable to determine whether I was commenting upon Ramana's understanding or (much more likely) on a seeker's mistranslation or misunderstood commentary.

Michael James makes similar statements in his translation and commentary on Uḷḷadu Nāṟpadu about Ramana modifying what he says according to the level of understanding etc. of the questioner, and also about the problems of translation and understanding of the translator. He says that:

> *when we read such books we need to use our understanding of the fundamental principles of his teachings as expressed by him in his own original writings … to judge for ourself whether or not each statement attributed to him actually reflects his real teachings.* (Ref. 471)

I have been studying and writing about Advaita, full time, for the past 20+ years and have spent the past 2–3 years writing specifically about confusions in Advaita Vedanta. Consequently, I am happy that my analysis of the problems described above is correct. Therefore, the only explanations for some of the erroneous ideas apparently propagated by some disciples of Ramana are that either:

1. They have failed to grasp Ramana's overall teaching.
2. Ramana did not fully understand the traditional teaching of Advaita or chose to propagate conflicting ideas, thinking that they would be more effective.

Obviously, I do not attribute much likelihood to the second of these. Accordingly, I can only assume that the problem lies in the reasons described, namely the lack of a coherent body of sequential teaching and the fact that most of the records of Ramana's talks rely upon memory and translation by people other than Ramana. Trying to put together a complete picture of his overall teaching corpus is thus extremely difficult. Someone who begins without a complete understanding of Advaita would have an almost impossible task.

It seems quite likely, then, that many of those teachers who claim to be 'disciples' of Ramana (even though they never met him) did not have an initial, deep understanding of Advaita and that they acquired what they believed to be an understanding purely through association with Ramana's actual disciples or through extensive reading. Translations of original Tamil texts may certainly have helped, but translations are inevitably filtered through the understanding of the translator. It might be speculated, for example that, if Ramana chose to use a metaphor to help explain something, this might conceivably be understood and translated in a literal manner.

Since Sri Ramanasramam was established at Tiruvannamalai, many writers of Ramana's teaching would have stayed, or even lived there. They would have interacted with and learned from many of the other residents. There would be an accumulation of many snippets and stories along with any elements of clear teaching. With no background of traditional Advaita, it would have been difficult to assimilate and filter all of this to form a coherent picture of Ramana's own understanding. And with memories of any direct personal interactions with Ramana passing from A to B to C ... the phenomenon of Chinese Whispers would not easily have been avoided. This, indeed, is an excellent example of why sampradāya teaching is so important.

All this is, of course, entirely speculative on my own part and I apologize to any writers and Ramana adherents for any mistaken notions. I am simply endeavoring to explain how the misunderstandings described in this book may have come about without compromising the brilliance of Ramana himself.

As an example, consider Ref. 470. This a translation from the Tamil by Robert Butler of material by Muruganar. The publisher notes for this book that *"it embodies the teachings imparted by Ramana to Muruganar,* ***through the medium of silence****, and through the practice of self-enquiry, in which the aspirant dwells upon the 'I' sense in order to investigate the nature of his own consciousness."* And yet, the website of Michael James notes that: *"Guru Vācaka Kōvai, which is the most comprehensive* *and reliable collection of the sayings of Sri Ramana, recorded in Tamil verses by his foremost disciple, Sri Muruganar."* Similarly, Ref. 455 purports to be a record of Ramana's 'sayings' but it was largely written by Muruganar in Tamil (*"1254 stanzas being Sri Muruganar's handiwork and 28 the Maharshi"*) and translated into English by Professor Swaminathan. ('Teaching' through silence was discussed above.)

From all of that, one is bound to conclude that much if not most of what was written by Muruganar was his own understanding rather than necessarily Ramana's. In his defense, Muruganar lived with Ramana for over 25 years, so one could reasonably assume that he gained a pretty good understanding of the latter's teaching. (It is said that he was also the only one whom Ramana believed to have obtained enlightenment from the teaching.)

Ramana never authorized anyone to teach in his name but lots of teachers claim him as their guru. (See Ref. 754 for a lineage chart.)

The bottom line is that we can never be sure about the understanding of another unless they have written it down in our language (which they knew and spoke fluently), using words which could not have any other connotation. Even then, there is always the loophole that our general understanding of Advaita is not yet adequate to appreciate the subtleties being expressed. To what extent this proviso may apply to things written and spoken by modern satsang and Neo-Advaitin teachers is up to the seeker to decide for him or herself.

Nisargadatta Maharaj

The situation regarding Nisargadatta is similar. He also taught via satsang, meeting with seekers and answering their questions. Some attendees recorded the sessions that they attended and subsequently compiled these into books. The most well-known of these was *I am That* (Ref. 5), translated from tape recordings in Marathi by one of his disciples, Maurice Frydman.

(Following information derived from Ref. 482) Frydman had a long association with J. Krishnamurti through the Theosophical Society (though not always in agreement with him) before becoming a disciple of Ramana. (He was the author of *Maharshi's Gospel* (Ref. 477), anonymously published by Sri Ramanasramam and posed many of the questions contained therein.) Frydman clearly had an eclectic background of Advaita from his early life before meeting Nisargadatta but no formal, traditional understanding. The same also applied to Nisargadatta himself.

Nisargadatta's teacher was Siddharameshwar Maharaj, belonging to the Navnath sampradāya, which derives much from Śaṅkara's teaching but also has elements from a bhakti tradition. He had no associated āśrama but simply gave talks and answered questions from visiting seekers in his small tenement above shops in Mumbai. He did not reference scriptures but simply spoke from his own experience (in Marathi). Frydman was already 71 years old when he became Nisargadatta's disciple. He stayed with him until his death 11 years later in 1976. The translation of talks that became *I am That* was eventually published in 1973 (Ref. 5).

He did not formally appoint any successor but, along with Ramana, he was clearly very influential in establishing satsangs as the preferred method of teaching Advaita. The main difference here (being honest rather than cynical), is that he did not charge money for his talks! Also (definitely being cynical this time), it seems that today's seekers seem not to want to commit to indefinitely prolonged traditional teaching and learning from ancient scriptures written in a language that they do not understand. Instead, they just want simple answers to life problems and an end to perceived suffering.

Other disciples, particularly Jean Dunn, also wrote books based upon Nisargadatta's talks (and it has been said somewhere that Jean was formally acknowledged as a successor) but, according to an interview given by Nisargadatta to David Godman, Frydman was said to be the only one who had truly understood the teaching. Certainly, no other book has achieved the popularity status of *I am That*. Other disciples such as Ramesh Balsekar, Alexander Smit and 'Sailor' Bob Adamson went on to become teachers in their own right. (See Ref. 755 for a lineage chart.)

Atmananda Krishna Menon

Sri Atmananda is regarded as the instigator of the style of teaching of Advaita known as 'Direct Path,' although the term may have originated with Ramana. The most well-known (English-speaking) current teachers who can be considered to use it are Francis Lucille, Rupert Spira and Greg Goode. Other important Dutch speaking teachers stem from Wolter Keers. One of his direct disciples, Ananda Wood, has written extensively about Atmananda and this material may be read at my website, beginning at Ref. 748. Sri Atmananda's principal work is the three-volume *Notes on Spiritual Discourses* (Ref. 13), which is also available as a PDF at my site. (See Ref. 756 for a lineage chart.)

Self-help, 'Spirituality,' etc.

I have lamented many times that the typical High (Main) Street bookstore rarely contains any books on Advaita. There will usually be a selection of 'New-Age' type books on crystals, angels, witchcraft, tarot-reading and the like. T.S. Eliot ridicules these in his *Four Quartets*:

To report the behaviour of the sea monster,
Describe the horoscope, haruspicate or scry,
Observe disease in signatures, evoke
Biography from the wrinkles of the palm
And tragedy from fingers; release omens

By sortilege, or tea leaves, riddle the inevitable
With playing cards, fiddle with pentagrams (Ref. 196)

He calls them the 'pastimes and drugs' with which we try to divert ourselves from the distress caused by private and public problems of the moment. What we are really looking for, he says, is *"the point of intersection of the timeless with time."* But the best that we can achieve is *"music heard so deeply That it is not heard at all, but you are the music While the music lasts."* (Ref. 196) This is the difference between a deep meditation and the gaining of enlightenment.

Most of the 'Spirituality' books help no one. They merely provide a diversion for a while and even many of their readers probably simply laugh at them. Some, however, seem to speak from a position of knowledge. They refer to past sages and sometimes even authoritative books, giving the clear impression that the author is familiar with them and has absorbed what they have to say. These are far more dangerous. A seeker may read them and believe what is said, turning them away from a possibly fruitful path into a blind alley.

A good example is the book *Waking Up* by Sam Harris, Ref. 490. I wrote a very long and mostly highly critical review of this at Ref. 492. Although it is good as a 'Self-Help' book, and thus justifies its place in the bookstore, it seriously misrepresents both the aims and the teaching of Advaita. What he writes makes it clear that he does not even understand what Advaita means by 'enlightenment.'

That book illustrates how some authors may claim the backing of Advaita in order to pursue their own ideas accumulated from whatever sources they may have sampled briefly. It takes many years before one knows sufficient to be able to write about it without the risk of misleading readers. And one cannot 'mix and match' from the various religions. Śaṅkara devoted significant effort to refuting the ideas of other sources such as Buddhism and Sāṃkhya philosophies. The phrase 'caveat emptor' is often used in commercial contexts; how much more should it be borne in mind in a spiritual context! Blind alleys may take up a lifetime of seeking.

Organizations

Apart from the traditional organizations just mentioned, there are a number of others that aim to attract seekers to an environment in which they can find systematic teaching in a controlled way, thus avoiding the haphazard nature of satsang meetings. They solicit regular attendance over a period of years, if not indefinitely.

If these are to work, however, there must be an actively participating, sampradāya teacher in charge, who has formally taught and authorized the teachers 'beneath' him. I have written about my own experience with the School of Economic Science (SES) elsewhere (Ref. 398). There, all of the teaching material is written by one person who only meets a qualified teacher every year or two to ask problematic questions that may have arisen. The majority of members are taught by students who have attended for a number of years, but who are still largely ignorant of the subtleties of Advaita. Accordingly, although their methods may make members more attentive and considerate individuals, it is not a satisfactory means for learning Advaita.

I have no experience of any other organization, so am unable to comment. However, it seems inevitable that the same limitations must apply with respect to teaching structure and syllabus. This is why, when I am asked to recommend teachers (which I frequently am, by questioners at Advaita Vision), I always suggest that the seeker look for their nearest Arsha Vidya or Chinmaya Mission group. Since the primary teachers in those institutions will have been formally inducted by a sampradāya teacher, the format and content of their teaching ought to be reliable.

One proviso that must be mentioned is something that I only recently encountered in the excellent paper by Phillip Charles Lucas (Ref. 521). Referring to the North American Chinmaya Missions in the last decade of the twentieth century, he suggests that they *"primarily serve Indian emigrant communities around the world."* And he speaks of the trend of Hindus in North America to attend Hindu temples and incorporate rituals into their daily lives.

I put this to Ācārya Sadananda of the Washington Chinmaya Mission, who is a direct disciple of Chinmayananda. He states that the aim of the organization has always been to appeal to *any* serious seeker, regardless of prior beliefs or background. When it was first established, numerous Americans and Canadians joined the courses and some even became saṃnyāsins. But the mission also installed and consecrated idols, so that existing Hindus also became interested.

Nevertheless, he does concede that there are now more Hindus than Westerners. He says that most of the Americans seem to be not so 'serious' and leave after a while. He believes that a similar development applies to the Ramakrishna organization.

Both Chinmaya and Arsha Vidya also have residential courses (typically of 2–3 years duration) with the intention of preparing future teachers. In this way, they 'simulate' the traditional sampradāya style of teaching.

List of Modern Teachers

Internet Resources

In the past twenty years, the information relating to Advaita that is available on the internet has multiplied dramatically. In 1995, a few discussion groups enabled interested seekers to share their understanding and discuss their experiences but there were few actual websites. Web search technology was also in its infancy, so that it was not easy to discover the little information that might be found. When writing *Back to the Truth* (Ref. 467), I compiled a list of these resources for an Appendix. On 23rd August 2006, typing the keyword "advaita" into the most popular search engine (Google even then) returned 936,000 results and that was three times more than the previous year. On 27th July 2021, when I began this section, there were 6,330,000 results. On 11th January 2024, there were 7,590,000. On 5th April, this had increased by another 310,000. This is an increase of more than 100,000 per month! More careful selection of search criteria can recover information about virtually any aspect of the subject. Even entire classical works can often be downloaded for study off-line.

With the advent of AI, it is now possible to ask quite sophisticated questions in Advaita and receive what appear to be detailed and intelligent responses. But beware! You cannot (yet) rely on the accuracy of these answers. Unfortunately, the engines can only extract material from the many sites that contain information and, as you will see from the list of teachers that follows, much of that material is either unreliable or just plain wrong!

The appendix that I produced for *Back to the Truth* aimed to provide a very brief introduction to the sort of material that might be found. The source was my own website — www.advaita.org.uk — part of whose purpose was to link to those sites that I had found to be particularly good in their related classification. As editor of the Advaita category for the Open Directory Project that existed then, the aim was that I should provide entries for all sites dedicated to Advaita, whether about specific teachers, organizations, publications, philosophy or history. It was, therefore, very appropriate that I should add this appendix to record a fairly complete set of resources relating to Advaita. Unfortunately, I ceased to act in that role probably at least 10 years ago and the Project was closed down by its owners (AOL) in 2018.

It would have been a considerable task to continue to try to keep this up to date and I have been kept busy writing new books and maintaining the new 'blog' site at www.advaita-vision.org. The old advaita.org.uk still exists and most of the resources that were referenced in the first edition of this book are still present but it is now woefully out of date. Many of the links will no longer work, either because the owner has moved or because it has been closed down. The site is also not cell-phone friendly. To redesign and code it to bring it up to date and make it flexible for all platforms would be a massive amount of work and I have neither time nor skills to do this (and certainly cannot afford to pay anyone else to do it). Sorry! (If any reader would like to take on this task, please contact me!)

Caveats and Reservations

I compiled this list of teachers by consulting all of the 'lists' that I could find via Google or other sources, together with all of the material that I have accumulated myself over the past 20 years.

My aim was to include as many teachers that I could find who were stated (by themselves or others) as 'teachers of non-duality.' I then endeavored to find out whether or not they claimed to be teaching Advaita. This I did by scanning through their own websites, book reviews, interviews etc. I freely admit that this was not a comprehensive process. To perform this task in a rigorous way would have taken a very long time. Accordingly, all of the following are possible:

- I have not included a teacher who does teach Advaita.
- I have included one who does teach Advaita but have said that it is 'Not Advaita.'
- I have included a teacher who does not teach Advaita but have failed to identify this.

If any of these are true, then I freely apologize to that teacher, but suggest that maybe they need to change or add to their website to make the actual situation clear.

I do not want to be accused of unfair or unreasonable comments. I have sometimes included quotations from the website's own material. For this, I can only be accused of 'out of context' quotation, although I did genuinely try not to do that. Nevertheless, any quotations are the teacher's own. If they no longer agree with what they said, then they should delete it so as to avoid misleading seekers.

There are lots of claimed 'spiritual' teachers, teaching 'wholeness,' 'love' and other nice words, but who are clearly not teaching Advaita. I have not been rigorous in including or excluding them all. As a general guideline, if I could find mention of the word 'non-dual' on their website or in articles, I have probably included them. Otherwise, I probably haven't. I have tended to exclude 'non-dual healers' and 'non-dual therapists' and others describing their practice using contradictory notions.

If, whilst reading through material related to a particular teacher, I came across a statement that I felt merited highlighting, I have often quoted this. I do so without any comment of my own, leaving it to the reader to form their own opinion. It may sometimes appear that I am deliberately choosing outrageous statements in an effort to be sarcastic or amusing. There may be something in that but, in my defense, the quotation is the teacher's own and I have endeavored not to take anything out of context to make it seem other than stated.

If there were indications that the teaching was in accordance with Advaita but I found quotations that contradicted this in any way, then I felt this justified including such quotations as examples of misleading teaching. These may appear elsewhere in the book.

Teachers may try to argue that, if they are teaching non-duality, then it must be the same as Advaita but this is not the case. Whilst it is true that the end-point of any non-dual teaching must be the same, the route for getting there may be quite different. Although I am unable to speak for any other route, what I can say is that the Advaita-path is possibly the oldest and most 'used,' having successfully shown many the way to understanding. Despite being so old, the fact that it does not eschew reason and experience also makes it very amenable to the modern mind.

Lists Consulted

Back to the Truth

Appendix D – Modern Teacher List (Ref. 467)

I no longer recall how I compiled that list — much the same way in which I compiled this one, I guess!

'Natural Awakening – Advanced Nondual Training'

https://www.nondualtraining.com/resources/community/

Links to past participants in 'Nondual Awakening: Advanced Nondual Trainings.'

The Urban Guru Cafe

https://urbangurucafe.com/

Podcasts with (100) non-dual teachers. *"What is pointed to in these podcast programs will not go stale or be dated. What is pointed to has never aged or changed one iota. Therefore these programs continue to serve as a vehicle for clear pointing."*

Open Circle Center

https://opencirclecenter.org/links-and-resources/

Satsang-givers and other teachers with local connections (Bay Area, California)

Meeting Truth

https://meetingtruth.com/Teachers.aspx

Teachers with upcoming events (Europe and US)

Extraordinary Wisdom

http://www.extraordinarywisdom.net/links.htm

Links of interest (women teachers)

Nondual Therapy Directory

https://nondualtherapydirectory.com/listings/

All types of session (emotional and somatic enlightenment; energy transmissions; face to face; non-dual self-inquiry; online; psychological; shadow work).

Past Conversation (2014 – 2017)

http://www.living-from-love.com/conversations-2014---2017.html

Buddha at the Gas Pump

https://batgap.com

Conversations with "Ordinary" spiritually-enlightened people. (702 so far at the time of writing, March 2024.)

The Journey of Awakening: The Unity of Mind, Body and Heart

https://journeyofawakening.purepresenceconferences.com/

(Recordings of) past speakers at the conference(s).

Association of Spiritual Integrity

https://www.spiritual-integrity.org/

*The mission of the Association for Spiritual Integrity*SM *(ASI) is to foster the fundamental role of strong ethical principles in the ongoing development of spiritual leaders and communities.*

The ASI is a voluntary, inclusive, international organization of spiritual leaders, teachers and guides.

Membership is open to anyone in a position of spiritual leadership who agrees to abide by the ASI Honor Code of Ethics and Good Practice.

Huge list of organizations (39) and individual members (638) of this body. But scarcely any appear to be in any way connected with Advaita, with interesting specializations such as 'Psilocybin Facilitator,' 'Trillium Awakening,' 'Earth and Sky Counseling,' 'Cacao Ceremonialist,' 'Priestess Warrior Lover,' 'Multidimensional Soul Light'... and so on.

Stillness Speaks

https://www.stillnessspeaks.com/

Stillness Speaks® is a resource for self inquiry and self exploration — the endless journey of self realization. We offer works of teachers and traditions, both historical and contemporary, Eastern and Western, indigenous and otherwise. Our approach is integral — all are welcome!

Non-duality is equated with Advaita (which, of course, is not true) and teachers such as Adyashanti are listed here (his influences are principally Zen Buddhism).

SAND (Science and Nonduality)

https://scienceandnonduality.com

This began quite a few years ago, organizing annual conferences with a variety of speakers, presumably endeavoring to reach a common understanding about the nature of consciousness and reality, assuming a focus of non-duality. A look at their website now shows that it has mushroomed into a mass of 'Events' (Community Gatherings, Webinars, and Retreats) covering lots of mystical, therapeutic, unscientific, nothing-to-do-with-non-duality activities. Notwithstanding the fact that science can intrinsically say nothing about non-duality (by definition), it does seem as though commercialism has overtaken the original intent of this endeavor. There are numerous articles at Advaita Vision about the role of science, but see in particular my article at Ref. 525.

Yes Vedanta

https://www.yesvedanta.com/

A major source of 'correct' Advaita – managed and written by Andre Vas – highly recommended.

20 Best Nonduality Blogs and Websites

https://blog.feedspot.com/nonduality_blogs/

The best Nonduality blogs from thousands of blogs on the web and ranked by traffic, social media followers & freshness.

The SAND site is listed at number 1, which is not good! But my own site at Advaita Vision is listed number 2, so I guess I will let them off...

What Am I really?

https://existenceawareness.wordpress.com/links-2/

Compiled by Bill East (died 2009?). So, some of the links are now out of date or nonexistent.

Everyone is Going Conscious

https://everyoneisgoingconscious.blogspot.com/2013/05/links-to-linkless-nonduality-in-world.html

Basically a blog with links to, and material from, the sites of non-dual teachers.

SpiritualTeachers.org

https://www.spiritualteachers.org

Teachers categorized from 5* down to 1* rating in the view of site owner, Shawn Nevins, influenced principally by Richard Rose and Douglas Harding. Some very intelligent criticism of a number of well-known teachers.

Hinduwebsites.com Advaita Vedanta

https://hinduwebsites.com/resources/advaita.aspx

Extensive list of sites relating to Advaita.

The List

This is organized alphabetically by the first name of the teacher. I decided to do it this way because quite a few are known principally by their Christian name, or by the name given by their guru, or assumed because it sounds 'spiritual' and thus more likely to attract seekers. (Apologies — I don't seem able to quell this cynicism! It is particularly engendered by the names of 'organizations' that are often established — 'Reach for the Truth,' 'Born into Light' and so on, or URLs of similar provenance.)

I have included key major teachers such as Ramana Maharshi for completeness, with links to the principal websites for these. Readers will recognize these and therefore not attempt to find out where they are next giving satsangs! Also, some of the teachers for whom I gave links at my website (www.advaita.org.uk) over 10 years ago are now dead. I have endeavored to indicate this when I know it to be so but offer apologies for any others. Of course, books written by some who have died or simply stopped teaching may nevertheless still be worth reading.

Key

No longer active	I was unable to find any current website for this teacher. Note that this does not mean that there isn't one, just that my search terms on Google failed to find one.
Not Advaita	I found a site for this teacher, or an organization referencing them and there were some written extracts/quotations from them. But I could not find anything to indicate that they understood, and were aiming to teach, Advaita.
	Note that, just because an entry does not specify 'Not Advaita' does not mean that it IS Advaita – it may just mean that I was unable to find sufficient material to decide one way or the other!

The format of each of the entries below is as follows:

1. **Name of teacher**
2. Name of organization established (if any), as indicated by the home page of their website. (This will obviously be omitted if there is none.)
3. **Link to website** (May be omitted if I couldn't find one.)
4. Name(s) of their teacher(s) and/or main background religion/philosophy, as stated at their website or links from other sites. (This will be omitted if I was unable to determine.)
5. Selected quotation(s) to give some idea of the nature of their teaching. Other quotation(s) may also appear elsewhere in the book if relevant to the topic under

discussion. I provide the references for quotations, usually from their website or published book, but occasionally from an emailed newsletter or communication. If no reference is given, it will be from the homepage of the website. (There will frequently not be a quotation. I did not want to include one just for its own sake!)

6. My comments (if any); often (usually!) just the words 'Not Advaita.'

The List

Adam Chacksfield

'Falling Open Together'

www.nondualcenter.org

A spiritual teacher who shares the openness of nonduality, the intimacy of love, and the aliveness of erotic life energy.

Website taken over by 'Free Credit Wallet Casino' last time I looked. Not Advaita!

Adyashanti

http://www.adyashanti.org/

Principally Zen.

Not Advaita. I have also listed many of his disciple-teachers but they will not usually be Advaita either.

Aja Thomas

https://medium.com/@barnashram

When you recognize that you are Absolute Consciousness, you will see that there is nothing else. There is no good and no bad, and that everyone and everything is a manifestation of That. It is all Absolute Consciousness, perfectly manifesting itself in the great drama of cosmic creation. (Ref. 93)

Sounds OK, but you have to join to read anything at the website. (I do not do this when such restrictions are encountered!) I posted one of his blogs in 2012, which commented on the (then) modern-day teaching of Advaita. (Ref. 758)

Alan Jacobs

Died 2020.

https://www.theculturium.com/eulogy-for-alan-jacobs/

Ramana Maharshi

Apart from the Source (Brahman) the world does not really exist. It is an appearance in Brahman (Consciousness), A sensual representation interpreted by the brain and so a creation of the mind (māyā). (Ref. 358)

Was chairman of the UK Ramana Maharshi Foundation. Also supported both Ramesh Balsekar and Tony Parsons, so not strictly traditional Advaita.

Alan Jolie

The Dawn Within. (Blogger, not a teacher.)

https://thedawnwithin.com

J. Krishnamurti, Rupert Spira.

The words for the discovery of our true nature — like enlightenment, realisation, awakening, liberation, etc — are all very significant. They all point to truth and have numerous things to say. Take 'enlightenment' for instance. Its original signification is 'to shine' or 'to make luminous'. So to enlighten means to put the light on. It means to cease being distracted by all that is objective in our experience and doesn't define us truly, and make what is already and absolutely ours here and now apparent. It doesn't mean to achieve, to reach, to attain, to get something new. (Ref. 668)

Intelligent, eclectic. Not particularly Advaita.

Alan Watts

Died 1973.

https://alanwatts.org/

Not Advaita. But two books worth reading are Refs. 250 and 359.

Alice Gardner

Facebook; original site no longer exists.

This is where our true nature can begin to interact with the world, and to offer itself to the world through us, as us. In this process we can't know how that is going to happen. One of the essential elements of our being able to bring our realization down into our human lives is a willingness to live and move without knowing the outcome, without knowing why to do things, sometimes without even knowing how. (Ref. 669)

Not Advaita.

Alicia St. Rose

https://donteatthemenu.com/

All of your problems, doubts and suffering are manufactured by the mind. This batch of shoddy goods comes rolling off the assembly line and you unknowingly purchase them wholesale!

You are not responsible for their origin, so you have no obligation to buy. Simply look, do not touch. (Ref. 670)

Nice quote but not Advaita. (She also does not claim to be a teacher.)

Amoda Maa

Timeless Truth for the Contemporary Seeker

https://www.amodamaa.com/

At the absolute level, consciousness is already awake. It is fully alive in its pristine awakeness as formlessness. But as it descends into the relative level, it easily gets lost in the identification with form. You, with your capacity for self-reflection, are the portal through which consciousness can become aware of itself. You, with your capacity to choose where attention goes, are responsible for consciousness returning to itself.

Many years ago — long before I set out on a spiritual path and long before I began the journey of inner inquiry and long before I had matured into the person I am today — I was spontaneously transported to a future world. [!!] [Note that the articles from which these quotations were taken have now been removed.]

Not Advaita!

Anamika Borst

http://www.anamikaborst.com/index-lazd.html

Leo Hartong

There is only This. Ever. Appearing as Everything. All the different understandings, e.g. traditional advaita vedanta, versus neo advaita, is never versus really, as both are appearances in This. (Ref. 673)

Not Advaita.

Ananda Wood

https://www.advaita.org.uk/discourses/ananda_wood/ananda_wood.htm

Atmananda Krishna Menon

In the Śvetāśvatara Upaniṣad, 2.14-15, the ego is compared to a dirty mirror, which shows up as an obscuring obstacle to the light that it reflects. But, by understanding ego's falsities and hence clearing them away, the ego ceases to be an obstacle and becomes instead a means to truth. (Ref. 216)

Writings and books available for download from Ref. 674.

Ananta Kranti

https://www.ananta-kranti.com/

Osho and *"a two and half year period of silence in a Zen style retreat in Japan (otherwise known as a Japanese prison)."*

Then I entered Primal De-conditioning, bringing conscious my childhood wounds and imprints, feelings/dynamics with my parents and waking up to how that plays out in my projections. (Ref. 675)

Not Advaita!

Andre Vas

https://www.yesvedanta.com

Swami Dayananda, Neema Majmudar.

Most Westerners first learn of non-duality through exposure to the "teachings" of Ramana Maharshi and/or Nisargadatta Maharaj — either directly through reading various books that contain collections of their conversations with seekers or indirectly through hearing their statements expounded upon by others who have understood — or, as is often the case, misunderstood — the words of the two spiritual titans.

While both of these men were undoubtedly brahmanisthas, or liberated beings — they were not shrotriyas, or qualified teachers versed in the methodology of the sampradaya, or Vedantic teaching lineage. In other words, though they knew who they were — they did not know how to effectively deliver the systematic, step-by-step, means of knowledge called Vedanta — that leads the qualified student to understanding one's true identity...

Mastery of any subject matter is like this. Be it mathematics, negotiation, analysis, or understanding nature of Self. This is what 99.99% of Ramana's and Nisargadatta's learners don't take into account. (Ref. 676)

Wise words!

Andrew Cohen

https://www.andrewcohen.com/

https://www.manifest-nirvana.com/

Manifest Nirvana is a monastery of the future, an evolutionary ashram, an integral temple, a church of verticality — a sacred intersubjective space that exists both as a nondual dimension beyond the world, and as a trusted spiritual home within it...

Manifest Nirvana is an integral hub, a meeting place and a developmental vortex to catalyze Second and Third Tier capacities in consciousness. (Ref. 677)

Not Advaita!

Andrew Taggart

Living Wisdom, Being Peace

https://andrewjtaggart.com/

Ranjit Maharaj

Eclectic Doctor of Philosophy, apparently blogging learned articles on all aspects of 'practical' philosophies since 2011.

Andrew Vernon

No obvious recent internet activity.

Ranjit Maharaj

Death is really only a concept. It has power because we give power to it. As long as we take ourselves to be small and insignificant individuals, we are subject to the fear of death. Our view of life is mistaken. We imagine ourselves to be subject to appearance and disappearance and we forget that for something to appear and disappear, a changeless background is necessary. Just as a river flowing to the sea is water when it begins as a tiny spring, is water when it passes through the country, and is still water when it merges into the vast ocean, so are we pure consciousness before "birth," pure consciousness during this life, and pure consciousness after "death". (Ref. 678)

Angelo Dilullo

https://simplyalwaysawake.com

Simply stated, waking up from the dream of separation means living a life of spontaneity, wonder, freedom, and unbroken peace. It means realizing your true, undivided nature and living out of an instinctual interconnectedness that is undeniable and immediately available at all times. It means expressing yourself authentically and without hesitation and feeling comfortable in your own skin no matter the situation. Ultimately, it is about the end of suffering in this lifetime. (Ref. 679)

Not Advaita.

Annamalai Swami

Died 1995.

https://sriannamalaiswami.org/

Ramana

It is not helpful to enquire why there is māyā and how it operates. If you are in a boat which is leaking, you don't waste time asking whether the hole was made by an Italian, a Frenchman or an Indian. You just plug the leak. Attempting to find the origin of māyā with your mind is doomed to fail because any answer you come up with will be a māyā answer. Establish yourself in the Self. Then watch how māyā takes you over each time you fail to keep your attention there. (Ref. 680)

Annette Knopp

Ramana, plus a variety of Eastern and Western sources, such as 'Psycho-Spiritual Integration & Trauma Resolution.' She is also an *"ordained Wisdom Keeper in the Order of Universal Interfaith (OUnI)."*

https://www.annetteknopp.com/

Throughout our entire life — from birth to death, in moments of great joy or utter darkness — we are intimately connected with the Open Ground of Being. When we live in conscious connection and understanding of this fundamental reality, our lives become infused with Love and Openness and we know ourselves to be home. (Ref. 681)

Not Advaita.

Annette Nibley

What Never Changes

No apparent activity since around 2014.

John Wheeler, James Swartz. *"Switched to traditional Advaita after meeting with James Swartz."*

So stop. Rather than looking for the truth, even the truth of "who you are," just stop, for one moment, and don't look for anything. Just stop trying, stop moving. Stay put, for once in your life. Admit that this is all there is. It doesn't get better. There is no other truth but this. Existence just is, and there is no purpose to any of it. (Ref. 682)

Arjuna Ardagh

https://radicalbrilliance.com/arjuna-ardagh/

Poonja

He has trained more than 2000 people to become Awakening Coaches over the last 25 years.

Arjuna and his wife, Chameli Ardagh, have created The Deeper Love, which teaches singles and couples how to integrate awakening consciousness into intimate relationships.

Not Advaita.

Artur

Welcome to the Ocean of Being. Website in German.

https://artur-sein.de/

Samarpan, Ramana.

Aruna Byers

Awakening Coach

https://www.awakeningcoach.com/

The first step towards the Ultimate Freedom begins as we discover our heart, and when its wisdom becomes more and more available to our mind, as this mind looks within the heart for guidance, acting on the heart's advice instead of confining its frame of reference to its own limited understandings. (Ref. 683)

Not Advaita.

Atmananda Krishna Menon

Died 1959.

https://www.advaita.org.uk/discourses/atmananda/atmananda1.htm

Self-forgetfulness is the cause of the creation of the world, and self-remembrance or withdrawal to the Self is the destruction of the world. (Ref. 13, Note 569)

Any question which has the slightest reference to the Absolute cannot be answered in the relative and the question does not arise in the Absolute. (Ref. 13, Note 1047)

Atman Nityananda

Advaita Atma Yoga Academy

https://atmannityananda.org/

Haidakhan Babaji (?), Sivananda, Ramana, Nisargadatta *I am That*.

Author, Teacher and Coach of Self-Knowledge, Spirituality, Nonduality & Tennis psychology.

The Academy activities aim to help people to know themselves in depth, to transform their minds and hearts, to develop inner harmony and a higher level of consciousness.

Not Advaita.

Bart ten Berge & Georgi Y. Johnson

https://www.iamhere.life/

Syllabus of the 7-Year Spiritual Psychology Education: What to expect from Module 1:

Awakening of sentient awareness through the employment of the felt sense through body, heart and mind; Depth access to the chakra system and exploration of the auric layers; Shifting into an inclusive dimension beyond polarity of up and down, through the language of the chakras.

Not Advaita!

Bernd

https://meetingtruth.com/Teacher/Bernd (Own website no longer exists)

In timeless awakening we are absorbed in ultimate truth. It's an endless love affair, an endless invitation. It's always here and now. And just because of that, we are invited to give everything.

Bharat (Melvin Rochlin)

Died 2018.

http://www.ombharat.com/

Osho, Poonja, Mira.

Also books on palmistry…

Bill Free

https://billfree.com/

Course in Miracles and Direct Path Advaita.

Bill Free is the founder of Pure Presence Productions LLC, a platform for thought leaders, wisdom teachers, and facilitators from nonduality, science, philosophy, and the arts to promote the expansion, understanding, and direct experience of awareness for beings around the world to awaken to their true identity.

Pure Presence Conferences is an open space for truth to flow in one big Satsang like the many faces of God in all its expressions including but not limited to A Course in Miracles, Advaita Vedanta, Buddhism, Christian Mysticism, Atheism, No-ism, Nonduality and more. (Ref. 684)

Not Advaita.

Bob Seal

https://advaitatoons.blogspot.com/

Nisargadatta, 'Sailor' Bob Adamson.

Non-dual cartoons.

Bodhi Avasa

THERE IS BUT ONE BEING IN ALL THINGS AND THIS ONE IS YOU

http://www.bodhiavasa.net/ and **https://bodhiavasa.com/**

When Oneness itself has lost sight of itself it begins to create identification with what is present and as the body/mind is present under all the circumstances of the human experience it is then quite natural that the body/mind is identified with and claimed to be what one is. The one that is doing the identifying is the impersonal, consciousness itself. Once realization takes place and the attention rests in the seeing of Oneness the seeking comes to an end. (Ref. 686)

Bok (Kip Bok Wood)

Wild Animal Zen

https://wildanimalzen.com

Adyashanti, David Hawkins, Eckhart Tolle, Byron Katie, Ramana Maharshi, Nisargadatta Maharaj, and Tulku Urgyen Rinpoche.

Does your experience of yourself come and go? My answer would be no. Does your experience of thoughts, feelings and perceptions come and go? My answer would be yes. Even your experience of having a body comes and goes if you pay attention. For example, when you are completely focussed on something you are working on, the experience of a body disappears. So we have to ask ourselves: If the experience of thoughts, feelings, and perceptions, and even of having a body, comes and goes, what is it that doesn't come and go? What is this experience of ourselves, this sense of me, that does not come and go but is always so? (Ref. 687)

Brian Piergrossi

http://brianpiergrossi.com

With the unrelenting sole intention of educating and facilitating the awakening of consciousness and creating the New Earth inside individuals and communities around the world, Brian Piergrossi is spearheading a movement integrating awakened spirituality, peak performance and human potential in our modern world. (Ref. 688)

[!!]

Bruce Joel Rubin

'Kundalini Yoga Meditation' – derives from Kashmir Shaivism.

https://www.brucejoelrubin.com/

At the age of five, Bruce Rubin had a spiritual experience playing in a sandbox in the middle of the afternoon… In 1965 he took a massive (and accidental) overdose of LSD and began a journey which lasted between 3 and 4 billion years… After 44 years of daily meditation, Bruce experienced what is referred to as a spiritual awakening. Oscar-winning screen-writer. (Ref. 689)

[!!]

Burt Harding

The Awareness Foundation

http://www.burtharding.com/

Ramana Maharshi

Each human says, "I am John or Mary" but in Reality there is only one 'I' known as God or LOVE (true pure awareness known as love). Spiritual awakening happens when we realize that this 'I' which we had taken to be 'me' is the true 'I' in its expanded state beyond the body. What I am giving you are words and cannot explain the inexplicable, however, as your heart opens you will begin to see what is obvious here and now. (Ref. 690)

Burt Jurgens

www.beyonddescription.net – flagged as a 'security risk.' No other website material found.

Book *Beyond Description: Notes on the Dissolution of a Seeker*; blurb by John Wheeler.

Canela Michelle Meyers

https://www.canelamichelle.com

Isaac Shapiro

When people come to satsang, if they offer up a scenario, I can support them to find the love in it. I am unable to see the love in other people's experiences or details, but they can. So I support them to find the love. Because we're all personally involved with our own details. It would be from the perspective of the person experiencing these happenings that he or she would be able stop and relax into seeing how it is love speaking. (Ref. 691)

Not Advaita.

Catherine Ingram

https://www.catherineingram.com/

Buddhism and Poonja.

Freedom is to be found here and now, not in some imagined future. The future never comes. Freedom is simply to know that what we are is pure awareness. We are not merely this body or the steady barrage of thoughts that we tell ourselves. We are the pure awareness in which everything is arising and passing, and all of it is arising as pure awareness itself. So this is to know yourself as your own source even as you are living it; to have the attention placed on the source or on the pure awareness instead of on these fleeting occurrences of body and mind; to know yourself as the ocean and not merely the individual expression or the wave. (Ref. 692)

Cee

Apparently no longer active.

Ramana and Nome.

You could say each moment is real as it is experienced, but how real is that? In other words, discriminate right here and now between what is arising and the pure Consciousness. As anything arises, discriminate between the arising and the pure Consciousness, and you can see how you, yourself, have to be the pure Consciousness which is more real than the arising. (Ref. 693)

Chadwick Johnson

The W.A.Y. Project (Who are you?)

https://chadwick-johnson.wixsite.com/theway

Mindfulness

Then one day I realized that I was not Chad. Chad was not original to me. I discovered, in prayer and meditation, that I was much greater than this ego called Chad. I remembered who I was (and AM) prior to the dream of Chad. (Ref. 694)

Not Advaita.

Charlie Hayes

The Eternal State ~ Advaita Nonduality

http://charliehayes36.tripod.com/

'Sailor' Bob Adamson, John Wheeler.

I assert with absolute confidence that no one, you or anyone else, was ever 'born' as a separate entity. It is all just language, AKA bullshit (that's a technical term!). To be 'born' is simply to assume a false sense of self. It's a 'case of Mistaken Identity!'. It is the delusion of taking a temporary thought, passing concept like a cloud coming and going in the sky-like Awareness-Consciousness that You ARE, to be real. (Ref. 695)

Chris Hebard

Stillness Speaks

https://www.stillnessspeaks.com/

Material from teachers from various traditions.

The greatest mystery of all: as your journey progresses, you will discover that there truly is only one teacher and that teacher is ultimately found within. Until then, we have many sages that guide us along ... or illuminate the way ... we are honored to offer a small sampling of these luminaries ... a list that will grow with time.

Not a teacher in his own right. Eclectic site. Didn't seem to be anything representing traditional Advaita. Direct Path well-represented.

Chuck Hillig

Living As The Source Of Who You Are

http://www.chuckhillig.com/

*Who you **really** are will never ... and **can** never ... get enlightened. Getting enlightened is not a big task for who you **are**. Getting enlightened is only a big task for who you are **not**.* (Ref. 517)

Colin Drake

No specific website apparent. Book *Beyond the Separate Self* and numerous others.

LSD, mescaline, Ramakrishna, Ramana Maharshi, Gangaji.

Every 'thing' that is occurring in consciousness is a manifestation of cosmic energy, for the string theory and the earlier theory of relativity show that matter is in fact energy, which is consciousness in motion (or motion in consciousness). For energy is synonymous with motion and consciousness is the substratum, or deepest level, of all existence. (Ref. 697)

Not Advaita.

Daryl Bailey

Dismantling the fantasy

https://www.darrylbailey.net/

Jiddu Krishnamurti, Alan Watts, Yoga, Buddhism, Taoism, Sufism, Christianity, and certain contemporary psychologies, Ruth Denison, Robert Adams, six years as a Buddhist meditation monk in the Thai Forest Tradition, under the guidance of Ajahn Sumedho, Ramesh Balsekar.

No matter how much you think you've created this basic happening, you haven't. It doesn't matter how many meaningless sounds get attached to illusions of form, all of this is formless and beyond any possible explanation. You can call it no-self, or God, or whatever you feel you have to; words really aren't that important.

Without forms and labels what is there to question? Where is there any you to describe? There is only an inexplicable, formless dance presenting itself. (Ref. 698)

David Brockman

Apparently no longer active.

Absolutely everything has just been created, including any concept of time or 'cause and effect'.

The oceans, mountains, sky, sun, sensations, thoughts, you, him, her, everything, absolutely everything that exists in experience has just been created. These words are the first and only words that you'll ever read; this moment is the first and only moment you will exist and live. Mind-blowingly amazing isn't it? (Ref. 699)

It certainly is...

David Carse

No active link.

Instead of looking outwards, look within. Whatever is not present in deep sleep does not exist.

As long as there is an 'I' to say "I am That", that 'I' is the ego. (Both quotes from Ref. 313.)

Neo-Advaita but see 'Recommended Reading' section.

David Ellzey

The Awakened Life

Author of *The Ocean of Now: How to Navigate the Unsure Waters of Our Challenging Times with Courage and Peace*

https://davidellzey.com/

Francis Lucille, Neelam, Rumi, and Nisagardatta.

(With his expertise as a coach, teacher, and author in emotional wellness and awakening consciousness), David has inspired nearly a quarter million people worldwide to awaken beyond these limitations. [!!!]

Not Advaita.

David Spero

http://www.davidspero.org

In the winter of 1996–1997 (the actual date remains vague), I was sitting in an ordinary motel room in Palm Springs, California. On this day, meditation went into unfathomable depths, penetrating into and beyond the very core of existence.

My thoughts evaporated and my head went from a spherical, physiological casing to an ocean of Divine Light within "seconds" — an ocean still and deeply active. This Light shone from the inside, the outside and from the beyond itself. "I" and "the world" dissolved forever into this immensity of warmly translucent, incandescent Light-Oneness. (Ref. 700)

Not Advaita.

Dhanya (Moffitt)

Swami Dayananda.

Teaches a few students in California.

Essays at Advaita Vision - https://www.advaita-vision.org/category/dhanya/ - and on various groups which discuss - non-duality on Facebook.

The non-dual Self (the atma) is completely here. It is You. More You than any changing thing you might have taken yourself to be. So completely and silently present, we miss it amidst the changing experiences which tend to captivate us.

Learn to distinguish between the changing and the changeless. Whatever is changing, be it the body, mind, or sense organs experiences, that is not you. What is ever changelessly present, underlying, as it were, all changing things, that is the Self. That is You! (Ref. 763)

Dhanya checked and commented on the draft of my 'Jungle' book (Ref. 441), so is highly reliable as a traditional teacher.

Dolano

http://www.dolano.com/

https://www.friendsofdolano.org/

Osho, Ramana, Poonja, Gangaji.

With the light of knowing who am I, it is easy and not complicated to liberate this mind. Only a willingness is needed of wanting to be free and taking 100 % responsibility rather than to complain.

A liberated mind is no more separate from your very nature, which is source, pure intelligence and unconditional love. Then mind is no more in a struggle, no more in the way, and your nature can come freely through. (Ref. 701)

Douglas Harding

Died 2007.

https://www.headless.org/

'The Headless Way.' Various practitioners listed but this is Not Advaita.

Eckhart Tolle

https://eckharttolle.com

When you become conscious of Being, what is really happening is that Being becomes conscious of itself. When Being becomes conscious of itself — that's presence. Since Being, consciousness, and life are synonymous, we could say that presence means consciousness becoming conscious of itself, or life attaining self-consciousness. (Ref. 45)

Not Advaita. His teaching disciples are, consequently, generally excluded.

Eli Jaxon-Bear

The Leela Foundation; married to Gangaji.

https://leela.org

Taoism, Tibetan Buddhism, Poonja, Enneagram.

Eli Jaxon-Bear presents the Enneagram of Liberation, a radical new way to use the Enneagram for deep insight and realization of your true nature.

Not Advaita.

Ellen Emmet

https://www.ellenemmet.com

Francis Lucille (but now in the "non-dual tradition of Kashmir Shivaism"). Married to Rupert Spira.

We explore our direct experience and allow it to reveal its essential reality. Our particular focus is the body, allowing it to be our mirror and our pathway, our prayer and our altar, and ultimately the shining expression of this shared identity.

Not Advaita.

Éric Baret

Articles at **https://scienceandnonduality.com**.

Jean Klein, Tantra.

Truth is not 'something' to be felt, or to be experienced; it is the constant experience of non-truth. It is a non-experience and that is why it never happened to anybody and that is why one cannot live in truth. One can only see that one lives in untruth. To be free is not an occupation. You are what you are. (Ref. 702)

Eric Putkonen

Nonduality & Enlightenment Simplified

https://www.nondualitysimplified.com/

If you are 100 percent devoted to the feelings and experiencing of the here and now, you might find thought slows or ceases. In that silence of mind, the inner silence and stillness is easier to notice. Abide in the silence and stillness. In that silence of mind, the revelation of Oneness may occur. (Ref. 703)

Not Advaita.

Eva Millauer

Embodiment as the One Heart.

https://evamillauer.com/

The practice of embodied oneness allows for an organic process of integration of any pattern that feels still separate. Mysteriously, when we approach anything from the reality that there is no separation, there is nothing that can not be aligned to that. We learn to see heart break, despair, anger, sorrow, grief and fear as welcome guides to uncover deeper levels of what we may have felt safer to disown in the past.

Not Advaita.

Felipe Oliveira

https://nothingwronganymore.com/

John Wheeler and Bob Adamson.

Efforts to 'be present' must yield only mind activity because what is being aimed at is a concept or an experience. Consciousness is always present; existing now. Present consciousness is not an experience. It is the spontaneous backdrop to all experience. You are this. (Ref. 704)

Florian Tathagata

No longer active.

When we speak about something called the ego we are actually speaking about something that does not exist; it is only a subtle movement of not wanting to have the experience we are having right now or wanting another experience that we like. If we do not label that subtle sense of I, we will not find much, simply a contraction. Can you meet that contraction without giving it a name? Because it has no reality; it has no substance. (Ref. 617)

Floyd Henderson

https://floydhenderson.com/

https://advaitavedantameditations.blogspot.com/

Nisargadatta, Native American Teachings.

This Teaching invites you to question everything. Faith in dogma requires that you question nothing. The "journey" only begins when questioning begins. The "journey" only continues if questioning continues.

In order to be reincarnated or to have a resurrection and life eternal, you would have to be a body and a mind and you would have to "have" a personality. (Both quotes from Ref. 705.)

Francis Lucille

http://www.francislucille.com/

Jean Klein, Krishna Menon.

Enlightenment is the sudden recognition that non-duality is, has always been, and will always be the reality of our experience. Self-realization is the subsequent stabilization in the peace, happiness and freedom of our natural state. (Ref. 706)

Fred Davis

https://awakeningclaritynow.com/

Fred Davis studied and practiced Eastern wisdom for twenty-five years prior to 2006 when his seeking ended, and his true awakening commenced. He is the creator and editor of Awakening Clarity Now and the founder of The Living Method of Awakening ... Hundreds of people on five continents have found the door to freedom using The Living Method. (Ref. 708)

I have had people wake up within just a very few minutes of beginning a session, and others who took well over an hour. (Ref. 709) [!!!]

Fred offers 'Skillful Means Classes' to 'Discover Oneness,' 'Online Sunday Satsangs' to 'Explore Your True Nature,' 'Recorded Video Courses' to 'Awaken to Oneness,' and 'Group Clearing Series' to 'Achieve Pure Clarity'... but no Advaita.

Gail Brenner

Sacred Space for Awakened Living

https://gailbrenner.com/

Consider the radical possibility of seeing everything through the eyes of love. Expand out of the mindset of separation and into the all-encompassing field of clarity and love...where everywhere you look you see yourself. It's humbling to the personal self and touches the heart endlessly. (Ref. 710)

Not Advaita.

Gangaji (Antoinette Roberson Varner)

http://www.gangaji.org/

Poonja

In its truest meaning the concept of enlightenment is simply the open heart, the open mind. The heart can bear it all because the heart is the living expression of consciousness, naturally imbued with the capacity to bear anything and everything that appears in consciousness, including every mistaken idea and definition that you are not that. Heart opening is wisdom and wisdom is mercy. It's impossible to be merciful to anyone else if you are closed to yourself. (Ref. 711)

Not Advaita.

Ganga Mira (Mira Decoux/Pagal)

https://www.gangamirasatsang.com/

Poonja

Who you really are is here, just now regardless of the states of your mind. You are ever your Self.

Gautam Sachdeva

https://www.gautamsachdeva.com

Siddharameshwar, Ramesh Balsekar, Eckhart Tolle.

True apperception 'happens' when an aspirant is totally absorbed – mentally, emotionally and intellectually, in what the master is saying. Yet, being totally absorbed mentally, emotionally and intellectually is not something one can 'do.' It happens quite naturally as, after all, we carry our life's experience with us. So when something strikes us and 'hits home,' it is because we can relate at the core of our being to what we have heard. What helps is when the thinking mind, always questioning, doubting, or focusing on the surface-meaning of the words, is quiet. The chances of true apperception happening are more in an unconditioned, trusting mind. (Ref. 712)

Geoffrey Neill

Also known as Janak Giri.

No longer active.

Gilbert Schultz

Seeing-Knowing

http://www.seeing-knowing.com/

There is no teaching or path to non duality. To create a path, you have to have distance between TWO different places. If you cut an orange in half, it is no longer a whole orange. It is not possible to put the two halves back into wholeness. The mind divides itself through words and definitions. All meaning requires differentiation. Understanding itself is inherently dualistic. The natural state is wordless and silent. A recognition of wholeness brings an apparent state of silent and wordless appreciation. (Ref. 713)

Not Advaita.

Gina Lake

Radical Happiness

https://radicalhappiness.com/

It's time to awaken out of the ego and its limiting beliefs and sense of lack and dissatisfaction. Gina Lake's books, her channeled messages from Jesus, the Christ Consciousness Transmissions, and her online courses will help you do that.

Not Advaita.

Greg Goode

https://greg-goode.com/

PhD in Philosophy; Francis Lucille and Sri Atmananda (Krishna Menon) as well as the Chinmaya Mission.

But our investigation will reveal in the most direct way that objectivity is false. We will see that no matter what kind of object is involved, objectivity is simply never our experience. The belief in objectivity and separation is simply unfounded. When this is deeply understood, partly due to the investigations we will undertake in this book, the misleading sense of objectivity will be understood as false and will eventually vanish. The entire structure that seems to keep us separate collapses, along with all suffering. (Ref. 714)

Direct Path Advaita.

Halina Pytlasinska

http://www.nondualityinfo.com/

Disciple (?) of Tony Parsons. *"[A] British psychologist and therapist who works with the collective unconscious using the social dreaming matrix method."* (Ref. 715)

Not Advaita.

Hans Laurentius

https://hanslaurentius.com/

Nisargadatta, Ramana.

Waking up and staying requires many alarms. Every confrontation is one. Every rejection, disappointment, disappointment is one. The true man uses these to free himself, the half-man uses techniques to continue to sleep quietly as soon as possible, or complains and seeks confirmation. What you are is determined by how you deal with things, not by what you pretend. Go to war with your ignorance, break off all walls, refuse excuses and sedatives, eating barbed wire and drink vinegar (to you speak!). (Ref. 716, translated from Dutch by Google.)

Not Advaita.

Harry Liantziris

No longer active.

Helen Amery

https://wildfigsolutions.co.uk

Francis Lucille, Rupert Spira.

A month-by-month journey. Join for the months you want so that you resolve the resistances in your system, enlighten your experience of life, and reveal more of your aligned expression. Each month is a complete journey in itself. The more months you're part of, the more enlightened you feel. (Ref. 717)

Not Advaita.

Helen Hamilton

https://www.helenhamilton.org

Nisargadatta Maharaj, Adyashanti, Mooji, Papaji, and others.

Self-inquiry then becomes this beautiful thing of just sitting with this question and allowing all the ways that life wants to answer. So nothing at all is excluded in that inquiry, in the terms of what answers we are going to accept. If there is a noise outside where you are living, that is also an answer, if you have an emotion, a positive or a negative emotion, that is also an answer. (Ref. 718)

Not Advaita.

Howard Cohn

Mission Dharma

http://www.missiondharma.org/

https://dharmaseed.org/teacher/82/

Theravada, Zen, Vipassana, Dzogchen, Poonja, Ramana. Counseling Psychology.

LOTS of video and mp3 talks available but couldn't find any transcriptions.

Not Advaita.

Igor Kufayev

https://igorkufayev.org/

"Advaita Tantra" [?]

Igor Kufayev is one of the most important spiritual teachers in Europe and the US. He is a tantric-energy-transmission lineage holder, rare among nondual teachers today, with each member of his long-standing community absorbing and radiating the ancient prana-shakti of his tradition.

Not Advaita.

Isaac Shapiro

http://www.isaacshapiro.org/

Poonja

We all have unconscious habits of attention, that are uncomfortable to ourselves, and the ones closest to us, and indeed to all with whom we are associated. All reality is experienced through these unconscious habits, which function as cognitive filters, and make it almost impossible for us to recognize them. Therefore it can be of enormous value, to have someone who is perceptive at this level, to assist us...

In the course of investigation, people spontaneously recognize the true nature of themselves, which many report as the experience of peace, unconditional love, compassion, or simply of being home. (Ref. 719)

Not Advaita.

Jac O'Keeffe

Truth for its own sake

https://www.jac-okeeffe.com/

Jac takes your understanding of unity consciousness to new levels by guiding you to experience it and the unified field for yourself. Here is your opportunity to go from a conceptual understanding to owning your own deep understanding and wisdom about all things Oneness! (Ref. 720)

Not Advaita.

James Braha

Astrology and Nonduality

http://www.jamesbraha.com/

'Sailor' Bob Adamson

Little wonder so few seekers ever realize their true self. If consciousness is who we already are, then seeking is the very opposite of what is necessary! If consciousness is who we already are, seeking of any kind obscures our true nature. The moment a spiritual search begins, one unwittingly plays a game of hide and seek where he or she simultaneously plays both parts! (Ref. 599)

James M. Corrigan

https://stilljustjames.medium.com/

We assume that since we are conscious of our selves that we are therefore 'conscious beings'. When I say that I am a conscious being, I mean that I am first and foremost conscious of me — my attributes, my thoughts, my feelings and my actions. Awareness, however, except as an intuitive thought about it, is not one of the things that I can be conscious of. I feel the consciousness of various phenomena, but what would it mean to feel the awareness of that consciousness? If awareness and the feelings that are imparted upon our conscious experiences are ours, here in this body, then to feel the awareness of that consciousness means that we would have to be 'outside' of our own selves. We would have to be a presence looking upon our 'selves' in a most intimate way to be sure, but as an onlooker nonetheless. (Ref. 519)

Not Advaita, but his book contains some interesting philosophical observations and is worth reading if you are that way inclined (i.e., can follow it).

James Eaton

Authentic Living

https://www.authenticliving.org.uk/

When our deepest beliefs, the ones we thought were rock solid and sacrosanct, are fundamentally shaken and crumble to dust, when our heart erupts and a molten lava flow of feelings begin to burn, how astonishing, that in the midst of these fiery energies — in no longer finding interest in the stories of fear, anger, hate or blame that try to take hold — there is nothing but gratitude and wonder for the immutable joy that is our very essence! (Ref. 600)

Not Advaita.

James Swartz

Chinmayananda

https://www.shiningworld.com/

Were it made known what it actually takes for self-realization, the spiritual world would shrink to the size of a pea overnight. (Ref. 416)

You may believe that all spiritual people are somehow … well … spiritual, but you would be wrong. Spiritual people are just worldly people dressed up in spiritual clothing. While they have a vāsanā for otherworldly intangibles, they are not necessarily immune to the assortment of everyday attractions favored by their worldly brothers and sisters: the pull of security, pleasure, power and fame. (Ref. 447)

Traditional Advaita in a satsang guise.

Jan Kersschot

Site still exists but appears blank (Flash used?). No recent activity apparent.

Life is a good movie: you don't realise you're in a movie because everyday life looks so real. That's why I call it a daydream. But when you have a good look at what this person really is, you may discover that it is a concept. I think it is one of the greatest discoveries you can make in life, really seeing that the ego is an idea that appears in the mind. What you think you are is built up by hearsay and memory… It is not "you" watching the movie, the movie is being watched by the Light and your ego or personality is just one of the thousand images that appear on the screen every minute. (Ref. 601)

Foreword to Ref. 759 is by Tony Parsons.

Not Advaita.

Jan Koehoorn

https://jankoehoorn.nl/

Alexander Smit (Nisargadatta); Dutch.

A satsang is a meeting where you can ask questions about your spiritual quest, about your self-examination. [No other quotable material at website.]

Jason Swanson

https://youare-seeing-oneness.blogspot.com/

There is no path or practice. Just know that the I AM is your true nature. It is not the words "I AM", what are the words "I AM" pointing to?

No longer active.

JC Tefft

Non-Duality and Pure Consciousness Awareness

https://jctefft.com/non-duality

The brain is merely the materialized aspect of functioning Mind appearing as form, that's all. The brain is thus an extension of Mind, a physical outcropping of Mind, one might say, that is hard-wired, so-to-speak, to the functionality of Mind, allowing for concepts of Mind to materialize and come forth, or not.

Not Advaita.

Jean Klein

Died 1998.

No website.

Atmananda Krishna Menon

The seeker and the sought are one... It means the seeker has nothing to find, for what we are fundamentally is not an object perceived in space and time... It should be very clear for you that there is nothing to find, nothing to obtain; it is in waiting that you are waiting. (Ref. 722)

Jeannie McGillivray

http://www.vitalaliveness.com

Ex Study Society.

The invitation for this gathering is to surrender unreservedly to the unknown, the Truth of this eternal moment, so that the light of awakeness may bring the entirety of our experience to the foreground. When we have the courage to be fully present in open awareness to the totality of ourselves, we stand at the edge of the known. (Ref. 723)

Appears to be no longer active. Not Advaita.

Jeannie Zandi

www.jeanniezandi.com

Jeannie's more dedicated courses are by application and require commitment, from 30 days (Holy Work Challenge) to 8 months (Holy Essentials I, II and III).

Not Advaita.

Jean-Pierre Gomez

No longer active.

Jeff Foster

http://www.lifewithoutacentre.com/

Jeff belongs to no tradition or lineage but has a deep respect for traditions and lineages. Jeff is not an 'authority' on life. His words are equal to the sound of a bird singing, or a cat miaowing. All are expressions of the One Life. And when all words have disappeared, as they do, all that's left is laughter. (Ref. 602)

Note that the above was from an interview in 2011. Jeff now claims that he no longer has anything to do with Neo-Advaita:

Oh, my friends, I do speak from experience. I was once a fully-paid-up member of this loveless cult. I left about six or seven years ago, sneaking off in the dead of night, ready and willing to be a living, breathing human being again with a beating heart, and ready and willing to listen deeply to my fellow humans, and the relief was so, so great. Don't drink the Kool-Aid. (Ref. 603)

(Still) Not Advaita.

Jeff Vander Klute

https://jeffvanderclute.com

Jeff is a co-founder of Sourcing The Way, and he is a member of the Evolutionary Leaders Circle, *the Global Compassion Council of* Charter for Compassion International, *and the* Association for Spiritual Integrity. *He serves on the board of directors for* Alliance for the Earth *and* Garden of Light, *and he was previously the board chair of the* Source of Synergy Foundation *and the Happiness Initiative (now* Happiness Alliance*).* (Ref. 604)

Not Advaita!

Jennifer Hadley

Power of Love Ministry

https://poweroflove ministry.net/

If you're looking for spiritual connection, to heal your mind, heart, life, relationships, finances, or build a spiritual career, we may have what you're looking for.

Not Advaita.

Jenny Beal

Cotswold Non-Duality Group

https://www.ouspenskytoday.org/wp/about-courses/cotswold-non-duality-group/

Ex member of Study Society; now following Rupert Spira, Francis Lucille, Greg Goode rather than Ouspensky.

Lots of articles to read here.

Jerry Katz

https://nonduality.com/

Site provides a list of his books (writing and photography). Discussion group now on Facebook.

The desire for nonduality is the desire for the impossible and the discovery of the worthwhile. The teaching of nonduality says the worthwhile and the impossible are not separate. (Ref. 605)

Widely read (and written) on Non-duality in general. But not Advaita.

Jessica Eve

The Glorious Both/And

https://www.theglorious bothand.com/

"'Rescuing' people from the perils of nonduality seeking!"

Many spiritual paths ask us to leave the ego, our personal sense of self, behind. The problem is not the ego, but that it doesn't see how beautiful it truly is!

Not Advaita.

Jim Dreaver

Global Realization Project

https://jimdreaver.com/

Jean Klein

Its/my mission is to bring the message of realization to the world, so that we can end conflict and the horrors of war between nations and live in genuine peace, harmony, and co-operation with each other.

It does this through teaching the simple, yet mind-blowing mantra "Who is this 'me' that gets triggered?" whenever we have an emotional reaction to anything or are suffering in any way. (Ref. 760)

Not Advaita.

Jim Gilman

The Silent Way – Advaita Vedanta for the Western Mind

https://www.thesilentway.org/

Swami Chinmayananda

The attitude of the witness means that we watch. Rather than to be involved as a participant, to witness means to stand apart as it were, and simply observe. How do we accomplish this? I often suggest to students that we approach it like a game. The rules of the game are these: "I" am the subject. Anything of which I can be aware, anything that is an object of cognition, is an "object." There is a distinction between the "I", the subject, and the entire world of objects. If I look at something, I am not the thing at which I am looking, I am the one doing the seeing. The subject is aware of the object. The object does not illumine itself. It must have a conscious observer for its existence to be known. (Ref. 606)

Advaita!

Jim Newman

There is no path; "this" is home. For no one.

https://www.simply-this.com/

The end of seeking is not the fulfillment of the individuals' need for answers about what life is, what death is, nor is it the satisfaction of the need for meaning and purpose. ***It is the end of the need to***

know, which is the end of questions and search for answers as the causeless end of the questioner which never was. *The end of something that never happened. There is already not two. Real separation is a dream.* (Ref. 607)

Not Advaita.

Jivanjili

One in None Sacha Center; Dutch.

http://www.jivanjili.org/

Zen, Osho, ShantiMayi.

In the silence we hear our inner voice the loudest; in the irresistible call of the Beloved One... your 'True Names' and bears no name. It is the wordless, all-pervading call of the silent essence in all experiences. (Ref. 761, Google translated from Dutch.)

Not Advaita.

Joan Tollifson

The simplicity of what is

http://www.joantollifson.com/

Zen, followed by Toni Packer + many other Advaita and Buddhist.

Nondual spirituality, as I see it, is about openness, presence, direct immediate knowing — sensing, awaring, feeling, perceiving, being the aliveness of this moment. No words are ever quite right. Sometimes this openness is even called not knowing, meaning not grasping or fixating. Rather than being about accumulating information, it's more about letting go, relaxing, surrendering. (Ref. 611)

John Astin

Well-Being in Every Moment.

https://www.johnastin.com/

Through this inquiry into the nature of moment-to-moment experience, what's revealed is that every experience — including those we consider to be "negative" and in need of fixing — is a vast, indescribable field of open-ended, cloud-like energy and intelligence.

Not Advaita.

John Baxter

Modern Psychology & Vedanta

https://non-dualpsychology.com/

If you lose the thread of Vedanta, it's probably not an intellectual issue, it's more likely an emotional issue. So if you are suffering so much emotional disturbance that you are unable to sustain your focus, or you need to requalify because you've lost your way, consider psychological help. (Ref. 610)

There may well be some truth in this but it is not Advaita.

John David (formerly Premananda)

http://www.johndavidsatsang.org/

Presence is simple. Presence is that which is when thought is no longer there. Presence is also Love, for when there is nothing to block we are Love. Presence is also Freedom because when mind is quiet there is nothing to take us away from this moment now. So keep coming back to the Source from which everything arises. (Ref. 612)

John de Ruiter

Unveiling Reality

https://johnderuiter.com/

Listen only to what directly speaks to what you know the truth of. You, awareness, being quietly grounded in what you directly know the truth of puts you into oneness. Nothing else does that. A teaching and a practice, on its own, isn't going to do that. Your response to what you know the truth of in a practice or in a teaching takes you within; it connects you within.

Not Advaita.

John Greven

No longer active.

Traditional Advaita — a kind of path using knowledge, reason, logic, investigation to dispel the clouds of false ideas so that the sun (Self) is realized. Neo-Advaita — a kind of path that pretends to ignore the clouds of false ideas and encourages seeing Oneness directly.... Neo, it seems, offers the opportunity of removing some traditional Advaita baggage that was born in a different era and culture. Ultimately, it is the One — not the temporal teaching or teacher — that removes the veil. (Quoted in Ref. 521)

Not traditional Advaita, obviously!

John Prendergast

The Deep Heart

http://listeningfromsilence.com/

Adyashanti and Jean Klein.

Explore the convergence of psychological healing and spiritual awakening that happens most clearly and powerfully in the depths of the heart.

Not Advaita.

John Sherman

https://www.justonelook.org/justonelook.php

The Just One Look Method is an extremely simple approach to mental suffering unlike anything you have ever tried. It will rid you of the root cause of your dissatisfaction with life and the painful yearning for peace and fulfillment that seems never to be fully satisfied.

Not Advaita.

John Wheeler

No longer Active.

An archive of his teachings, with lots of video material, is available at Ref. 696.

Joi Sharp

www.satsangwithjoi.com

The Unbound Self

Supporting the Embodiment of our Universal Self through the application of Neuroscience, Mindbody Science and Quantum Mechanics.

Not Advaita.

Jon Bernie

https://www.jonbernie.org/

Zen, Jean Klein, Poonja, Robert Adams, Adyashanti.

To awaken is really to become fully alive — to live fully each moment in being. In that beingness you find, finally, the meaning and purpose of your life.

Judith Blackstone

The Realization Process

https://realizationprocess.org

Tibetan Buddhism

When we realize nondual transparency throughout our whole body, we uncover ongoing, effortless nondual reality. (Ref. 613)

Not Advaita.

Judy Cohen

https://www.irreverentmind.com/

(Website flagged as a security risk.) *"Integrate non-duality with your everyday life. Live what you know."*

Not Advaita.

Karen McPhee

Living Now

www.karenmcphee.com

Karen offers an invitation to return to your innate wholeness and rest in the heart of being. Her private and group sessions support *awakening to true nature and integrating all aspects of self into a state of embodied wholeness. - Single Session: $120 for an hour; Intuitive soul sessions help you connect more deeply with spirit to illuminate your path of highest freedom and fulfillment.*

No actual examples of what she 'teaches.' But not Advaita.

Karen Richards

No specific website.

Awakening is not the end — far from it. If anything, it can be likened to a beginning-less beginning of true experiencing — life seemingly offering a deeper opportunity to experientially surrender to what has been recognised and abide with increasing conviction as that. (Ref. 614)

Not Advaita.

Karl Renz

http://www.karlrenz.com/

For being what you are no work or development is required. All concepts, of way, development and even cognition, appear with the first I-thought. This first idea creates time, space and thus the entire universe. And as long as this I-thought appears to be real ... there appears the desire for unity and herewith the longing for a way out, for an end of suffering.... By being what you are, or better, as you are, absolute, prior to all and nothing, all concepts are destroyed. (Ref. 520 quoted in Ref. 521)

Not Advaita. For a specific criticism of this teacher, see Ref. 522.

Katie Davis

No longer active.

In 1986, Katie Davis radically and spontaneously awakened to the ultimate reality of who we really are without practices or teachers. She had never meditated or even heard of enlightenment, Advaita Vedanta, Non-duality or Self-realization. Katie had no intellectual reference whatsoever for what had occurred. (Ref. 615)

Not Advaita.

Kavi Jezzie Hockaday

https://www.kavijezziehockaday.com/

I am Kavi Jezzie Hockaday, a visionary poet harnessing the power of words to unveil the profound essence of life, while offering transformative experiences that awaken the deepest chambers of the heart.

Not Advaita.

Kavitha Chinnaiyan

Svatantra Institute: Ecstatic wisdom in a chaotic world.

https://svatantra.institute/

An initiate in Śrīvidyā and nondual Śaiva Tantra, she is a disciple of Śrī Caitanyananda Natha Saraswati (Haran Aiya) and has studied Tantra, Advaita Vedanta, Yoga and Āyurveda with teachers across the globe. (!!)

Direct Path (Greg Goode), Tantra and 'Path of the Goddess' (?).

Svatantra is the goal of radical self-discovery through understanding, digesting and earnestly applying the simplified concepts from Eastern traditions. Svatantra is only possible when we become willing to not use these concepts to bypass pain or hardship but to sincerely understand the cause of our suffering.

Not Advaita.

Kenneth Madden

https://www.kennethmadden.net/

Nothing is on offer here and this communication is clearly expressing that you are already that which you seek, you are already whole and complete. There is absolutely no hope to be found here as hope is an emphatic rejection of what is in favour of what could be. When what is being suggested here resonates and is realized fully (not in a conceptual sense) life is seen as it really is once more; indescribably full and in absolute freefall. (Ref. 724)

Not Advaita.

Krishna Gauci

https://www.krishnasatsang.com

Osho, Poonja.

Doing hatha yoga, pranayama, prayer, mantra, japa, kirtan, puja, kundalini yoga, prostrations, sitting meditation, samatha, vipassana, visualization and every other practice are fine, but practice in itself can distract you from the direct experience of the Self. Effort that requires you to create a goal for something that doesn't exist now furthers the duality and separation that it seeks to solve. (Ref. 616)

Not (Traditional) Advaita.

Leo Hartong

No longer active.

By labeling the world around us, we apparently gain the power to manipulate it to a certain degree; but through this practice, we also get hypnotized into seeing the world as a collection of separate objects, facts, and events, instead of as a single occurrence. (Ref. 22)

[See 'Recommended Reading.']

Leonard Jacobson

http://www.leonardjacobson.com

At the deepest level, you are pure consciousness, beyond form and content. You are powerful beyond imagining. You are eternal but you are on a journey through time. (Ref. 618)

If we are fully present, there are no thoughts. If there are no thoughts, then quite literally, there is no time. (Ref. 619)

Lisa Schumacher

Meeting in the Heat of Peace

https://satsangwithlisa.org/

Gangaji

Upon hearing Gangaji say, "Be your Natural Self," Lisa's Heart caught on fire and she fell into a deep bow of surrender, consumed in the profound realization that Love is All.

Not Advaita.

Louise Kay

Embodied Awareness: Explorations in Truth

https://www.louisekay.net/

Through the practice of Embodied Awareness you can awaken to your True self, discover your purpose and live a fulfilled life of joy, passion and creative expression.

Not Advaita.

Lynda Cole

No longer active.

Madhukar

http://www.madhukar.org/

Ramesh Balsekar

I've been looking at the statistics (such as they are) on the incidence of enlightenment throughout recorded history and, by means of certain rigorously scientific procedures, I have come up with the most up-to-date estimates of enlightenment probability yet available. It doesn't look good, I can tell you. In fact, the chances that you or I will finally "get it" this lifetime are pitifully small. My findings suggest that only 1 in 3,972,913 seekers will become enlightened in this current lifetime. Expressed another way, a seeker such as you or I should realistically expect to search for 24,765,538 years before enlightenment occurs. (Ref. 185) [I assume that this is not intended to be taken seriously!]

Mandi Solk

https://www.healingbyrevealingsoul.com/

Christian Science, Ramana, Poonja, Mooji.

Mandi also provides 'Halo Gazing' sessions: Once I have received your photo(s) I have to wait until the time is right for the Halo to be revealed to me. It's usually within a few days of receiving them, but if it takes a little bit longer, please be patient. You can be assured that it will be done. I have to wait for divine guidance so that I can perceive 'through God's glasses'.

I don't recall coming across this in any Advaita text that I have read...

Marcelo Bermann

https://awakenedself.org/

Prasad, Ramana.

Awarded Akashic Certification (2019).

For those, like me, who do not know what this means, Britannica says that *"Akashic record, in occultism, a compendium of pictorial records, or 'memories,' of all events, actions, thoughts, and feelings that have occurred since the beginning of time."*

Wow! Not Advaita!

Maria Felipe

https://mariafelipe.org/

ACIM (A Course in Miracles) – Not Advaita.

Marianne Djihi

Advaita Yogacentrum

https://www.advaita-yogacentrum.nl/

Kashmir Shavism, Jean Klein.

Dutch. Meditation and Yoga – Not Advaita.

Mark McCloskey

http://www.puresilence.org/

A gentle, loving, inner peace and silence is here and now in this moment. It has always been this way. It is always here. It is right here within you and all around you, a stillness, an apparent void, a seeming nothingness out of which everything arises, exists, and eventually returns.

Mark West

No longer active.

Marlies Cocheret (de la Morinière)

http://www.marliescocheret.com/

Osho, Adyashanti.

Marlies brings a potent invitation into the deep silence that we are. She has devoted her life to the Beloved. The kindness of her gentle and direct teaching guides us home like a lighthouse. She loves to be with people in the precious unfolding of Love and Truth.

Not Advaita.

Mary McGovern

http://graceisnow.blogspot.com/

Invited readers only!

Martinus Cosmology. (No, I hadn't heard of it either! Based on the vision of Danish philosopher Martinus Thomsen.) Definitely not Advaita.

Maury Lee

Enlightenment For No One

https://nomaury.blogspot.com/

Ultimately, the ego is not who we are, just an identity built of constructs, thoughts and feelings. Unfortunately, the ego doesn't realize it's just a bunch of concepts. And as those concepts are internalized and habituated, we develop feelings to go with them. Feelings are just automatic value judgments. (Ref. 620)

Meike Schütt

Meetings in Truth

https://meikeschuett.com/

Isaac Shapiro

It is the felt sense of connection that provides the space to notice those movements. The usual judgements crumble away, emotions and sensations are invited to discharge in the arms of love provided by the space of peace.

Not Advaita.

Metta Zetty

http://awakening.net/

Metta Zetty is an ordinary woman whose understanding of the nature of Reality has been profoundly transformed by an extraordinary experience of spontaneous awakening. In this timeless moment of intuitive recognition, Metta experienced a sudden, stunning insight into the nondual nature of Reality.

Not Advaita.

Michael Damian

A psychologist who offers 'Psychospiritual guidance.'

https://www.michaeldamian.org

As you come to know your real nature, the superstructure of mental identity and imagination loses its support and gives way to light — the light of intelligent, aware spirit. The world of things remains but is now illumined and uplifted in your presence. The world becomes an intimate to you, so that you feel no real divide between your bodily form and other forms. On the level of form they are distinct and you honor that fact, but distinctions do not imply a fundamental separation. In fact, the distinctions only highlight the unified background of consciousness. (Ref. 515)

An intelligent, 'non-denominational' description of 'who-we-really-are.' It is not Advaita (but doesn't claim to be).

Michael James

Happiness of Being

https://www.happinessofbeing.com/

Ramana, Sadhu Om.

Michael usually gives presentations and leads discussions at the Ramana Maharshi Foundation UK, in London.

Though this state of true knowledge — the state in which we are fully awake to the absolute reality of our own self — transcends all our ordinary three states, it nevertheless underlies them at all times, including the present moment. Therefore, in order to experience this fundamental state of true knowledge, all we need to do is to scrutinize and know our essential consciousness 'I am' at this precise moment. (Ref. 621)

This may be a representation of Ramana's teaching but it is not Advaita according to Śaṅkara. Turīya is not a 'state' and cannot be experienced. Also, who could "know our essential consciousness"?? There are more queried quotations in the body of the text. Note that I am really not singling out Michael for criticism. It is simply that, at the time I was writing this book, I was also criticizing the introduction to his latest book. And many of the examples happen to coincide with the frequent misunderstanding of current teachers.

Michael Stark

https://onenoumenon.blogspot.com/

Another blog of poems.

Not Advaita.

Mike ?

https://discoveringnonduality.com

Discovering Nonduality

Influences include Rupert Spira, A. Ramana, Ramana Maharshi, David Godman, Craig Holliday, Eckhart Tolle, Shunyamurti, Richard Rohr, and Swami Satchidananda.

What's true for me may not be truly true. What I mean is there is Truth, and it's not relative. We may believe whatever we want, yes. We have that freedom and that right, and no one can tell us otherwise. That is true. But that does not mean it's True. Truth is not just whatever we decide to believe.

A 50-minute session is $135.

Miranda Macpherson

Living the way of Grace

https://mirandamacpherson.com/

Ego Relaxation frees you to live an authentic life. Relish the gift of your existence. And make a meaningful contribution to our world.

Not Advaita.

Mokshananda

https://meetingtruth.com/teacher/Mokshananda

A disciple of Gurumayi and Adyashanti, he teaches, together with Marlies Cocheret at Free Water Sangha in Santa Cruz, CA. He can be booked as a speaker through 'All American Entertainment.'

(Not to be confused with Brother Mokshananda, the last disciple of Paramahansa Yogananda, author of *Autobiography of a Yogi* and teacher of Kriya Yoga.)

Buddhism rather than Advaita.

Mooji

http://www.mooji.org/

Ramana

If the world as it is ordinarily perceived and experienced inside the human mind and ego was indeed real, then one would be pressed to declare. 'Oh my God, we really are in deep shit.' Luckily for us the shit is only really inside our heads and can easily be flushed out by satsang. Find out where the nearest satsang is — urgently. (Ref. 401)

Mukti

http://www.muktisource.org

Paramahansa Yogananda; Wife of Adyashanti.

Not Advaita.

Nathan Gill

Died 2014.

Consciousness has absolutely no problem whatsoever with a personal 'I' being present. Only Consciousness appearing as the seeker believes — or has been led to believe — that there is a problem with the personal 'I'. The seeker believes that he or she needs to be rid of the personal 'I', that non-doership or non-identification are important, but the whole thing is Consciousness arising in and as your awareness now. (Ref. 63)

Nathan Spoon

Ganapati-Advaita Ashram in Charlotte, NC.

http://ganapatiadvaitaashram.blogspot.com/

No blog since 2010.

Neelam

Fire of Truth Satsanga

http://www.neelam.org/

Poonja

Presence is already here. The reason it does not seem to be available all the time is because our attention does not rest here. The practice is coming here, to know your true nature over and over again. Develop a better habit, training our attention to be here. Break through this misunderstanding, this belief that there are times Presence is not here. (Ref. 725)

Not Advaita.

Nic Higham

The Wholeness of Experience – Non-duality Informed Counselling and Coaching

https://nisargayoga.org/

Nisargadatta

Non-dual realisation is the clear and complete awareness of the reality of experience. It happens that your experience is reality. Your experience is made of it, consists solely of, and nothing whatsoever other than actuality itself, reality itself. So you are always immersed in the naked presence of reality.... You're already seeing that. (Ref. 593)

Nick Gancitano

The Self-Inquiry Center

https://www.self-inquiry.com/

Ramana

Self-Inquiry is the Direct Path and a proven solution to help you live a fulfilling life by becoming conscious of patterns that detract you from authentic happiness. Whether you simply desire 'stress relief' or you're an experienced yogi seeking Enlightenment in this lifetime, you'll find what It Is you are looking for…

Nick Roach

https://www.nickroach.uk

Barry Long

I failed to find a suitable quotation, but he does promote Ref. 125 at his site, so that may be thought to give an indication.

Not Advaita.

Nirmala

Nondual Spiritual Mentoring

http://www.endless-satsang.com/

Neelam, Adyashanti.

Nirmala and his wife, Gina Lake, offer Christ Consciousness Transmissions (CCTs) in five weekly online gatherings on Thursdays, Saturdays and Sundays at 11 am Pacific time, and also on Tuesdays and Saturdays at 5 pm Pacific time. Read more about these transmissions that facilitate awakening.

Listen to a channeled message from Jesus where he introduces himself and Christ Consciousness Transmissions.

Not Advaita.

Nisargadatta Maharaj

http://www.nisargadatta.net/

Experience, however sublime, is not the real thing. By its very nature it comes and goes. Self-realization is not an acquisition. It is more of the nature of understanding. Once arrived at, it cannot be lost. (Ref. 5)

This quotation is from his most famous work *I am That* — a book that has inspired many to take up Advaita! The problem with much of the material, however, is that most (if not all) of it is translated and therefore susceptible to confusion. It is also mostly in the form of question and answer — and therefore, again, susceptible to confusion. His later material also became increasingly difficult to follow, verging on Neo-Advaita or meaninglessness. For example:

This 'droplet' of knowingness is a result of the food essence body; in understanding it, you are out of it. If this last step is taken, knowing that I, the Absolute, am not that 'droplet', the consciousness, it has to happen only once. There is no more involvement with the play of the consciousness. You are in a state of no return, the eternal state. (Ref. 345)

This may be a problem of Q&A circumstance/recording/translation etc., as discussed earlier.

Nome

Society of Abidance in Truth (SAT)

https://satramana.org

Ramana

What is real is the innate. What is natural is innate. Determine what is innate in you. All that is not innate should be discarded as not so.

What is innate is transcendent of all doing. What is innate cannot be gained or lost. What can you lose? Everything you can lose. What of that which is not a thing? What is not a thing must be discerned nonobjectively. (Ref. 595)

Nonduality Institute

We are a non-profit center dedicated to the scientific study of nondual awareness.

https://nondualityinstitute.org/

I had to include this, although it is obviously not a 'teacher.' The idea that science could 'study' non-duality is just so incredible! They say: *"Such unitary experiences are possible because of the background presence of nondual awareness – an open, awake cognizance that precedes conceptualization and contextualizes and unifies both extrinsic task-positive and intrinsic self-referential mental processes, without fragmenting the field of experience into opposing dualities."* And that explains everything – not!

It appears to be very serious, with a board of scientists with impressive qualifications. Everything about it is fine, if you are interested in neuroscience etc., except for this one aspect that baffles me: If reality is non-dual, then the aim is clearly nonsensical; if it is not, then they are wasting their time anyway.

Norman Scrimshaw

Awakening to the Heart: A Mountain Sanctuary for Heart-Centered Community Gatherings & Events.

https://awakeningtotheheart.com/

Adyashanti, Neelakantha Meditation, Yoga, Sound Healing.

Not Advaita.

Nukunu

https://nukunu.net/

Osho and Pooja; philosophy and psychology degrees.

The truth, Enlightenment, is not something you understand with your mind, it is "something you are". The mind cannot understand it. It is the fourth dimension "Turiya" in sanskrit. (Ref. 726) [!!!]

Not Advaita.

OM C. Parkin

https://www.om-c-parkin.de/en

Ramana, Poonja, Gangaji.

Freedom is about consciously recognizing the unconscious desire to be limited, the desire to be in prison... Although it is admittedly contradictory and incomprehensible, the moment that suffering is obviously here, the desire for suffering must also be present... Or do you really think it is God who wants you to suffer?... But who is "God"? God is just your *idea of God. You can always only hold your own idea of God responsible and pretend not to be responsible for it yourself.* (Ref. 622)

Everybody can ask questions or share their heart in Darshan. Each of OM's answers has the clear and sharp flavor of uncompromising Truth. Penetrating straight through the questions, OM focuses directly at the questioner himself, dropping deeper than thoughts or feelings can do. (Ref. 727)

Not Advaita.

Osho (Previously Bhagwan Shree Rajneesh)

Died 1990.

https://www.osho.com/

A tradition is nothing but the footprints of enlightened people in the sands of time — but the footprints are not enlightened. (Ref. 83)

Apparently, Osho's intention was to offer to people as many different spiritual viewpoints as possible, thus he talked on Zen, Sufism, Jesus, Tantra, Krishna, Yoga, Hassidism, Vedanta, Buddha, Mahavira, Socrates to name just a few.

He very clearly reveled in his notoriety, quite intentionally going out of his way to upset the establishment in order to expose the false notions at the base of their opinions and beliefs. His daily talks to his followers were recorded and much of the material has now been transcribed into books. Many of these are extremely readable and full of profound and thought-provoking observations, as well as many very funny jokes! But don't expect the material to teach traditional Advaita!

Pamela Wilson

http://www.pamelasatsang.com/

Robert Adams, HWL Poonja, and Neelam. She can be booked as a speaker through 'All American Entertainment.'

Satsang is a gathering of people to honor Truth, to rest from the conflict and confusion of the world, and take refuge in the Heart.

Not Advaita.

Paul Morgan-Somers

The non-dual formless nature of life

https://innate-evolution.teachable.com/p/non-duality

interview: **https://batgap.com/paul-morgan-somers-transcript/**

After a series of spontaneous experiences as a teenager he left his sleepy village near the coast of West Wales and spent the next 5 years in a Vedanta Centre Monastery playing in the love and wonderment of what Is, and sharing time with representatives of most of the world's religions.

And now he provides a course on 'Non-Duality and the spiritual nature of life' for £114. (Need to sign-up to watch videos.)

Peter Brown

The Yoga Of Radiant Presence is the actual nature and process of reality itself, so is intrinsically the most fundamental, essential, and efficient spiritual engagement possible…

Died 2022.

http://www.theopendoorway.org

What you are actually is beyond words, but it would be not untrue to say you are nothing whatsoever other than pure, infinite, disembodied consciousness/intelligence; a field of miraculous infinite light; God dreaming itself; an infinite point of pure potential; or the infinite implications of nothing whatsoever. (Ref. 623)

Peter Francis Dziuban

https://consciousnessisall.com/

Book *Consciousness is All*. Free chapters for download.

Infinite doesn't mean forever in time, but is the complete absence of time, because time, too, would be measurable. Infinity is not even a circle or endlessly repeating loop, for that, too, has form, an inside and outside. Infinity has no form or limits — exactly as the Consciousness You now are has no form or limits. They are the same One. (Ref. 728)

Not Advaita.

Peter & Pearl Sumner

No longer active.

Philip Mistlberger

ACIM (A Course in Miracles), Osho, Buddhism etc.

http://www.ptmistlberger.com

The longing for freedom eventually directs us to set out on a path — usually called 'the spiritual path'. The basis of this path is the intention *to realize truth. The path actually goes from nowhere to nowhere, in the sense that what we are really doing is re-discovering our true nature — a true nature that is already the case, underlying the layer of dust created by our mind.* (Ref. 134) [See 'Recommended Reading.']

Philip Renard

http://www.advaya.nl/

Advaita, Dzogchen and Zen; Da Free John, Alexander Smit.

The Absolute is uninterruptedly the case. Although it cannot be experienced, it constantly bestows reality to everything that is being experienced. This bestowing quality is in a way being 'transmitted' by the Self, the 'primordial Experience', which in its turn bestows temporary reality to the manifold experiences. (Ref. 625)

Poonja

Died 1997.

https://avadhuta.com and **https://www.satsangbhavan.net/**

The awareness that is realization is beyond the mind. Far, far beyond the mind. It is the business of the mind to keep you unaware of what you really are. It fills you so completely with doubts and fears, it gives you the notion that there is nothing beyond the mind. By continuously generating doubts and fears it accomplishes the trick of preventing you from being aware of who you really are. It keeps you ignorant of the fact you are already realized; that you have always been realized. It is the function of the mind to keep you in the darkness of the past. When there is no mind, there is no past and no time. When there is no mind, the ultimate truth of who you are shines uninterruptedly, unimpeded, and unobscured by wrong ideas. (Ref. 626)

Prajnaparamita

https://www.prajnaparamita.nl/en/

Alexander Smit, Poonja, ShantiMaya.

Many do not realise that when you are your own teacher, you will be taught by your ego. Can you see — for yourself —your manoeuvres away from being profoundly touched? Do you allow yourself to be disturbed in your comfortable habits? Can you see your blind spots? It is certainly true that one can see into the nature of existence quite deeply by reading books, self-enquiry and meditation, but awakening is so subtle and so total. Is there enough urgency in you to bring the journey to resolution without needing to protect anything? (Ref. 627)

Premamanda

See John David.

Pyar (Trolle)

German.

http://www.pyar.de/

Samarpan (Osho) + many traditions.

My heart is burning together with you and discovering again and again that we are nature as body, clarity as spirit and love as a soul.

To become deeper and deeper aware changes our thinking, feeling and acting. We discover and unfold our effectiveness with joy in ourselves and can shape a living future for all of us and this beautiful blue planet. (Translation by Google.)

Not Advaita.

Rajneesh

See Osho.

Ramana Maharshi

Died 1950.

Official – https://www.sriramanamaharshi.org/

Unofficial – http://www.ramana-maharshi.org/

In a state of deep sleep we lay down our ego, our thoughts and our desires. If we could only do all this while we are conscious, we would realise the Self. (Ref. 729)

Not a sampradāya teacher and some teaching (or what is translated and recorded) is contrary to traditional teaching. Nevertheless, much of it is often tremendously helpful to seekers.

Ramesh Balsekar

Died 2009.

http://www.rameshbalsekar.com/

The understanding, which is itself Truth, happens only when there is immediate and distinct (and therefore 'true') perception. It happens only in the absence of reason and logic, which are in duality. In such understanding the comprehender (the 'me' as an individual entity) is totally absent and the mind is in total surrender. Understanding, as such, can only spring out of absolute silence, the stillness that prevails when action ceases and conflict ends. (Ref. 514, quoted in Ref. 366.)

This is precisely the sort of 'explanation' that leads to mistaken notions about all sorts of issues relating to Advaita.

- Perception relates to the sense organs. It operates in duality. Everything that is 'perceived' is a form of Brahman but, until Self-knowledge is established, is thought to be a separate entity and named as such.
- You cannot 'perceive' the truth. Advaita means 'not two'; 'seeing' the truth would be duality.
- Self-knowledge does not exclude reason. Doubt causes the seeker to ask questions of the teacher as part of manana. Answers are naturally subjected to reason.
- It is in the mind that the understanding takes place — it is *not* absent!
- Finally, the understanding springs out of the explanations provided by the teacher, *not* out of silence!

Randall Friend

http://avastu0.blogspot.com/

'Sailor' Bob Adamson

What we must be able to see is that the 'thing' as it appears is not absolute reality — that means the rock isn't a completely separated existence. It didn't arrive anew as a new thing. But this is absolutely our root belief — each appearance is a thing — by that we MEAN a new and separate existence. So we believe there are an infinite number of independent existences — coming and going, being born and dying. Birth is the creation of a new existence and death is the ending of that separate, independent existence. But if we really look into this idea, we find that idea to be false, in fact it's not really even difficult to realize this. (Ref. 730)

Randall is now holding talks on Non-duality in 'Second Life,' the online 3D virtual world — http://secondlife.com.

Ranjit Maharaj

Died 2000.

The world is nothing but a long dream, take it for granted.

There's nothing there, so what is there to say? As long as the body is there, he acts, no doubt. He calls his mother "mother", and his wife "wife", but still he knows. If somebody asks him, "What is your name?", he gives his name, but he knows, "I am not this." (Ref. 731, quoted Ref. 732.)

Same guru as Nisargadatta – Siddharameshwar Maharaj (died 1936).

Raphael

Āśram Vidyā Order

http://www.vidya-ashramvidyaorder.org

Advaita, Plato, Neo-Platonists, Orphism (Pythagoras and Parmenides).

Brahman is the substratum of all possible phenomena and therefore of the whole of life, life which we erroneously call objective and subjective, visible and invisible, inferior and superior, one and manifold. (Ref. 629)

Richard Sylvester

http://richardsylvester1.wordpress.com/

Tony Parsons

A way of searching may lead to a person being more comfortable. That is fine but it is all that you get – a person who is more comfortable in their prison. If you are in prison, it is better to be comfortable but that doesn't get the person out of the prison they perceive themselves to be in.

Nothing will get the person out of their prison because the person is the prison. When the person drops away, it is seen that there never was a prison in the first place. (Ref. 487)

By whom is it seen, Richard??

Rick Linchitz

No specific link.

Satyam Nadeen

There was a realization that there was never any such thing as Rick. There's only consciousness unfolding. And there was complete peace and relief. That peace never left. In this 'story' it seemed that the Rick character had had experiences before that in meditation, was deep peace and unbelievable ecstasy, but those were always seen as an experience happening to Rick and they were always seen as something that if Rick worked harder he could go get and get back. This was different. This was much quieter, less spectacular. It was a simple disappearance of any belief in the reality of individuality. It was not an experience happening to Rick, just a disappearance of anyone who could have an experience. (Ref. 630 presented at Ref. 733.)

Who had this realization and experience, Rick?

Rishi Rajiv

https://www.rishirajiv.org

Poonja

Jiva is itself free. It is part of the Same. Individually you call it jiva or atman. Cumulatively in every being it is the same, you call it paramatman. Param means Absolute. It is That which is in everybody. The moment it relates with the individuality, it becomes Atman, the Soul, the Self. But it is not separate from That. Because of the form-oriented identification, this mind comes, and jiva goes in the trap of the form oriented likes and dislikes. And that's where the mind and the identification come. That is what we call as Atma, or we call as Gopi in another word. (Ref. 631)

Robert Adams

Died 1997.

http://www.robertadamsinfinityinstitute.org/

Ramana

"Begin at the beginning." Revered by what Robert Adams refers to as fundamental precepts of "all true religions" of the world. The result is a "Direct experience of God", resulting in extended periods of peace, an awakening of loving kindness, compassion, humility and

a realization of a sense of brotherhood with all. Living in natural spiritual integrity, one's life is guided by The Power That Knows the Way.

And the website points out five times on the home page that the "Robert Adams Infinity Institute is a nonprofit 501(c)(3)" (whatever that means).

Why not awaken now? What are you waiting for? Make up your mind that you're going to awaken right now, and allow your mind to turn into your Heart, which is Pure Awareness. Do it! Some of you are still asking, how do you do it? Through Silence. (Ref. 155)

Robert was one of the earliest 'Satsang' teachers. He was not a Neo-Advaitin but a Ramana adherent. All of his material is readable and some of it is quite good. But this is not traditional Advaita. In the past, there have also been complaints that he lied about his background with Ramana. I have not personally investigated this. And it does seem that the objectives of the organization established after his death are questionable.

Robert P. Meizer

Wherein I Explain – that it's inexplicable

https://mu.thelemistas.org/bobbymeizer/

Nisargadatta Maharaj – Bob Adamson – John Wheeler – Bobby Meizer.

The ego believes it is fighting for its very existence here so it tries its best to be stubborn, but in the end it must lose. It's finite, limited by definition. The Absolute. No contest. (Ref. 632)

No longer active.

Robert Saltzman

https://dr-robert.com

'Depth psychologist' and psychotherapist.

I know nothing about ultimate matters: nothing about submission to the will of God, as in Christianity and Islam; nothing about realizing one's identity with Brahman, as in Hinduism; nothing about what happens when you die, and nothing about how all of this got here — none of it. (Ref. 633)

Not Advaita.

Robert Wolfe

Died December 2022.

https://livingnonduality.org/

Ramana

... every meaning that we give to something is reducible to the recognition that only one thing is ever happening: an expression of Be-ing. Everything is simply that one Truth. This is what is meant by "true nature". (Ref. 508)

Robin Dale

No website. No longer active?

There is only This. If you think you're enlightened, throw it away and begin again. The idea of 'enlightenment' is like a big ugly monster with a pretty face, inside you. Like the idea of the Abyss is a big warm openhearted angel with an ugly face. (Ref. 516)

Not Advaita.

Rodney Stevens

https://radianceofbeing.blogspot.com/

Since you ARE awareness, there can be no roads or journeys or techniques to it. But that is precisely what 99.99% of the gurus, meditation mega-stars, and spiritual teachers want to do: Give you a mantra, a technique, or a process to reach some form of "enlightenment."

Sorry, it is not going to happen. Has it happened for them? Absolutely not! Talk with someone who has a living understanding that he or she is awareness itself. Only can that person be your guide, your pointer to the eternal.

Not Advaita.

Roger Castillo

https://www.rogercastillo.org/

Ramesh Balsekar

'You' can't do anything. All the movements and functioning of the body-mind including thoughts and emotions are happening automatically without 'anyone' doing them — 'you' have never done anything...

(Blog seems to contain more about Coronavirus than Advaita!)

Roger Linden

The Elusive Obvious

http://www.rogerlinden.com/

J. Krishnamurti, Tony Parsons.

Liberation is the complete and permanent evaporation of any sense of a separate self. It's not an intellectual appreciation or an intuitive insight into the nature of reality. It's the breaking of the vacuum seal or the bursting of a bubble. It is the end of seeking and the realisation that there is only wholeness. What remains is silent, spacious awakeness, consciousness, within which the wondrous translucent immediacy of life is appearing. And the experience is tender, peaceful joy — it's love. (Ref. 430)

Rory B. Mackay

https://www.unbrokenself.com

James Swartz

As a component of the subtle body, the ego is essential to our functioning in the world. Without an ego, you'd never get anything done. Whenever somebody called your name you'd be unable to respond because the part of you that identifies with that name would be absent.

So, the ego does serve its purpose. It's neither necessary nor possible to "kill" it. All that's really necessary is to dethrone the ego; to divest it of self-identification; to see it as nothing more than an instrument allowing us to function in the world rather than the sum total of who we are. (Ref. 635)

True!

Rosemarijn Roes

https://www.rosemarijnroes.nl

It is a paradox. Writing a book about what is. Nothing can be explained, it is about nothing. There is only writing, words coming from nothing, are nothing. And yet there can be a recognition, or there can be a falling away of some beliefs. It is talking in two worlds, who do not meet. The me world and that what is. For the me there is only the real and solid world.

What a challenge to meet nothing. Where it is about nothing is everything, nowhere to go. Where each knowing is pointless and control is seen as an illusion. What a freedom. The answer on a longing. (Ref. 524) [Apologies for the fact that, although this was formatted as poetry, since it took up so much space and didn't rhyme, I reformatted it.]

Not Advaita.

Roy Townsend

https://devgrah.blogspot.com/ – Not active since 2015.

If a person says they are enlightened they are most probably not as that shows they still think there is someone to become enlightened. The true enlightened couldn't answer with a yes or no to that question as they know there isn't actually anyone here who could possibly become enlightened in the first place.

Once enlightenment happens first we know who we really are and then know that the person we thought we were doesn't exist — he (in my case) is an illusion only. By saying I am an illusion I don't mean this body/mind, I mean the 'me' I thought was in control of this body/ mind. There isn't anyone in control of this body, it's programmed to look after itself.

[See the section on 'Who Is It Who Is Enlightened?' above.]

Rupert Spira

The Essence of Non-Duality

https://rupertspira.com/

Francis Lucille

The mind, body and world are experienced to be unreal as objects but real as awareness, just as the fields in a film are unreal as fields but real as screen. (Ref. 432)

I wrote a long review of Rupert's first book at Ref. 637. I gave it 5* but also criticized many aspects.

Sadananda, Acharya Kuntimaddi

Advaita Vedanta and Forum, Ācārya at Chinmaya Mission, Washington, DC.

http://advaitaforum.org/

Swami Chinmayananda

See 'Recommended Reading' section.

'Sailor' Bob Adamson

Nisargadatta

https://www.sailorbobadamson.com/

The idea of enlightenment or self-realisation as a onetime event or a lasting and permanent state or experience is an erroneous concept. Understand-ING or know-ING is alive in the immediacy which can never be negated. The emphasis is on the activity of know-ING which is going on as the immediacy now — not the dead concept I understand or I know.

Salvadore Poe

http://www.salvadorepoe.com/

Numerous influences, culminating with Dolano.

In my own experience, when the purely subjective "I" is known, it is not that the "self" or "I", the body/mind vanishes, as some modern teachings suggest, but that it instantly expands from the contracted sense of a personal "I" to the infinite "I", which is firmly set in now.

The body mind, with its sensations, thoughts, etc., still appear, but they are no longer, in that moment of knowing/being the sole locus of experience, as it is in our normal contracted state of being. Now they are part of the "all". (Ref. 596)

If one is ready, the message is simple. Stop. Turn around. Have a shift of knowing. Instead of knowing only the objective world – inclusive of the five senses, thoughts, emotions and sensations, all passing experiences – come to know yourself as the knowing of all of that, which is not an experience and does not change. It is peace already. This is a 180 degree turn around, from subject/object, to pure subject with no object, in which all objects ever-changingly appear. It is the self-effulgent light of knowing, knowing only itself. It is existence knowing itself. It is I knowing myself. It is knowing and being, which are one and the same, no separation, not two. (Ref. 597)

Quite good!

Sandy Jones

https://celestialsongspirit.blogspot.com/p/celestialsong.html

There is an invisible Eternal Light behind the appearances of this world. This Light is the Infinite Mind of God, the Ineffable One. Everything going on in our world is happening, appearing, being seen and experienced by way of God's Infinite Being, the Awareness you are, the One and Only Light of Divine Consciousness. (Ref. 734)

Not Advaita.

Satyam Nadeen

Apparently converted from Michael Clegg by four years in prison. Ramana, Nisargadatta, Poonja and Ramesh Balsekar.

All he said in his opening chapter was "Consciousness (Source—All That Is—God) is all there is." WOW!!! He said it and I could actually see it, know it, feel on fire with it, and begin to live it. (Ref. 735 quoted in Ref. 736)

Satyananda

https://www.satyananda.org/

Ramana

Primal Yoga aims at providing depth to the practice of yoga: the primal depth that yoga is aiming at, which is firstly harmony in the body, followed by harmony in the mind, Samadhi and Self-Realization. It is a slow yoga, not a yoga of varieties, of positions. It is a yoga of observation, meditation and development of awareness in consciousness. (Ref. 641)

Not Advaita.

Science and Nonduality Conference (SAND)

https://scienceandnonduality.com/

Organized by Zaya and Maurizio Benazzo.

Where we come together to explore beyond ultimate truths, binary thinking, and individual awakening while in deep reverence of the beauty, complexity, pain, and great mystery that weave the infinite cycles of existence.

Occasional contributions from teachers of Advaita (e.g., Rupert Spira) but mostly Not Advaita.

Scott Kiloby

Enlightenment Embodied

http://www.kiloby.com/

Detox and addiction treatment.

Scott's inquiry tools have brought freedom to thousands worldwide. [!] *Learn the basics for free in five days.* [!]

Needless to say, not Advaita.

Shakti Caterina Maggi

Awakening to Life

https://www.shakticaterinamaggi.com/

Her key teachings are the love for transcendence, or spiritual awakening, followed by its deep integration, into everyday living, so that each moment can be met as a precious opportunity for spiritual growth. Her students are left with the joy of an open heart and an authentic sense of freedom within the recognition of our being as one with everything. (Ref. 598)

Not Advaita.

Sharon Landrith

Clear Light Sangha

www.sharonlandrith.com

Adyashanti

Not Advaita.

Sheilan

What if this is all an illusion?

http://infinitelivingteachings.wordpress.com/

Ramana Maharshi, Ramesh Balsekar, Wayne Liquorman.

Earth is a school, and we in the 3rd dimension are participating in a collective dream. This teaching dream is about to change to a new lighter dream in higher dimensions. At the end of this dream, the main players who are bringing forward the light are being revealed in what is called the Great Awakening. (Ref. 642)

Not Advaita!

Shunyamurti

SAT Yoga Institute

https://www.satyoga.org

Ramana, many Eastern and Western philosophies, *"and profound exploration of the dimensions opened by entheogens"* [i.e., LSD etc.].

As we approach the final collapse of the global social order, it is imperative that the healthy seeds of the next age begin to sprout. This means that a critical number of souls must reach the level of Being necessary to assure continuity of consciousness. We must develop the virtues that will enable survival — including benevolence, moral strength, perseverance, love, wisdom, and joy.

Not Advaita!

Sitara

https://advaitavedanta-sitara.de/

Osho, Dolano, Gangaji, Swami Paramarthananda.

Satsangs in German.

Blogged for some years at my own site. Many essays available at her site (in German).

Advaita is the only philosophy that goes beyond this ubiquitous orientation towards 'becoming.' Not that the acquisition of certain skills or the elimination of certain identifications would be devalued but Advaita points out that becoming by itself will not lead anyone to the True Knowledge, the only goal of every pursuit — simply because that goal is never away in space or time from the seeker. (Ref. 667)

Soham

https://soham.one/home.aspx?sflang=en

Osho, Gangaji, Shivkrupanand ('Samarpan' meditation).

For over twenty years, I have intuitively known that total and complete liberation would happen for me in this lifetime and not only for me personally, but for everyone who is energetically connected to me. With this in mind, Satsang has been happening and I have been meeting thousands of people, promising all the while that being with me will ensure the awakening of everyone who is with me.

Not Advaita.

Sruti

https://batgap.com/sruti-transcript/

Gangaji and Mooji.

Lots about Cystitis and pain. Couldn't find anything about Advaita.

Stephan Bodian

Wake up to your life.

https://www.stephanbodian.org/

Zen, Dzogchen, Jean Klein and Adyashanti.

I'm still waking up to different dimensions of reality that I hadn't even seen so clearly before. So I feel incredibly grateful to be on this journey, but I never could possibly ever say that it's done. (Ref. 643)

Not Advaita.

Stephen Wingate

https://selfknowledge2.wixsite.com/self-knowledge

Nisargadatta, ACIM, Dzogchen, Neville Goddard, The Teachings of Abraham, The Seth Teachings, Carl Jung, New Thought, Ernest Holmes, Joel Goldsmith, Adyashanti, Eckhart Tolle and many others.

You exist. You are aware. Is a teacher needed to know this? A teacher may remind you of what you are, and what you are not, and point you back to this fundamental truth time and again until you realize it for yourself, or until you get sick and tired of hearing it and you move on to another teacher who tells you the same damned thing! (Ref. 502)

Not Advaita.

Stephen Wolinsky

https://stephenhwolinskyphdlibrary.com

Nisargadatta, Zen and others.

Founder of Quantum psychology.

Not Advaita.

Steve Hagen

https://www.dharmafield.org/

Not Advaita (Zen).

Steve Taylor

https://www.stevenmtaylor.com/

Wakefulness is a state of expansive and intensified awareness. In my research, I have found that this state incorporates four different aspects or domains. The first domain is perceptual awareness. When a person awakens, the world around them becomes more real, beautiful, fresher, vivid, and alive. Things considered ordinary become more beautiful and fascinating. It's as if a veil falls away, and suddenly, an extra dimension of reality is added to the world. (Ref. 737)

Not Advaita.

Stuart Schwartz

Merging into the Infinite.

http://www.satsangwithstuart.com/

Robert Adams

In satsang one has the taste of no mind, this loosens the construct of ones held identity and allows the process of facing ancient murky emotions to surface and be faced. You could say that it is the process of excavation that catapults one to the heights of nothingness. (Ref. 644)

Sue Cawthorne

https://uk.linkedin.com/in/sue-cawthorne-0a8b0966

Reiki Master/teacher, Non-dual Awareness coaching/ teaching, Mindfulness/teacher/coach, trained Crystal Healer.

Non-duality coach [!] *at Pure Awareness, Bath, England, United Kingdom. Founder and Director at Soul Alchemy Academy.*

Not Advaita!

Sundance Burke

No longer active.

When the function of thinking is known as having absolutely no role to play in our Self-realization, it naturally and spontaneously subsides to reveal a deeper sense of who we are. (Ref. 645)

Not Advaita.

Suzanne Foxton

https://nothingexistsdespiteappearances.blogspot.com/

Links inactive; no recent writing.

I was washing some dishes. I took a knife from the sink. The knife became an amazing wonder; it was exactly right; it was the most knifish knife that ever knifed; it was life, knifing. A kind of vision engulfed me, or replaced me; my mind needed to supply visuals, so I seemed to see a sort of cosmic winking in and out... (Ref. 738)

Not Advaita!

Swami Abhayananda

https://www.themysticsvision.com/

Christianity, Ramakrishna, Vivekananda, Muktananda.

The evolution of the soul occurs over many lifetimes, with its summit being the full openness to self-surrender in the Love of God, and the subsequent realization of its supreme identity. And because the evolution of the universe reflects the evolution of each soul, the stellar and planetary positions, which signal that soul's enlightenment, will coincide perfectly with that moment in the soul's evolutionary summit. (Ref. 646)

Not Advaita.

Swami Atmananda Udasi

Ajatananda Ashram

https://ajatananda.org/

Ramana, Nisargadatta, Krishna Menon, Poonja, Swami Chidananda, Abhishiktananda (Henri Le Saux), Swami Ajatananda (Marc Chaduc).

'Pure Consciousness' is all there is. It is another name for the divine Being or Presence. It is the ultimate Reality, beginningless and endless. It is beyond time and space. It is one without a second, or indivisible oneness, yet it is the source of everything, the foundation of all what is manifested. It is Bliss. It is most Benevolent. It is beyond description though it has been formulated in diverse ways at diverse

times by all the great religious traditions of the world, and directly known and experienced beyond words by the sages. It cannot be grasped by the intellectual mind, but can only be recognized as our True Nature through 'no mind', that means at the level of the Heart. The recognition of our True Nature or Self is the end of suffering. (Ref. 647)

This is all good, clear, traditional Advaita until the reference to 'no mind' and 'Heart' at the end. Here, the influences of his teachers are apparent.

Swami Dhyan Giten

https://swamidhyangiten.wordpress.com/

Psychology

Our intuition is the inner teacher, the inner guide, the inner master. The old Indian scriptures say that the outer spiritual teacher is helpful to find your own intuition, your own inner teacher, your truth.

Intuition is to create a trust in yourself and in your intuition, your inner guide, the inner master. Intuition is to learn to listen to the still, small voice within, and that will guide you. (Ref. 648)

Not Advaita.

Swami Muni Narayana Prasad

Narayana Gurukulam

https://narayana-gurukula.org

Narayana Guru

Death is an occurrence by which all the specific attributes of an individual disappear. It is not a process of becoming nothing. What really exists cannot become non-existent. (Ref. 130)

See 'Recommended Reading' section.

Swami Parthasarathy

https://www.vedantaworld.org

A man who adds new meaning to the phrase 'Business Guru' – *TIME* Magazine.

Over the last 50 years, A. Parthasarathy has been addressing organizations and corporations in USA, UK, Europe, Russia, China, Malaysia, Singapore, Australia, UAE, South Africa, and India.

But note that, prior to his 'business interests,' he wrote Refs. 16, 123, 282, and 387, all of which are worth reading. His recorded talks on Bhagavad Gīta stimulated my early interest in Advaita.

On realization of the Self, the individual merges with Brahman. The erstwhile 'experiencer' who has hitherto been 'experiencing' the 'world of objects' becomes Brahman. Distinctions such as the 'experiencer', the 'experienced' and the 'experience' are found only in terrestrial experience. When you become one with Brahman these distinctions vanish. Thereafter Brahman alone exists. Nothing else. (Ref. 16)

[This example shows that even traditional teachers may communicate confusing ideas.]

Swami Premodaya

International Centers of Divine Awakening [honestly!]

https://www.i-coda.org

See also **https://www.spiritualteachers.org/swami-premodaya/**.

Osho, Gangaji.

Bodhisattva Shree Swami Premodaya invites you to step directly into awareness and recognition of the vast and unending divine reality – which is beyond all joys or sorrows, beyond any beliefs or ideas, beyond this body and its apparent life and death, and even beyond the most exquisite experiences or states of mind. (Ref. 649)

Not Advaita.

Swami Sarvapriyananda

Minister and spiritual leader of the Vedanta Society of New York (Ramakrishna Order). Excellent talks available (video/ audio) on YouTube/Spotify etc.

https://www.vedantany.org/

Well ultimately, Maya is nothing different from the absolute, whose power Maya is, and so ultimately the answer would be this seemingly dualistic universe which seems to be as far from God as possible is actually nothing other than God. You would not say that it is God, but it's nothing other than God. There's a very interesting distinction.

Mary Hale, one of the disciples of Vivekananda in the late 19th century, she wrote in a poem to Vivekananda: 'you have taught us that all is God' and Vivekananda wrote back: 'I have never taught such strange doctrine that all is God'. And she said: 'you said it'. He said: 'no, I never said that all is God. God only is, the all is not', which is an important distinction in nondualism. (Ref. 650)

Swami Satchidananda

Integral Yoga

Died 2002.

https://swamisatchidananda.org/

(https://integralyoga.org/)

A jīvanmukta may be doing anything. He or she need not be sitting in samādhi in some cave; this person may be in Times Square, but is still a jīvanmukta. A jīvanmukta is involved in the world for the sake of humanity without any personal attachment. (Ref. 11)

Yoga philosophy. See 'Recommended Reading.'

Swami Satchidanandendra

Died 1975.

https://adhyatmaprakasha.org/

The one unique feature of Śaṅkara's traditional interpretation is that it holds that the main purport of the Vedantic texts is to reveal Brahman or Atman by culminating in the Intuition of Brahman without any intervention of any action to be done either before or after that intuition. (Ref. 651)

Known as SSS or even SSSS (Sri Swami Satchidanandendra Saraswati). Not actually a sampradāya teacher but an ardent advocate of traditional teaching according to Śaṅkara. Not all traditional Advaitins agree with his views and there has been much argument upon a number of topics. See my book, Ref. 398.

Swami Saurabhnath

https://www.facebook.com/swamisaurabhnath/

A disciple of Nath Tradition in Maharashtra, India.

Unable to locate any online samples of writing. He has several books, including a comprehensive Bhagavad Gita translation and commentary.

Swami Virajeshwara

Died 2014.

https://hamsaashramam.org/

'I' is nothing, it is naught, a cipher. A non-entity. It does not exist. 'I' is a mere nonexistent ego. It has no existence, no place on earth. All this was in deep samadhi. That was it. (Ref. 739)

Swami Virajeshwara's guru was Swami Vidyananda Saraswathi, who was a disciple of Swami Sivananda Saraswathi of Divine Life Society, Rishikesh.

Tim Freke

https://timfreke.com/

To wake up, we are told, we must eradicate many of our natural human characteristics. We must stop desiring things to be different and acquiesce to the way things are. We must sever all personal attachments and be detached and aloof. We must become selfless saints who are never angry and fearful. We must become holy ascetics who deny ourselves the pleasures of the flesh. From the lucid both/and perspective none of this is true. Thank goodness. It's okay to be human. (Ref. 408)

Not Advaita.

Timothy Conway

https://www.enlightened-spirituality.org/

Influenced by many traditions. Advaita includes Ramana and Nisargadatta.

The pseudo-advaitin labors under and suffers a chronic compulsion to always absolutize everything onto the 'ultimate' or 'final' truth-level of discourse (paramārtha-satya)... Basic humaneness, warmth and tender loving care vanish in a preference for a cool, robotic demeanor and a slavish adherence to speaking 'Absolutish' and always having to sound 'profound.' (Ref. 522)

Lots of essays and a page with lots of funny jokes! His highly-critical, long article, and compendium of contributions from others on the topic of Neo-Advaita (Ref. 522) is referenced by many.

Timothy Schoorel

http://www.7freedom.com/index.htm

Website was flagged as a 'Potential Security Risk,' when I tried to access it.

To believe that consciousness is ultimately a function of the human being, that it is created by the human brain, is a very anthropocentric thought. It is like believing that the earth is the center of the universe, or that the sun moves around the earth. It is believing that the human being is what existence was built around. This paradigm-shift takes us away from the human being to an understanding of consciousness as such. (Ref. 652)

Tom Das

Liberation and Non-Duality

https://tomdas.com/

This really is an Advaita site! But, the 'Disclaimer' page states that: *"This website is for general information and entertainment purposes only"*! And *"having an email dialogue with him, is NOT a replacement for or substitute for face-to-face, in-person, qualified medical, psychological, psychiatric or legal advice, diagnosis or treatment."*! And finally: *"Using Tom Das's services and reading his website is entirely at your own risk WITHOUT warranty or guarantee of any kind, either expressed or implied, including without limitation any warranty for information given, advice, or opinion."*

Ramana Maharshi

Does that mean that not everything is consciousness? No! Perhaps everything is consciousness! Perhaps it isn't. The point is that we do not know. Everything may or may not be consciousness. We don't know. It's actually a scientific question and we currently don't have the evidence either way. It may be impossible to know, as how would you know that there is nothing beyond consciousness?... (Ref. 653)

Not always Traditional Advaita.

Tom Fitzgerald

http://www.tomfitzgerald.org/ – site last updated 2009

"Tom did not become attached to one particular philosophy or group as he wished to honor his own true path."

Tom is a spiritual teacher with an ability to tune into a person's energy field and bring into awareness the beliefs and feelings that are preventing them from being in the now. This awakened state of present being awareness enables a person to access the ultimate truth of their being. (Ref. 656)

Not Advaita.

Tom Thompson (and Bonnie Thompson)

The Awakened Heart Center for Conscious Living

https://www.theawakenedheartcenter.com/

"A student of human psychology and a practitioner of the yogic pathways and enlightenment traditions."

Conscious Living is an all inclusive way of life. It is based on the Enlightenment Pathways of the East and the Human Potential teachings of the West. It includes the possibility of radical awakening along with the integration of body, emotions, mind and spirit; living skillfully and effectively in this world; and being in loving, empowering relationships. (Ref. 657)

Not Advaita!

Toni Packer

Meditative Inquiry

(1927–2013)

Founder of Springwater Center.

Zen. Not Advaita.

Tony Parsons

https://www.theopensecret.com/

The mind loves the idea of enlightenment being some kind of distant, virtually unobtainable, perfect place of permanent bliss, free from suffering and full of omniscience, omnipresence and lots of other important 'omni's' stomping around, shouting the odds and saving the world. And of course, because all this glory and specialness has to be attained, it seems there has to be a long haul through the dark night of the soul, endless past karmas, original sin, right-thinking, right action and preparation for the bardos. "It is a tale told by a fool, full of sound and fury, signifying nothing." (Ref. 660)

Quotations should be "told by an idiot."

Unmani - Liza Hyde

http://www.die-to-love.com/

Osho, Dolano (Zen).

The job of the teacher is not to give you some kind of special spiritual experience, but to encourage you to see that all experience is spiritual, regardless of the labels of the mind that seem to separate spiritual from mundane. The teacher can not give you awakening. It is always about the readiness of the student to wake up out of beliefs about yourself, the teacher, and even awakening itself. (Ref. 661)

V.V. Brahmam

http://www.brahmam.net/

Founder and president of the Bhagavan Sri Ramana Maharshi Ashram, Andhra Pradesh, India.

Site features many hours of audio and video recordings of satsang. He speaks extremely slowly and then is translated into Tamil (?). I was unable to find any transcriptions or other written material. There are also lots of photos of him…

Vasant Swaha

https://vasantswaha.net/

Osho, Poonja.

I have no teaching, for how can you put silence, love, freedom into a teaching? It is a living experience.

Not Advaita.

Vijai Shankar

Academy of Advaita

https://www.academy-advaita.com/

The spoken or written words are not borrowed from another author or source or have been spoken by any other author. The words are not borrowed from any written scriptures either. The Academy of Advaita archives wisdom for not only this generation but also for future generations yet to come. [!!]

Not Advaita!

Vince Flammini

https://vinceflammini.com/

Any instruction other than to leave everything alone, to relax, to just rest as you are, is dangerous. It is dangerous because it points us back into the shadow realm of thought, technique, manipulation, alteration, effort, and theory…

Isness is you-ing you. What a relief! There is nothing to do but rest as we are. (Ref. 662)

Not Advaita.

Vishrant

https://www.vishrant.org/

Osho

Since awakening in 1999, he has served as a vehicle for higher consciousness and enlightenment who shows seekers a pragmatic way towards creating a mind that will support Truth and Love… Vishrant teaches that serving heart is the "beauty way", which he calls The Way of the Heart.

The one who wants enlightenment can never wake up. Enlightenment does not happen to the ego. It is not real. What we really are is pure awareness. When that awareness becomes aware of itself and stays aware of itself, that is enlightenment. (Ref. 663)

Volker Hinten

Advaitaweb; Dutch

https://www.advaitaweb.nl

Alexander Smit

Also strongly promotes mindfulness, which is not Advaita.

Wayne Austin

Heart Whispers

http://www.heart-whispers.com/

Gangaji, Ramana.

Everything is happening Now. Walk in the Mystery. In the end, all we need know is that: All is well. Ultimately, everything is reduced to Silence. (Ref. 530)

Not Advaita.

Wayne Liquorman

The Advaita Fellowship: Seekers of Truth

http://advaita.org/

Ramesh Balsekar

This Advaita, as I talk about it, is not actually a philosophy, because it does not hold any tenets. It is simply a collection of pointers and concepts, and it posits that none of them are true in an absolute sense. This teaching is not about conveying the truth. It is about prying away the limitations and misconceptions about how things are. (Ref. 510)

Wayne is very inventive with metaphors and is undoubtedly one of the best satsang teachers.

(Yukio) Ramana

Radical Awakening and the Opening to Heart Consciousness.

http://radicalawakening.org/

Poonja

In a private Radical Awakening session, you are guided to such a powerful place of awareness, something shifts so deeply in consciousness that things are never again perceived in the same way. Issues are viewed within the backdrop of heart, which is realized as always pure, and always present. (Ref. 665)

Not Advaita.

Zoran Josipovic

See Nonduality Institute above (he is the founder), and Judith Blackstone (his wife).

https://realizationprocess.org/zoran-josipovic/

The Empathic Ground is the relational healing aspect of the Realization Process. It is a series of attunement practices that can be practiced by two people or by groups of people. The practices deepen and refine contact between people, and enable them to receive and respond to each other with less projection and less fear. (Ref. 666)

Not Advaita.

Recommended Reading

Before letting you peruse the list below, I cannot resist recounting a story I read (from the Ramana Maharshi organization) indicating what Ramana said about reading lots of books. He asked whether, on looking in the shaving mirror in the morning and seeing that we needed a shave, we would then go to look in lots of other mirrors for confirmation. Similarly, if we read a book explaining that we are not who we thought ourselves to be and that we should endeavor to find the real 'I,' why then read lots of other books telling us the same thing? We should simply start to do something about it now! Just as the mirror cannot shave us, the book cannot enlighten us.

Fortunately, this guidance is not entirely reasonable. It is possible to learn an awful lot from books. Unfortunately, one can also be seriously confused. Many of the books on Advaita do not correctly present the teaching of Advaita. The 'bottom line' is simple — there is only the non-dual reality and 'you' are necessarily That. But it is how you reach that conclusion in a manner that leaves no room for doubt that is the difficult part. Most modern books (by satsang and Neo-Advaitin teachers) simply repeat the bottom-line message in as many different ways they can think of and hope that one of them will sink in. What you need is a carefully developed and reasoned approach that will clear your doubts as you progress. And there are not many of these around.

I feel I can make this statement because, since I wrote my first book, I have acquired (and often read!) very many books on Advaita. I feel reasonably safe in claiming that I probably have the most extensive collection in the UK, outside of the major universities — probably around 1500 after including electronic versions. See http://www.advaita.org.uk/library/library.html for the list of books (which is not complete as I have not been updating this site for the past 10 years or so). I may not have read them all (OK, I haven't), but I have at least skimmed all of them to determine whether they were worth the time and effort (for me). I have read very many and certainly all of the ones mentioned below.

Also, as you would expect, my own understanding of Advaita has matured over the past 25 years and I now realize that some of the books that I might have previously promoted, I should not have done. I am also now able to recommend some about which I was previously unaware, and some which have only recently been published.

Note that some of the books recommended below may be difficult to find. Many are published by Ashrams in India and some of the ones I have purchased in the past were in very limited editions (one as low as only 200 copies). One compensating factor is that, if a book is published in India, it is going to be relatively cheap. (Of course there is the clear danger that, if you purchase such a book in the West, they will mark up the price to the Western equivalent, and thereby make a much improved profit!)

Warnings

As I already noted, finding a good (qualified in the way I have described) teacher is difficult. Having found one, access to him or her is likely to be, if not impossible, at least drastically life-changing. Probably 99% of seekers, even if they consider themselves to be 'serious,' are unlikely to be prepared to give up job, home, friends, and relatives to move halfway around the world in order to be able to attend lessons given by a particular teacher.

Consequently, most seekers are obliged to look to books as their source of Self-knowledge. Here, 'access' to them is trivial. Nearly all can be purchased online, from one source or another. Unfortunately, choosing which to buy is, if anything, *more* difficult than choosing a teacher! The reason is simply that one is most unlikely to be able to walk into the nearest bookstore, pick up a promising book, and look through to discover if it is readable and informative. Even the best city-bookstores near me rarely stock *any* books on Advaita. I am only aware of one, and that is in London. The only time I have ever seen one of my own books on sale in a bookstore, other than the one in London (Watkins, Cecil Court), was over 20 years ago in Amsterdam, where I saw the first edition of *Book of One* in a shop window! The only 'spiritual' books one is likely to find are ones recently promoted by Oprah on the radio. (Hence the success of Eckhart Tolle's *Power of Now* for example, which one *still* finds in most bookstores!)

If you have a 'spiritual bookstore' in your area, you are very lucky but, even then, it is far more likely that you will find books on talking to angels and learning from your past lives than you will find good books on Advaita. (This even applies to Watkins!)

Many (most?) of the books that you will find on Amazon fall into one of two categories: academic or popular-spiritual. The former are aimed at students of philosophy-religion and usually written by a professor in those areas. Occasionally, these may be very good indeed, but more often (it seems) the author has studied the subject in order to be able to teach it rather than because they wanted to become enlightened. Consequently, such texts will be lacking in direct, personal Self-knowledge and will merely pass on the sentiments of whichever sources happened to have been studied. They are usually written in an 'academic' style, which is often impenetrable. And they may even seem to convey understanding which is contrary to traditional Advaita.

Nevertheless, 'academic' is usually preferable to 'popular-spiritual'! These latter are usually written by someone who claims to have 'spontaneously awakened' following some dubious and frequently ignominious event. Subsequently, they 'wanted' to pass on their newly-revealed knowledge to others, totally uninfluenced by the fact that such a process might be an easy way of making a living. Cynical this may appear to be, but I have read some of these books! Accordingly, one needs to be very careful indeed when considering this genre. Nevertheless, it must be conceded, there are some gems amongst the gravel!

Categories

I will recommend books in the following categories:

- Books for beginners
- Traditional Advaita
- Satsang
- Direct Path
- Neo-Advaita (Yes — I do recommend some of these!)
- My own books.

General Guidance

There are direct links from the library and other locations at my website (www.advaita.org.uk) to purchase these books from Amazon in both the US and the UK, or from India in some cases. Please use the links as they generate a small amount of commission which I can then use for purchasing more books for the library! (Incidentally, if any reader knows of a worthy location to which I can donate the books on my death, please contact me (via the website). They would have to collect them and should provide some justification — i.e., I do not want to give them to a private owner but to a library or university, for example. And hopefully not for a few years yet!)

Possibly the best guide to the likely long-term value of a book is to look at the Contents page and the index. My library of books is sorted by category, and I have just looked through the shelves of books by satsang and Neo-Advaitin authors. Out of the 41 books there, only two of them have an index. Interestingly, both are by Wayne Liquorman, who is actually quite good for a satsang teacher. Out of the 36 versions of the Bhagavad Gīta that I have, a surprising 18 have an index (although two of these *are* in Sanskrit!). And this relative figure is probably similar for other traditional texts (but I am not doing any more counting).

If there is no index, then (terrible though it may seem), I recommend using a soft pencil to mark passages that you find of value (positive or negative) and putting an '*' at the top of each page that has been marked. When you have finished the book, if you are really motivated, you can add the flagged elements to a spreadsheet. (I have been somewhat halfhearted about this and my spreadsheet has only 5300 entries. I use a very good search engine – dtSearch – for finding material on my computer (around 10GB of Advaita-related files).) If you want to find out about a particular topic, you can then look it up in the spreadsheet and immediately locate the book and page that tells you about it.

If we are talking about 'general' books, i.e., not a particular Upaniṣad or other special text, an even better initial guide probably comes from looking at the 'Contents' pages. A book that is worth looking at more closely will list the sort of topics that are relevant in Advaita in the sort of order that one might expect them to be introduced to a seeker. Thus, they will cover the 'starting' position of identification with body etc.; look at the practices that one needs to prepare the mind; probably deal with the main prakriyās of traditional Advaita; and end up with topics such as the nature of reality, creation and, of course, the 'conditions' of enlightenment and jīvanmukti.

Satsang-type books do, in fact, usually have a Contents page of sorts. But they are often just a list of the (essence of) the questions that have been asked by attendees of the satsang. Where this is not the case, the subject is often anyone's guess, with the words used presumably having been chosen to provide humor rather than information.

Without naming any names, some examples of chapter headings that I found are: 'Miss Scarlet in the Billiard Room with a Wrench'; 'The Sky over the Sea of Emotion'; 'Thieves in an Empty House'; 'There is no need to Wait for the Bus'; 'The Devil Claims Responsibility'; 'Intergalactic Beans'; 'Laughing at the News'; 'I feel like a dog chasing its tail'; 'We are the Latest Models.' (I will offer a prize of a signed copy of the first edition of this book to the first person who can name the books from which these headings are taken.)

I. Best Books for Beginners

I have been asked many times, by seekers posting questions to my website, which Advaita books I would recommend. Eventually, after I had pondered this question for the nth time, I wrote out a list, aiming to cover the best of those books in all of the following categories. This was extremely difficult and I cannot claim to have entirely succeeded. Nevertheless, here they are. I decided to separate them into books by Indian authors and ones by Westerners.

All the best commentaries on scriptures and most on 'special' topics are by Indians but most of the general introductions are by Westerners.

Indian

1. **Vedanta: The Solution to Our Fundamental Problem** by D. Venugopal (Ref. 394). Rather than explaining key topics, this one provides a complete presentation of Advaita, beginning with an explanation of life's problems and then describing the steps that a seeker takes in Advaita to realize his or her true nature, and that of the world appearance. The complete book is serialized at my website, beginning at Ref. 740 — there are 62 parts — but you really should buy it! The author is a direct disciple

of Swami Dayananda and understands the teaching in depth. It is both readable and authoritative.

2. **Introduction to Vedanta** by Dr. K. Sadananda (Ref. 438). This was originally written as a series of essays to provide introduction to the key concepts in Advaita. The essays were edited by myself and published originally on my website. They were then collected together and published in this book, which fulfils the aim superbly. Dr. Sadananda is now an ācārya with Chinmaya Foundation and teaches in Washington, USA.
3. **The Living Gita: A Commentary for Modern Readers** by Sri Swami Satchidananda (Ref. 357). A supremely readable commentary. This is Yoga philosophy rather than Advaita but beginners will not really see the differences and it is so readable and inspirational that I overlook this! The other 40 or so versions I have are not so likely actually to be read.
4. Three general books on Advaita by Swami Dayananda are highly recommended: **Self-Knowledge** (Ref. 186) is based on nine talks on ātma vidyā given in May 2003; **Dialogues with Swami Dayananda** (Ref. 112) is collected from various sources and was originally published in 1988. Both of these are very readable and suitable for any level of student. They are short but contain key topics presented with exceptional lucidity. Finally, **Introduction to Vedanta: Understanding the Fundamental Problem** (Ref. 363) provides exactly what it says – an introduction to some of the key concepts, explained in simple terms for the beginner. 'The fundamental problem,' 'The Informed Seeker,' and 'Ignorance and Knowledge' form the core of this very clear exposition. It also uses all of the correct Sanskrit terms so that these will be understood when moving on to more general reading.

5. **Vedanta Treatise: The Eternities by A. Parthasarathy** (Ref. 123). Swami Parthasarathy has written several books, including one on the Gītā, one on Śaṅkara's Ātmabodha, and a commentary on several of the Upaniṣads. The *Vedanta Treatise* was his attempt to summarize Vedanta from his readings of the classical texts and from his studies with his own guru, Swami Chinmayananda. A new edition was produced in 2004. He also ran a school in Bombay, which provided a three-year residential course on Vedanta. And his children/disciples run an organization in London, which teaches Advaita 'for management.' This is an excellent introductory book. It tends to be more practical than theoretical, emphasizing bhakti and karma yoga aspects more than those of jñāna. The quotation on his Bhagavad Gītā cassettes was that it "is a technique, a skill for dynamic living, not a retirement plan." As you will have noted, I deprecate such 'misuse' of Advaita, but this does not detract from the value of the book.

Western

1. James Swartz is one of the very few teachers who follow traditional methods but in a more modern, satsang-style context. He is a direct disciple of Swami Chinmayananda. In particular, his book **How to Attain Enlightenment** (Ref. 416) can be recommended. It is full of quotable statements expressing the essence of Śaṅkara's teaching in pithy, often witty aphorisms. The reader is in no doubt that the writer knows what he is talking about. It is Eastern philosophy for the Western mindset. There are lots of books out there written by satsang teachers and some of them are quite good. This is not one of them — it

is written by an accomplished traditional teacher and it is excellent.

2. The best book *about* the teaching of Ramana Maharshi (in my view) is **Be As You Are** edited by **David Godman** (Ref. 17). Short, but full of the clear explanations of probably the best known teacher of the past millennium. David Godman researched many sources and combined the material so as to provide fuller answers to the various questions, which are sorted into topic. It has to be noted that Ramana, like Ramakrishna, was not a sampradāya teacher. Whilst his answers tally with the traditional ones for the most part, there are potential confusions, such as his idea that the mind has somehow to be 'destroyed' in order to realize the truth.
3. **A Natural Awakening** by Philip Mistlberger (Ref. 134). It seems that many teachers attempt to subvert the traditional teachings by diluting them with ideas from Western psychology in order that they may satisfy the modern seeker looking for a 'better life.' In order to address the perceived needs of these Western students, what seems to be needed is a teacher who understands both psychology and Advaita. He will then be able to address the psychological issues authoritatively in their own context whilst at the same time expanding the students' awareness into being able to see the truth behind their seeming problems. Philip Mistlberger clearly has the ability to teach in this way.

I invariably pencil in notes in the margins of books whenever I encounter particularly useful explanations or helpful metaphors so that a very good indicator of the value of a book can be gained by the number of such annotations. Based upon this, I can state categorically that this is a very good book indeed!

It should be noted that his teaching has now moved more towards ACIM than Advaita.

4. **Awakening to the Dream** by Leo Hartong (Ref. 22). Leo's teaching is usually regarded as Neo-Advaita, influenced as he has been by both Tony Parsons and Nathan Gill. Nevertheless, it retains some of the best traditional metaphors and styles. It is a marvelous exposition of non-dual teachings, straight from the heart. It draws on quotations from a wide variety of sources (not just Advaita), but is highly recommended!
5. **The Book of One** by Dennis Waite (Ref. 84). Someone pointed out that I was not recommending my own book for beginners and that I really ought to be. Modesty aside, I obviously think that what is said here is worth reading or I wouldn't have written it. I will not try to write a subjective-objective review of it, however, and refer anyone interested to the section of my website devoted to extracts, endorsements etc. Suffice to say that it is a general introduction to Advaita in all its aspects.

II. Traditional

There are traditionally three types of scriptures referenced by this philosophy. They are called the prasthāna-traya (prasthāna means 'system' or 'course' in the sense of a journey; traya just means 'threefold'). The first of these is śruti, which refers to the Vedas, incorporating the Upaniṣads. Śruti literally means 'hearing' and refers to the belief that the books contain orally transmitted, sacred wisdom from the dawn of time. The second is smṛti and refers to material 'remembered' and subsequently written down. In practice, it refers to books of law, in the sense of guidance for living, which were written and based upon the knowledge in the Vedas. Most often it is used to refer to just one of these books — the Bhagavad Gītā. Finally, there is nyāya prasthāna, which refers to logical and inferential material based upon the Vedas, of which the best known is the Brahmasūtra of Vyasa. This work was extensively commented on by Śaṅkara in the Brahmasūtra Bhāṣya, which analyses the theory and arguments behind Advaita and counters all of the objections that might be posed to that mode of interpretation and rejects other philosophies.

In *Back to the Truth* I recommended quite a few scriptural resources but most of these were simply translations of the original Sanskrit. I would no longer recommend these unless you have a large library and are thus able to compare translations. The problem is that Sanskrit words have many potential meanings, often totally unrelated. When translating a sentence, one has to take into account the entire context, and understand the purport.

My book *Confusions in Advaita Vedanta* (Ref. 398) highlights numbers of instances where a respected teacher or academic has mis-translated a word so that the sentence takes on the meaning that accords with a prior misunderstanding of the topic. Accordingly, it is really advisable: a) that a naïve seeker only read scriptural texts that are well commented and explained; and b) that the seeker is pretty sure that the writer has a correct understanding of that scripture.

Of course, it is rather difficult to satisfy oneself on that second condition unless one already has a trusted opinion on the subject! Having read or referenced many versions of practically all of the key scriptures, I can offer some advice.

For me, the 'gold standard' of scriptural commentary is the talks by Swami Paramarthananda. These used to be available to download, but I understand they may only be purchased in India on DVDs, since they are really only intended as study-aids for those attending his classes. However, many of the talks have been transcribed and the complete set for many of the main scriptural texts may be downloaded from Ref. 741. The transcriptions are usually very good, although representation of Sanskrit words is variable. The talks on the more advanced texts may contain quite a lot of Sanskrit, but this is not usually a problem if you are familiar with the main terms.

Swami Dayananda was, in my view, the best teacher of traditional Advaita in written form and one of the few to teach in the West. He was able to explain the most difficult aspects clearly, using modern language and often amusing metaphors. He died in 2015.

One other, very important, point is that the reader must be careful to choose only those texts that are at, or just ahead of, his or her current level of understanding. The more advanced texts not only assume a correspondingly greater prior understanding of the basics, but they also contain much more Sanskrit! Note that you do not need to know Sanskrit as a spoken or written language – it is the vocabulary with which you need to become familiar. This really only happens with familiarization – the more times you encounter a word, the sooner it will 'sink in'!

1. Upaniṣads

There are very many translations and commentaries on these, either singly or in groups. There are not so many versions of the 'Complete' Upaniṣads, if it could be agreed what this means exactly, since there are certainly more than 100 separate ones. Upaniṣads such as the Bṛhadāraṇyaka or Chāndogya can run to as many as 1000 pages, including commentary, while some like the Tejabindu are only a few pages. Some of the minor ones are based on Yoga philosophy rather than Advaita. Since the text of all of them is often obscure, the seeker should always go to the ones with Śaṅkara bhāṣhyas first. Even then, look for ones with commented explanations of Śaṅkara's comments as well, since his own comments are often quite difficult to follow.

Choosing a commentator on Śaṅkara's commentary is not an easy task unfortunately. If you cannot obtain a recommendation from someone whose opinion you trust, you just have to get whichever version you can find (that you can afford) and hope for the best!

Books containing many Upaniṣads tend only to translate the Sanskrit of the Upaniṣad itself, rather than providing explanatory comments. These cannot be recommended, since the particular English word used to translate a Sanskrit word becomes critical when there is no further help in understanding. This is not to say, however, that single Upaniṣads with commentary will always be reliable. It is virtually impossible to render the intended meaning exactly in a translation so it is almost always the case that the English contains elements of the translator's own understanding of Advaita. If this understanding is incorrect, then the translation may be erroneous and confusing. My book at Ref. 398 contains examples of this from even highly respected teachers and writers. Obviously the same applies to translations of Śaṅkara's commentaries.

A. Collections of Major Upaniṣads

The only one to which I frequently refer is the collection of eight of the major Upaniṣads, translated by Swami Gambhirananda and including some of the commentary by Śaṅkara, entitled unsurprisingly **Eight Upaniṣads** (Ref. 336). It comes in two volumes. But you should note that only a little of Śaṅkara's commentary is covered. If you want to be sure you understand what he says about a verse, you need to go to a single-Upaniṣad version which contains the complete Bhāṣya.

B. Single, Major Upaniṣads

If you want to look at individual Upaniṣads, the major ones are the Kena, Kaṭha, Īśā or Īśavāsya, Muṇḍaka, Māṇḍūkya, Praśna, Taittirīya, Aitareya, Chāndogya, and Bṛhadāraṇyaka. All have commentaries by Śaṅkara (which is why they are called 'major'). Of these, I would recommend the first four to begin with. The last two are very long but they are the oldest and the ones most often quoted, especially the Bṛhadāraṇyaka. But neither of them makes for easy reading! You can safely ignore the Praśna and Aitareya (I have hardly looked at them). The Māṇḍūkya is possibly the most important, with its commentary (Kārikā) by Gaudapada, but it is very difficult so should not be attempted straight away.

i. The very best commentaries I have encountered are those by Divyjñāna Varadarājan. There are four (so far): **Kaṭha**, **Muṇḍaka**, **Māṇḍūkya**, and **Taittirīya**. The last two of these are in two volumes and are more advanced. All four are based on lectures given by Swami Paramarthananda (and Swami Dayananda in the case of the last two). All of them provide word-by-word translation of both the Upaniṣad and Śaṅkara's Bhāṣya, as well as explanatory summaries of what is said. Unfortunately, they are difficult to get hold of, being published in limited numbers in India. The books indicate Arsha Vidya Gurukulam in Coimbatore, India as a source; alternatively try emailing Selva Nilayam at sntpl@dataone.in. Having just checked the AV website, there is presently no reference to the books but a few copies may be available at Amazon or Exotic India.

ii. For the **Kenopaniṣad** (Kena), I also recommend the one with commentary by Swami Muni Narayana Prasad (Ref. 260). It is not examined verse by verse as most treatments are. Instead there are many topics, such as 'What is Mind?,' 'The Unknowability of Truth,' and the meaning of the text is unfolded in a wider context. Although the correct Sanskrit terminology is used, it is a more modern interpretation.

iii. The **Māṇḍūkya** and its **Kārikā** by Gaudapada are essential if you want to learn about OM, states of consciousness or the ajāti theory of no-creation. Ref. 35 has some of Śaṅkara's commentary and is translated and commented by Swami Nikhilananda. It is, however, quite difficult and really only for the serious student. It is partly because I found it so difficult at the time I attempted it (over 35 years ago), that I decided to write my own commentary, after attempting to read everything that has ever been written on these texts (and available in English!). Accordingly, I am bound to say that the most accessible version is **A-U-M: Awakening to Reality** (Ref. 379). If you wanted to read only one book to discover the 'bottom line' on Advaita philosophy, this would probably be it.

iv. The 'go-to' version of **Bṛhadāraṇyaka** is that translated and commented by Swami Madhavananda (Ref. 1), and that for the **Chāndogya** is the one by Swami Gambhirananda (Ref. 405). Neither of these is exactly bedtime reading but of the various other versions that I have, these are the ones I consult most often by far. And that tends to be the purpose of these particular Upaniṣads. I did once read the Chāndogya all the way through (Swami Krishnananda version, Ref. 23) but found it hard going – and that version is actually readable, with very little Sanskrit in the commentary itself. But these Upaniṣads are the ones containing the most extensive commentaries of Śaṅkara and he expounds some of his most significant teaching in them. This can be understood when you realize that one of his main disciples, Sureshvara, wrote a commentary (vārttika) on Śaṅkara's commentary (bhāṣya) on the Bṛhadāraṇyaka that occupies 14 hardback books on my bookshelf (that's fourteen – not a typo)!

2. *Bhagavad Gītā*

There are many different translations and commentaries on this classic work, where 'many' may be literally hundreds. Some merely translate the Sanskrit, with varying degrees of accuracy and artistic license. Others provide several pages of commentary on each verse. I own around 37 different versions, some of which take up several volumes, so I am reasonably well-positioned to comment.

i. The one that I reference most frequently is that translated by **Swami Gambhirananda** (Ref. 396), which also contains most (?) of Śaṅkara's Bhāṣya. It is authoritative and probably the best for serious seekers. Of course, since it adheres closely to the language of the original, it may not be thought 'readable' by modern standards!

ii. The best version by far, if you have the time, the money, and the incentive, is the **Bhagavad Gītā Home Study Course** by Swami Dayananda (Ref. 419). The written version comes in nine hardback volumes, beautifully presented and a joy to read. It is also available on DVD as an online PDF version, which is naturally much cheaper but, if you can afford it, the books are totally worth the outlay. They take the text one verse at a time, but Swami Dayananda takes every opportunity to expand on them so as to cover the essentials of all of the teaching of Advaita. And you do not have to be an advanced student to begin with.

iii. Swami Dayananda has also written **The Teaching of the Bhagavad Gītā**, which is a slim paperback (Ref. 31). This is really using the Gītā to present an overview of Advaita, and it gives verses as illustrations rather than covering the entire book, verse by verse. It is, nevertheless, a very good book and I can thoroughly recommend it. (Indeed, anything by Swami Dayananda can be recommended.)

iv. If you want word-by-word translation of each of the verses, there are only three versions that I am aware of.

a. The version by **Winthrop Sargeant** (Ref. 417) is the one most readily accessible. It has both original and Romanized Sanskrit, together with the meaning and grammar for each word. There is no commentary, however.
b. Another, also without commentary, is by **Kailash Nath Kalia** (Ref. 418). It is published in India so will be much cheaper if you can find a copy. The presentation is the same as the Sargeant one.
c. The third version containing word translation is by **Nitya Chaitanya Yati** (Ref. 420). This also contains a (modern) commentary as introduction to and summary of each chapter. This material seems to be readable (but I have not read the book so cannot comment on its merits. The author studied prasthāna traya with Nataraja Guru and taught the Gītā at Portland State University). The translation itself was by Nataraja Guru. Since this was published in India in 1993, it is quite likely that you will now have to search for a second-hand copy. If you want to study the Gītā in depth, it is really essential to purchase one of these unless you are proficient in Sanskrit.

3. *Brahma Sutra Bhāṣya*

This is the third branch of the prasthāna-traya – you will need a specialist bookstore to locate it. Note that, since you will presumably only be interested in the Advaitic interpretation, you will want the one with the Bhāṣya by Śaṅkara. There are also versions by Ramanuja (Viśiṣṭādvaita) and Madhva (Dvaita), although you are less likely to find these without searching on the internet.

i. The most popular version is again the one with commentary by **Swami Gambhirananda** (Ref. 34). It is an exceedingly difficult book to read and, though it contains some of the most profound philosophical analysis, it is certainly not for the beginner. This may also be found on the internet in PDF format.

ii. A version which is almost readable is that by the Advaita scholar **V.H. Date** (Ref. 40). Unless you really want the most accurate rendition, or are buying it just for reference, this is probably the best choice. It is in two volumes. It may also be found on the internet in PDF format. Do bear in mind, however, that it cannot be relied upon for strict adherence to the words, or even the understanding of Śaṅkara.

iii. Two versions that are much abbreviated, and therefore easy to read, are those by **Swami Sivananda** (Ref. 36) and **Swami Vireswarananda** (Ref. 421). This latter version may also be found on the internet in PDF format.

iv. An old version which is often referenced by other, older texts, is the one by **George Thibaut** (Ref. 422). It is again in two volumes. It may be downloaded from the internet in DJVU format. (A free DJVU reader for Windows can also be found.)

v. For those who want to read all of the academic arguments over key topics in the text, and compare what is said by each of the main commentators, there is a 3-volume version by **B.N.K. Sharma** that is sharp, sometimes funny but very difficult. It is only available in hardback and very expensive! (Ref. 423)

vi. It is generally acknowledged that the first four sutras of the work are the most significant and many versions address only these (there are 555 in total). One text which does so in an impressive manner is the one by **Sankaranarayanan** for Chinmaya International Foundation (Ref. 424). Each sutra and every comment by Śaṅkara has full Sanskrit text, transliteration, word for word meaning, English translation and annotated commentary. It is presented in a beautiful, large size, hardback edition of two volumes. Needless to say, it is very expensive and difficult to obtain, having been printed in only 2000 copies. (I understand that I managed to obtain the only copy made available in the UK!)

4. *Prakaraṇa Granthas*

This is the term used to refer to authoritative commentaries on the scriptures and which are not themselves part of the prasthāna traya. It is frequently used in respect of the works attributed to Śaṅkara such as Upadeśa Sāhasrī, Vivekacūḍāmaṇi etc. The word grantha literally means 'tying or stringing together' though can itself mean composition or treatise.

- **Ātmabodha** (Knowledge of Self)

This is one of the classic works on Advaita attributed to Śaṅkara.

Highly recommended, though only available from the author's organization 'Vedanta Life Institute,' **Sri Parthasarathy** provides original Sanskrit with word for word translation (Ref. 16). The book is also liberally sprinkled with excellent metaphors and stories.

The version by **Raphael** (Ref. 372) is short, with a good, clear, modern translation and commentary. It lacks Devanagari, but has Romanized Sanskrit and uses Sanskrit terms throughout. There is an extensive glossary.

- **Vivekacūḍāmaṇi** (Crest-Jewel of Discrimination)

This is probably the most famous of the books attributed to Śaṅkara but is almost certainly not written by him. Nevertheless, it provides an excellent summary of Advaita.

Swami Dayananda Saraswati – **Vivekacudamani: Talks on 108 Selected Verses** (Ref. 58). This is the book that I would recommend to all those who think that they already understand

Advaita. The explanations are crystal clear, often entertaining and presented with deep wisdom. There is only one possible problem in that there is a lot of Sanskrit and no glossary, so you have to note carefully as each new word is introduced.

The version I would recommend is one by **John Grimes** (Ref. 383). This has word-by-word translation of each verse, extensive commentary on many of them, and an academic introduction. It may, however, be difficult to obtain. The first (only?) edition was published in India and the copyright page indicates that it is 'For sale in Asia only.' As with the Bhagavad Gītā, if you go into a bookstore looking for this, do not automatically pick up whichever version happens to be there! You could be misled or at least confused by what you read.

This is really another text for which the talks of **Swami Paramarthanda** are incomparable. Although many would consider Vivekacūḍāmaṇi to be a text for beginners, the way that he presents this is as 'revision' for those who already understand most aspects of the teaching, i.e., as nididhyāsana. All is covered in considerable depth – 167 hours' worth of teaching + 3 of question and answer. A transcription PDF is again available from Arsha Avinash (Ref. 742).

- **Upadeśa Sāhasrī** (A Thousand Teachings)

This is one of the few books that all scholars seem to agree was definitely written by Śaṅkara. It requires some effort on the part of the reader but covers the subject of knowledge of the Self with thoroughness and obvious authority.

a. The version that I reference most frequently is that translated by **A.J. Alston** (Ref. 400). It just contains transliterated Sanskrit and a translation but Alston is so good that this is often all one needs.
b. The version from Sri Ramakrishna Math, translated by **Swami Jagadananda** (Ref. 104), presents the Devanagari

and English translation. One very useful extra is that footnotes are provided listing the Upaniṣads from which each of the very many references in the text derives.

c. The version by **Sengaku Mayeda** (Ref. 425) is worth mentioning because the index in Volume 1 contains every Sanskrit word together with a list of every verse containing it. Translation of all the text occurs in Volume 2. But this is a hardback book and so will be very expensive if you want both volumes.

- **Dṛgdṛśyaviveka** (An Inquiry into the Nature of the 'Seer' and the 'Seen')

A somewhat more obscure book, also attributed to Śaṅkara, is worth looking out for. It merits re-reading and study. It addresses the topics of the illusory self, the universe, māyā and samādhi. The version translated and annotated by Swami Nikhilananda (Ref. 73) is the version with which I am familiar and can highly recommend. It is available from the Vedanta Society of Northern California for a mere $2.50.

- **The Yoga Sutras of Patanjali**

Note that this is *not* Advaita. However, the mental preparation required in order to study Advaita with a qualified teacher, as recommended by śruti and Śaṅkara, has much in common with the practices documented in this text. These 'yoga' practices are the so-called Aṣṭāṅga (eightfold) Yoga, defined as 'the system of concentration and meditation based on ethical discipline.' In some modern texts, it is also referred to as Rāja Yoga (rāja = royal), and was suggested (possibly by Vivekananda originally) as being one of the paths to enlightenment. This is not correct. There is only one 'path,' namely jñāna yoga.

However, the translation by **Swami Satchidananda** (Ref. 11), with its many stories and metaphors, is able to communicate the ideas very clearly and the book is well worth reading. Each sutra is given in Sanskrit, with word-by-word translation, followed by extensive commentary where necessary to bring out the meaning. There is much of practical value in this book.

- **Yoga Vāsiṣṭha**

This is another classic. It is available in a number of editions, most of them transcribed by **Swami Venkatesananda**, and of varying sizes. Having completed writing the first volume of my book on *Confusions in Advaita Vedanta,* I can no longer wholeheartedly recommend Yoga Vasishtha. Vidyaranya quotes extensively from it in his work *Jīvanmukti Viveka,* and some wrong ideas are communicated thereby (from the standpoint of traditional Advaita). The problem is that, unless one is aware of the 'correct' teaching according to Śaṅkara, it is all too easy to pick up wrong ideas from later teachings.

Yoga Vasishtha itself was probably written before Śaṅkara in fact. But neither author refers to the other so either they were unaware of the other's existence or they disagreed with their teaching. Since Śaṅkara is very ready to refute others in his own writing, the former is much more likely.

- **Naiṣkarmya Siddhi**

This is an important work by Sureshvara, a direct disciple of Śaṅkara. It translates as 'The Realization of the Absolute,' and that is the title of the translation by **A.J. Alston** (Ref. 434), which is the one I would recommend.

- **Pañcadaśī**

This is a well-known text on Advaita probably written in the fourteenth century CE, possibly by Vidyaranya. (The word pañcadaśī means 15 – the number of chapters.) Much of what is said here corresponds closely with traditional teaching and is well explained using many metaphors. But there are some misleading 'extensions,' notably in respect of adding samādhi to śravaṇa-manana-nididhyāsana; talking about the guṇas in relation to māyā and avidyā; and referring to the ātman as being 'covered' by the five sheaths. The version with which I am most familiar is the one translated by **Swami Swahananda** (Ref. 435). Despite its relative popularity, I would not recommend the text for other than relatively advanced seekers because of the likelihood of confusion.

- **Tattvabodha**

There are various other texts, purportedly written by Śaṅkara, but probably not. Tattvabodha is worth mentioning as it defines lots of the terms used in Advaita and is therefore a useful reference. The book called **Insights into Vedanta** (Ref. 436) is a considerably 'enhanced' version by Swami Sunirmalananda. There are diagrams and lots of commentary – a very substantial read. The only proviso is that there is probably more here about Ramakrishna and Vivekananda than Śaṅkara. Accordingly, it is possible to pick up wrong ideas.

- **Post-Śaṅkara**

There are also other books written by Post-Śaṅkara teachers that are highly regarded. These include such texts as **Brahmasiddhi** (Mandana Mishra), **Iśṭasiddhi** (Vimuktatman), **Vedānta Siddhāntamuktāvalī** (Prakashananda), as well as those already mentioned by Vidyaranya. But, even assuming you manage to find these in a bookstore or on Amazon, it is probably best to avoid them. They are exceedingly difficult to read; their ideas diverged from those of Śaṅkara, and confusion is almost inevitable.

5. *Philosophical Treatments*

There are many books which address specific philosophical aspects of Advaita in an academic manner. Most of these are probably only attractive to those actually studying the subject at university but some are so well written and approachable and contain so much useful background material that they are worth attempting by anyone wanting to understand Advaita.

- **Methods of Knowledge according to Advaita Vedanta**

This is the book by Swami Satprakashananda (Ref. 27). The cover description states: "The book deals with an exposition of the six means of valid knowledge leading to Self-realization."

This is excellent – very readable, yet comprehensive and authoritative. I have not come across such lucid explanations of the most abstruse aspects of Advaita anywhere else. It also explains the differences between Advaita and other branches of Indian Philosophy. Everything is set out in point-by-point explanation. And it has probably the most comprehensive index of any book I have seen! **BUT...** Swami Satprakashananda was a disciple of Ramakrishna and was a strong adherent of wrong ideas regarding experience and samādhi and believed that one has to 'see God directly' in order to gain enlightenment. If you read this book, be careful to reject all such ideas!

- **The Method of the Vedanta**

Subtitled *A Critical Account of the Advaita Tradition* by Swami Satchidanandendra, translated by A.J. Alston (Ref. 24).

This is a huge book, requiring considerable commitment but, if you want to understand clearly what Śaṅkara believed and how his message has been modified or even distorted by subsequent interpreters, then it is essential reading. Śaṅkara's basic method is presented as that of adhyāropa-apavāda, attribution and subsequent denial. His commentaries on the prasthāna traya are examined in detail. Then, following a brief look at pre-Śaṅkara Advaita, there are chapters on each of the major teachers and schools that followed him, in which the same topics are reexamined, and the differences outlined.

Fortunately, the translation is by A.J. Alston (see below) so is always understandable. This book will be republished by Shanti Sadan when existing supplies run out so that they are the point of contact if you are unable to obtain it elsewhere.

- **A Śaṅkara Source Book Vols. 1–6**

Most of Śaṅkara's writing is scattered throughout his various commentaries on the prasthāna traya, the only major authenticated work being the Upadeśa Sāhasrī (see above). These writings are available in a number of translations with commentaries by others, but the translations are often difficult to follow and rarely what might be called "readable."

A.J. Alston (died 2004) was the brilliant translator of *The Method of the Vedanta* (see above). His ability to render the often-abstruse philosophical arguments of Śaṅkara into comprehensible and readable English is without parallel in my experience. Accordingly, this set of books (Ref. 437) is invaluable to serious students of Advaita.

Each book is divided into clear sections and subsections. Each topic is introduced and explained by the author, who then selects relevant passages from Śaṅkara's text which address the topics. It took Alston 37 years to complete this task and Advaitins everywhere can now reap the rewards. These are also published by Shanti Sadan, if you have difficulty finding them.

- **Advaita Vedanta: A Philosophical Reconstruction**

Written by Eliot Deutsch (Ref. 82), this reads like an academic Western Philosophical text and presents Advaita from an objective analytical viewpoint. This might tend to put off many potential readers but should not necessarily do so. Whilst it may seem dry at times and does require some effort to read, it presents some difficult concepts in a very clear manner, and is an essential addition if you are building a library of key texts on the philosophy.

III. Modern Age Teachers

This covers the now classic dialogues of sages such as Nisargadatta Maharaj and Ramana Maharshi and selections from the growing numbers of books written by present day satsang teachers, including the more radical, absolutist Neo-Advaitins. The first four sections separate out the different approaches of 'satsang,' 'Direct Path,' 'Neo-Vedanta,' and 'Neo-Advaita.'

1. Books by Original 'Sages'

These refer to those modern era teachers who are generally recognized as having been the 'original' in a particular 'lineage.' Those well-known to most seekers were: Ramakrishna Paramahamsa, Nisargadatta Maharaj, Ramana Maharshi and Atmananda Krishna Menon. There are few books actually written by any of these teachers. Most of the material that we have is in the form of transcriptions (which are often also translations) of talks, lectures or question-answer sessions. As such, none of them can be used for graded, progressive teaching material. At best, you may hit upon a particular problem that has been worrying you and find a clear explanation and resolution to the problem. But this is extremely hit and miss unless there happens to be an index.

Ramakrishna

He did not belong to any teacher lineage. Here is what I said about him in Ref. 398:

> *Ramakrishna had a particular facility for using stories and metaphors to explain otherwise difficult topics. But he was not a traditional teacher of Advaita. He did not belong to a sampradāya. His 'enlightenment' was based upon his experiences. He was a 'mystic', as is freely admitted by the author of this book. (A 'mystic' is defined by the Oxford English*

Dictionary as someone who attains unity with the Absolute as a result of "the spiritual apprehension of truths that are beyond the intellect". I.e. Such a person usually claims enlightenment as a result of an 'experience' rather than from gaining Self-knowledge through listening to traditional teaching; i.e. all of the preparatory spiritual sādhanas must have been done in previous lives. Subsequently, their own 'teaching' tends to be based upon this 'direct knowledge' as opposed to the 'indirect knowledge' of scriptures. Consequently, they are not śrotriyas [someone well-versed in the scriptures] *thus not qualified for teaching, since they have not learned the traditional methods from another qualified teacher.)*

I used to recommend the Bhagavad Gītā version by Swami Chidbhavananda (Ref. 118). It is readable, and has lots of quotes from Ramakrishna. I can still recommend it, as long as you are aware of the above proviso! You can purchase a book of **Sayings of Sri Ramakrishna** (Ref. 50), which has very many quotes and stories (over a thousand), sorted into topics and well-indexed.

Vivekananda

He was the direct disciple of Ramakrishna and was largely responsible for introducing Advaita to the West. Unfortunately, he picked up some wrong ideas from various sources, even whilst he was successfully 'marketing' it to the West. (See Ref. 439 and my own book Ref. 398.) In particular, he did not accept the authority of scriptures and he believed that one had to gain 'direct experience' of the truth after merely understanding it intellectually. Nevertheless, there is clearly much of value in his talks and, together, Ramakrishna and Vivekananda were responsible for setting up the world-wide organizations in place today. These have produced some of the most important traditional teachers of the past century, some of whose books I have recommended above.

His talks and essays are recorded in the 9-volume *Complete Works* (Ref. 191). I would not personally recommend these. As well as the distortions of the traditional teaching, his tone is too 'proselytizing' for me.

Atmananda Krishna Menon

This is the teacher principally credited with having devised the Direct Path approach to teaching Advaita. It was he who influenced the better-known Jean Klein and latterly Francis Lucille, Rupert Spira, and Greg Goode. Two books, **Ātma Darshan** (Ref. 360) and **Ātma Nirvritti** (Ref. 361) are very short, originally in verse form in the Malayalam language, and translated by the author. Simple, straightforward and logically presented, yet presenting all of the key issues of Direct Path Advaita. His better known **Spiritual Discourses of Sri Atmananda** was compiled by his disciple, Nitya Tripta, from his talks over the years. This is now available in three volumes or downloadable from my website (Ref. 13) and is the reference text for students of Direct Path.

Nisargadatta Maharaj

I am That, a collection of questions and answers given by him (Ref. 5), is possibly the best known book by a modern sage. In fact, the material is translated from the original Marathi by Maurice Frydman and so is subject to the pitfalls of this process (knowledge of both languages, prior understanding of the subject). But it has proven extremely popular and there is no doubt that it is a powerful book, shaking up existing ideas about who we are and the nature of the world. There are a number of other, later books, translated by another disciple – Jean Dunn. It has to be said that these do not have the same impact, and in the last one (Ref. 345), compiled from his final talks, he is beginning to sound like some of the modern Neo-Advaitin teachers.

Ramana Maharshi

Talks with Sri Ramana Maharshi (Ref. 49) is the classic book of conversations recorded by Sri Munagala S. Venkataramiah over the period 1935–9. Previously published in three volumes, they are now available in a single book of over 600 pages, published by Sri Ramanasramam. Very readable, yet full of wisdom. It has a comprehensive index and glossary. Many of his books, including this one, are available for free download in PDF format at https://selfdefinition.org/ramana/.

Maha Yoga by "Who" (Ref. 39). The author, only identified as "Who" on the title page, was Sri K. Laksmana Sarma, who studied for over 20 years with Ramana. He defines Maha Yoga as *"the Direct Method of finding the Truth of Ourselves."* The key topics addressed are happiness, ignorance, world, soul, god, the nature of the Self and the means for realizing this, and the role of the Sage and devotion. Some difficult concepts are explained with transparent clarity, and the entire book is readable and authoritative yet written with obvious humility. Highly recommended. It may be downloaded from Tom Das's website at Ref. 745.

Be As You Are by David Godman (Ref. 17) is the best book about Ramana — see 'Best Books for Beginners' above.

Other classic collections of material by or about Ramana Maharshi may be downloaded from Sri Ramanasramam at Ref. 746.

Swami Dayananda

A more recent sage, but one every bit as important, was Swami Dayananda (founder of Arsha Vidya, not the older teacher of the same name from Arya Samaj), who died in 2015. Not only was he a brilliant teacher himself, but also through his Ashrams, the guru of numbers of other excellent teachers. The book which provides a comprehensive coverage of Advaita philosophy is his **Bhagavad Gita Home Study Course**, already recommended above. He also wrote many short books on subjects relating to life in general, how to handle fear, stress, relationships etc. And many of his talks have been collected together into the 3-volume **Talks and Essays of Swami Dayananda** (Ref. 393).

2. *Books by 'Satsang' Teachers*

This category covers those teachers who do not clearly fall into one of the other categories: i.e., they are not Neo-Vedantins, Neo-Advaitins, or Direct Path; although, strictly speaking, these other categories also teach in a 'satsang' format. And they cannot be classed as traditional (meaning 'in accordance with the teaching of Śaṅkara'), irrespective of many claims to the contrary.

Nisargadatta Maharaj and Ramana Maharshi might be considered as the key sages who popularized this style of teaching. The dialogues in books may or may not be edited and, consequently, the quality of questions and answers is variable.

Given that a good teacher will be addressing responses directly to a specific seeker at his or her level of understanding, it necessarily follows that these may not be suitable for any particular reader and the context is also usually lacking. Accordingly, 'satsang dialogue' books are intrinsically not a good medium for teaching Advaita.

The redeeming facts are that there are many basic questions that repeatedly arise in satsang and such answers are generally understood by all. Also, some teachers are very good at explaining even difficult topics so that their material is often worthwhile regardless. The books recommended in this section are not all of this type but, where they are, they do not suffer too much from the drawbacks.

Osho

Some would have taken exception to including **Osho** in the list of 'recent sages' above. Accordingly, I have given him prime position in this section. He is certainly able to transmit key topics in a very clear manner, interlaced with many (often rude) jokes to keep one awake. But, whilst the philosophy that he propounded was usually in accordance with that of Advaita, he drew his inspiration from many other sources, including Buddhism, Sufism, and Hassidism. There are so many books by him that it is very difficult to recommend just one or two (even assuming that you have read them all). They are principally transcriptions of the talks he gave over many years or of the question-and-answer sessions that he held with his disciples or 'sannyasins,' as he called them. Many are based around a particular classical work such as an Upaniṣad.

All (?) books by **Osho** are available at http://oshoworld.com/. They are displayed about 250–300 words at a time and could theoretically be copied and printed. But this would take a very long time – they are clearly intended to be read online.

The Mustard Seed (Ref. 166) is based upon the Gospel according to St. Thomas, the Christian work discovered amongst the Dead Sea Scrolls. Although this document may not be universally accepted amongst Christians, he uses it to bring out very clearly the non-dual teachings of Christ. It is quite a long book – nearly 500 pages – but it is nevertheless amazing how many topics are covered. Always readable and provocative, it is often very funny too.

Also highly recommended are **Heartbeat of the Absolute** (Ref. 96) and **I Am That** (Ref. 83). Both are discourses on the Īśā or Īśavāsya Upaniṣad. The former is based on talks given in April 1971. The latter is published under Osho's previous pseudonym, Bhagwan Shree Rajneesh and is based upon talks in October 1980. If asked to choose between them, I would probably prefer *Heartbeat* (although *I am That* contains more jokes!).

Wayne Liquorman

Wayne is the owner of the advaita.org website, and consequently, I was obliged to be satisfied with advaita.org.uk back in 2002(?)!

He was the long-term disciple of Ramesh Balsekar and still publishes new Ramesh quotations each week. His books take the form of question and answer, presumably from his regular, worldwide, satsangs, but are presented under topic headings and usually indexed. I extracted quite a few worthwhile references from Ref. 113, **Acceptance of What Is: A Book About Nothing**, so can definitely recommend it as both entertaining and actually instructive.

'Sailor' Bob Adamson

Living Reality: My Extraordinary Summer with "Sailor" Bob Adamson by James Braha (Ref. 346). This does not consist of satsang transcriptions and therefore does not consist solely of dialogue. It is not even compiled by Bob but by one of his disciples, who himself puts most of the questions. Hence these are much more coherent and focused. Thirdly, James has provided valuable commentaries between sections, in which he is able to summarize and express his own understanding of the topics under discussion. Finally — and this is the factor that especially recommends it — the whole book is presented as a real-life adventure, in which we share the excitement of a prolonged visit by an enlightened teacher. 'Sailor' Bob spent a full five weeks in the author's home giving private and public talks, and we get an intimate and fascinating account of the entire experience.

John Wheeler

Awakening to the Natural State by John Wheeler (Ref. 70). This is not drawn from satsang material but from emails and from personal discussion of the author with 'Sailor' Bob. Additional comments and clarification have been added and the quality is generally high so that this book can definitely be recommended.

Joan Tollifson

I feel I have to mention her. I actually only have one of her books – **Painting the Sidewalk with Water** (Ref. 413) – and I don't believe I have ever read it cover-to-cover. But, for the past few months, I have been receiving her frequent emailed newsletters. I have read a number of these, and she is a very good writer. Her influences are many, beginning with Zen, so that what she teaches cannot be guaranteed to be in accord with Advaita. Also, much of her recent writing has been triggered by current events, such as the Israel-Hamas conflict. Nevertheless, I would expect that whatever you might read of hers would be intelligent and thought-provoking in the right direction.

James Swartz

See 'Best Books for Beginners' above.

3. Books by Direct Path Teachers

Jean Klein

He was probably the first of the Direct Path teachers following on from Sri Atmananda. In fact, according to Douwe Tiemersma (Ref. 456), *"Jean Klein came from the tradition of North Indian Shaivism (Shaivism of Kashmir), where the paths of Advaita and energetic yoga are combined."* There are a quite a few books, all in the form of short questions followed by longer answers on topics typically raised by those seeking answers to spiritual questions. These books were originally published by Element around 1990 but have been largely republished by Non-Duality Press. A good example is **I Am** (Ref. 19). He often brings a refreshing lightness to the mind with its tendency to become mired in irresolvable logical analysis. This book in particular is full of insightful observations.

Francis Lucille

He was the first teacher I turned to when I left the School of Economic Science in the UK (documented in Ref. 398). We exchanged emails a few times and I attended a couple of his residential courses at Rupert Spira's farmhouse in the UK. He had a book available in spiral-bound format that I found helpful at the time – **Eternity Now: Dialogues on Awareness** (Ref. 8). It contained transcriptions from some of his audiocassette discussions with David Jennings (who utilized the teachings of Advaita in his psychotherapy practice) together with additional material, such as answers to my email questions. Being Direct Path, there is nothing of the traditional bhakti or karma methods here. A book of the same title has been published much more recently and I assume that it is essentially the same. (Ref. 442) The questions are answered in an incisive and uncompromising way that will appeal to those who feel that they have to use their minds and intellects to analyze everything.

Rupert Spira

Also a student of Francis, he has since become a well-known teacher in his own right and has a number of published books.

His first was **The Transparency of Things** (Ref. 392), for which I wrote a very extensive review at Ref. 536. Here are my concluding remarks:

> *I suggest that this book is going to be of most interest to seasoned seekers, who may find new and insightful views into some of the familiar topics in Advaita. I fear that those who are not already used to the manner of speaking about Non-Duality will quickly discard the book – it will simply be too difficult for them. It requires both serious interest and genuine commitment to stay with it. But, for those who are prepared to make the effort there is much to savor and I recommend it highly to them. I personally found it to be a*

delight and a frustration (in equal measure!) and, on that basis, perhaps I ought not to award more than 4. But there is so much good stuff in here, and it towers above most other modern books on the subject, that I have few qualms about awarding 5*.*

Greg Goode

He is another modern teacher using the Direct Path approach. His first book was **Standing as Awareness** (Ref. 443), for which I wrote the original Foreword (which may be read at Ref. 537). (It was rejected by the publisher and replaced by one from a less 'traditional' source!)

Part of my version was as follows:

Anyone who has read Sri Atmananda's books or the notes on his discourses will know that following his reasoning processes is not always easy. The reader may well feel that what is needed is for the ideas to be reformulated for the modern Western mind. Jean Klein's books do achieve this to some degree but, since they are mainly answers to questions raised at his satsangs, they lack continuity and editing. The topics in this book, on the other hand, are culled from the many talks that Greg and his dinner companions have held over the past ten years and the material is carefully organized to present particular points in a coherent manner. This it does in a brilliant and readable way and, consequently, all of the material is valuable and relevant. Francis Lucille's book, 'Eternity Now', is very good and was written in a similar manner to this, being based upon 'prepared' questions. But, in this book, Greg excels in clarity of presentation and any reader should find it both stimulating and valuable.

Greg has since written **The Direct Path: A User Guide** (Ref. 444) to provide lots of practical 'experiments' to guide the seeker through the concepts discussed in the earlier book.

4. Books by Neo-Vedanta Teachers

Since the largest organizations stem from Vivekananda and Ramakrishna, most of the published scriptural translations and commentaries are by their ashrams. Inevitably therefore, when you look for particular scriptures, you are very likely to end up buying these. Fortunately, these are OK for the most part, since they are, after all, translating original material and comments by Śaṅkara. You just have to be wary that, if you encounter something that appears to contradict your prior understanding, this may be because the author has imposed some prior (mis) understanding gained from their teachers. See the 'Traditional' List above.

5. Books by Neo-Advaitin Teachers

It might come as a surprise that I am recommending some books by these teachers. It shouldn't. I have already pointed out that the 'bottom line' of both traditional and Neo-Advaitin teachers is the same – as, indeed, it must be! The problem relates to the way in which they get there. A few Neo-Advaitins do, in fact, use some of the same prakriyās and metaphors as are found in more traditional teaching. And, because they speak to a modern audience, their approach and language is more in tune with them.

i. **Awakening to the Dream – Leo Hartong** (Ref. 22). The two authors that I particularly recommend are Leo Hartong and David Carse. Neither are teaching now, as far as I am aware, but their books live on. But a strong caveat is needed here! Books by Neo-Advaitins have the same ultimate status as their live teaching. They really serve as 'appetizers' to point you towards a terminus of understanding, but not to take you there. You may very well enjoy them (probably far more than you will enjoy a traditional text!) but, although they engender a positive frame of mind, they do not instill understanding in any lasting sense. As an unpublished review by Matthew West put it:

Whilst it is noted that Awakening to the Dream receives a five star rating from 35 customer reviews on Amazon, some of which remark on the simplicity of the book's message, the clarity with which the subject is handled, the ease at which results are attained and express gratitude toward the author for the knowledge imparted; from a subjective point of view (and, of course, there is no subject) one is reminded of the spectacle of the emperor's new clothes. No offence intended but a body stripped of garments (or subject stripped of substance) doesn't necessarily appeal to everyone. (Ref. 743)
[Note that there are now 293 ratings, averaging 4.6 stars!]

ii. **Perfect Brilliant Stillness – David Carse** (Ref. 313). Ref. 744 provides links to my own brief review of David's book, two other reviews and a long response from David, together with a link to a sample chapter from the book. There is also a very positive recommendation in *Back to the Truth*.
iii. **Already Awake: dialogues with Nathan Gill** (Ref. 25). Nathan was another teacher of Neo-Advaita and this book is an excellent example of the style. For the most part, what he says is clear and (that adjective applicable to many modern teachers) 'uncompromising.' One can certainly imagine that a mature seeker might have some remaining vestiges of confusion removed by these words. But, unfortunately, it does occasionally fall foul of that bane of Neo-Advaita – gobbledygook – when there is an attempt to pass off the duality of vyavahāra as the non-duality of paramārtha. (For example, *"The seeing through is not dependent on any happening in the play, although it may*

appear that understanding arises in the story of the character prior to knowing being revealed.") As long as this problem is recognized, I can definitely recommend this book.

Bibliography

Apologies for the length of this and also for the fact that lots of the references are simply 'N/U' – not used. There are several reasons for this:

- I used the bibliography from *Back to the Truth* as a starting point. This was because I had originally intended that this would be a second edition of that book. When I changed track to write this book, many of those references became redundant.
- I searched the internet for quotations from all of the teachers that are mentioned and the sources for these are given as references.
- As noted in the introduction, it became apparent some way into the writing that I would have to restrict this book to 'finding a teacher.' Accordingly, those references relating to topics in Advaita also became redundant. (They will reappear in the next book!)
- Some of the internet references were superseded when I found better quotations.
- One or two of the quotations have actually been removed from the site that was originally referenced. I have left these in the text but readers must note that, if the cited reference is 'N/A,' then the quotations are no longer attributable!

1. Bṛhadāraṇyaka Upaniṣad, translated by Swami Madhavananda, Advaita Ashram, Kolkatta. Electronically available from http://www.celextel.org/ebooks/upanisads/brihadaranyaka_upanisad.htm.
2. N/U.
3. N/U.

4. N/U.
5. I am That, Sri Nisargadatta Maharaj, translated Maurice Frydman, Chetana (P) Ltd., Bombay, 1981. ISBN 085655-406-5.
6. N/U.
7. Pointers from Nisargadatta Maharaj, Ramesh S. Balsekar, Chetana (P) Ltd., 1983. ISBN 81-85300-19-4.
8. Eternity Now: Dialogues on Awareness, Francis Lucille, Truespeech Productions, 1996. No ISBN.
9. Presence-Awareness: Just This and Nothing Else, Talks with 'Sailor' Bob Adamson, edited by John Wheeler, Non-Duality Press, 2004. ISBN 0-9547792-4-X.
10. N/U.
11. The Yoga Sutras of Patanjali. Translation and Commentary by Sri Swami Satchidananda, Integral Yoga Publications, 1990. ISBN 0-932040-38-1.
12. N/U.
13. Notes on Spiritual Discourses of Shri Atmananda: Taken by Nitya Tripta, 2nd edition, Non-Duality Press, 2009. Vol. 1 (Notes 1–472) – ISBN 978-0-9563091-2-9; Vol. 2 (Notes 473–1121) – ISBN 978-0-9563091-3-6; Vol. 3 (Notes 1122–1451) – ISBN 978-0-9563091-4-3. Electronically available from http://www.advaita.org.uk/discourses/downloads/notes_pdf.zip.
14. N/U.
15. The Truth Is, Sri H.W.L. Poonja, Yudhishtara, 1995. No ISBN.
16. Ātmabodha (Knowledge of Self) by Sri Adi Shankaracharya, A. Parthasarathy, Vedanta Life Institute, 1980. No ISBN.
17. Be As You Are: The Teachings of Sri Ramana Maharshi, edited by David Godman, Arkana, 1985. ISBN 0-14-019062-7.
18. N/U.
19. I Am, Jean Klein, compiled and edited by Emma Edwards, Non-Duality Press, 2006. ISBN 978-0-9551762-7-2.

20. N/U.
21. N/U.
22. Awakening to the Dream: The Gift of Lucid Living, Leo Hartong, Trafford, 2001. ISBN 1-4120-0425-X.
23. Chandogya Upaniṣad, Swami Krishnananda, The Divine Life Society, 1984. No ISBN. Electronically available from http://www.swami-krishnananda.org/.
24. The Method of the Vedanta: A Critical Account of the Advaita Tradition, Swami Satchidanandendra Saraswati (Holenarasipur, Karnataka, India), translated by A.J. Alston, originally published by Kegan Paul International, 1989. ISBN 0-7103-0277-0 edition now listed and distributed by Shanti Sadan, www.shantisadan.org.
25. Already Awake, Nathan Gill, Non-Duality Press, 2004. ISBN 0-9547792-2-3.
26. N/U.
27. Methods of Knowledge According to Advaita Vedanta, Swami Satprakashananda, Advaita Āśrama, 1965. ISBN 81-7505-065-9.
28. N/U.
29. N/U.
30. N/U.
31. The Teaching of the Bhagavad Gītā, Swami Dayananda, Vision Books Pvt., 1989. ISBN 81-7094-032-X.
32. N/U.
33. N/U.
34. Brahma Sūtra Bhāṣya of Shankaracharya, translated by Swami Gambhirananda, Advaita Ashrama, 1996. ISBN 81-7505-105-1.
35. N/U.
36. Brahma Sutras, Swami Sivananda, The Divine Life Society. Electronically available from http://www.swami-krishnananda.org/bs_00.html.
37. N/U.

38. The Supreme Yoga: Yoga Vasiṣṭha, Swami Venkatesananda, Chiltern Yoga Trust, 1976. ISBN 81-208-1964-0.
39. Maha Yoga or The Upaniṣadic Lore in the Light of the Teachings of Bhagavan Sri Ramana, "Who," Sri Ramanashramam, 1937. No ISBN. Electronically available from http://www.ramana-maharshi.org/.
40. Vedanta Explained: Śaṅkara's Commentary on the Brahma-sūtras, V.H. Date, Munshiram Manoharlal Publishers Pvt. Ltd., 1973. No ISBN.
41. N/U.
42. N/U.
43. N/U.
44. N/U.
45. The Power of Now: A Guide to Spiritual Enlightenment, Eckhart Tolle, Hodder and Stoughton, 2001. ISBN 0 340 733500.
46. N/U.
47. The Open Secret, Tony Parsons, Connections, 1995. ISBN 0 9533032 0 9.
48. N/U.
49. Talks with Sri Ramana Maharshi, Sri Ramanasramam, 1955. No ISBN.
50. Sayings of Sri Ramakrishna, Sri Ramakrishna Math, 1987. No ISBN.
51. N/U.
52. N/U.
53. N/U.
54. N/U.
55. N/U.
56. N/U.
57. N/U.
58. Vivekacūḍāmaṇi: Talks on 108 Selected Verses, Swami Dayananda Saraswati, Sri Gangadhareswar Trust, 1997. No ISBN.

59. N/U.
60. N/U.
61. N/U.
62. N/U.
63. Self Enquiry, August 2000, Vol. 8, No. 2 (Quarterly Review of the Ramana Maharshi Foundation UK). ISSN 1357 0935.
64. N/U.
65. N/U.
66. N/U.
67. N/U.
68. N/U.
69. N/U.
70. Awakening to the Natural State, John Wheeler, Non-Duality Press, 2004. ISBN 0-9547792-3-1.
71. N/U.
72. N/U.
73. Dṛg-Dṛśya-Viveka: An Inquiry into the Nature of the "Seer" and the "Seen", with English translation and notes by Swami Nikhilananda, Sri Ramakrishna Ashrama, 1976. ISBN 090247927X.
74. N/U.
75. N/U.
76. N/U.
77. N/U.
78. The Teachers of One: Living Advaita – Conversations on the Nature of Non-duality, Paula Marvelly, Watkins Publishing, 2002. ISBN 1 84293 028 1.
79. N/U.
80. N/U.
81. N/U.
82. Advaita Vedanta: A Philosophical Reconstruction, Eliot Deutsch, East-West Center Press, 1969. ISBN 0-8248-0271-3.
83. I Am That: Discourses on the Isa Upaniṣad, Bhagwan Shree Rajneesh, Rajneesh Foundation International (now

Osho International Foundation), 1984. ISBN 0-88050-580X.

84. The Book of One: The Spiritual Path of Advaita 2nd Edition, Dennis Waite, O-Books, 2010. ISBN 978-1-84694-347-8. Extracts may be read at http://www.advaita.org.uk/discourses/thebook/thebook.htm.
85. N/U.
86. N/U.
87. N/U.
88. N/U.
89. N/U.
90. N/U.
91. N/U.
92. N/U.
93. In This Moment! Teachings on the Nature of Consciousness, Aja Thomas, ATMA Institute, 2002. ISBN 978-0962010835.
94. N/U.
95. N/U.
96. Heartbeat of the Absolute: Commentaries on the Ishavasya Upaniṣad, Osho, Element Books, 1994. ISBN 1852304766.
97. N/U.
98. N/U.
99. N/U.
100. N/U.
101. Vedanta Sutras of Narayana Guru, Swami Muni Narayana Prasad, D.K. Printworld (P) Ltd., 1997. ISBN 81-246-0085-6.
102. N/U.
103. N/U.
104. Upadeśasāhasrī of Śrī Śaṅkarācārya, translated into English with explanatory notes by Swami Jagadananda, Sri Ramakrishna Math, 1989. ISBN 81-7120-059-1.
105. N/U.
106. N/U.
107. N/U.

108. N/U.
109. N/U.
110. N/U.
111. N/U.
112. Dialogues with Swami Dayananda, Sri Gangadhareswar Trust, 1988. No ISBN.
113. Acceptance of What IS: A Book About Nothing, Wayne Liquorman, Advaita Press, 2000. ISBN 0-929448-19-7.
114. N/U.
115. N/U.
116. N/U.
117. N/U.
118. The Bhagavad Gītā, commentary by Swami Chidbhavananda, Sri Ramakrishna Tapovanam, 1986. No ISBN.
119. N/U.
120. N/U.
121. N/U.
122. N/U.
123. Vedanta Treatise: The Eternities, A. Parthasarathy, 2004. ISBN 8187111577.
124. N/U.
125. N/U.
126. N/U.
127. N/U.
128. N/U.
129. N/U.
130. Karma and Reincarnation, Swami Muni Narayana Prasad, D.K. Printworld (P) Ltd., 1994. ISBN 81-246-0022-8.
131. N/U.
132. N/U.
133. N/U.
134. A Natural Awakening: Realizing the True Self in Everyday *Life*, P.T. Mistlberger, Tigerfyre Publishing, 2005. ISBN 0-9733419-0-4.

135. N/U.
136. N/U.
137. N/U.
138. N/U.
139. N/U.
140. The Essential Teachings of Hinduism, edited by Kerry Brown, Rider, 1988. ISBN 0 09 978530 7.
141. N/U.
142. N/U.
143. N/U.
144. N/U.
145. N/U.
146. N/U.
147. N/U.
148. N/U.
149. N/U.
150. N/U.
151. N/U.
152. N/U.
153. N/U.
154. N/U.
155. Silence of the Heart, Robert Adams, Acropolis Books, 1999. ISBN 1-889051-53-5.
156. Kathopanishad, Swami Chinmayananda, Central Chinmaya Mission Trust, 1994. No ISBN.
157. N/U.
158. N/U.
159. As It Is (US Edition), Tony Parsons, Inner Directions Publishing, 2000. ISBN 978-1878019103.
160. N/U.
161. N/U.
162. N/U.
163. N/U.
164. N/U.

165. N/U.
166. The Mustard Seed, Osho, Element Books, 1994. ISBN 1-85230-498-7.
167. N/U.
168. N/U.
169. N/U.
170. N/U.
171. N/U.
172. N/U.
173. N/U.
174. N/U.
175. N/U.
176. N/U.
177. N/U.
178. N/U.
179. N/U.
180. N/U.
181. N/U.
182. N/U.
183. N/U.
184. N/U.
185. Enlightenment May Or May Not Happen: Talks on Enlightenment with Ramesh S. Balsekar, edited by Madhukar Thompson, Neti Neti Press, 1999. ISBN 0-9665245-1-9.
186. Self-Knowledge, Swami Dayananda Saraswati, Arsha Vidya Gurukulam, 2003. ISBN 0-9748000-0-7.
187. N/U.
188. N/U.
189. N/U.
190. N/U.
191. Complete Works of Swami Vivekananda, Swami Vivekananda, Advaita Āśrama, 1999 (8th edition). ISBN 8185301468.

192. N/U.
193. Self-Knowledge: Śaṅkara's Ātmabodha with Notes, Comments, and Introduction, Swami Nikhilananda, Sri Ramakrishna Math, 1947. ISBN 0911206116. (Introduction electronically available from http://www.anandamayi.org/om/ab2.htm.)
194. N/U.
195. N/U.
196. Four Quartets, T.S. Eliot, Faber and Faber Limited, 1979. ISBN 0-571-04994-X.
197. N/U.
198. N/U.
199. N/U.
200. N/U.
201. N/U.
202. N/U.
203. N/U.
204. N/U.
205. A Course in Consciousness, Stanley Sobottka, 2000. Electronically available from https://courseinconsciousness.neocities.org/.
206. N/U.
207. N/U.
208. N/U.
209. N/U.
210. N/U.
211. N/U.
212. N/U.
213. N/U.
214. N/U.
215. N/U.
216. Interpreting the Upaniṣads, Ananda Wood, Zen Publications, 2009. ISBN 978-81-88071-52-4. Electronically available from https://www.advaita.org.uk/discourses/ananda_wood/ananda_wood.htm.

217. N/U.
218. N/U.
219. N/U.
220. N/U.
221. N/U.
222. N/U.
223. N/U.
224. N/U.
225. N/U.
226. N/U.
227. N/U.
228. N/U.
229. N/U.
230. N/U.
231. N/U.
232. N/U.
233. N/U.
234. N/U.
235. N/U.
236. N/U.
237. N/U.
238. N/U.
239. N/U.
240. N/U.
241. N/U.
242. N/U.
243. Annamalai Swami: Final Talks, edited by David Godman, Sri Annamalai Swami Ashram Trust, 2000. No ISBN.
244. N/U.
245. N/U.
246. N/U.
247. N/U.
248. N/U.
249. N/U.

250. N/U.
251. N/U.
252. N/U.
253. N/U.
254. N/U.
255. N/U.
256. N/U.
257. N/U.
258. N/U.
259. N/U.
260. Kena Upaniṣad, Swami Muni Narayana Prasad, D.K. Printworld (P) Ltd., 1994. ISBN 81-246-0034-1.
261. N/U.
262. N/U.
263. N/U.
264. N/U.
265. N/U.
266. N/U.
267. N/U.
268. N/U.
269. N/U.
270. N/U.
271. N/U.
272. N/U.
273. N/U.
274. N/U.
275. N/U.
276. N/U.
277. N/U.
278. N/U.
279. N/U.
280. N/U.
281. N/U.
282. N/U.

283. N/U.
284. N/U.
285. N/U.
286. N/U.
287. N/U.
288. N/U.
289. N/U.
290. N/U.
291. N/U.
292. N/U.
293. N/U.
294. N/U.
295. N/U.
296. N/U.
297. N/U.
298. N/U.
299. N/U.
300. N/U.
301. N/U.
302. N/U.
303. N/U.
304. N/U.
305. N/U.
306. N/U.
307. N/U.
308. N/U.
309. N/U.
310. N/U.
311. N/U.
312. N/U.
313. Perfect Brilliant Stillness, David Carse, Non-Duality Press, 2005. ISBN 0954779282.
314. N/U.
315. N/U.

316. N/U.
317. N/U.
318. N/U.
319. N/U.
320. N/U.
321. N/U.
322. N/U.
323. N/U.
324. N/U.
325. N/U.
326. N/U.
327. N/U.
328. N/U.
329. N/U.
330. N/U.
331. N/U.
332. N/U.
333. N/U.
334. N/U.
335. N/U.
336. Eight Upaniṣads with the Commentary of Śaṅkarācārya, Volume 1, translated by Swami Gambhirananda, Advaita Āśrama, 1957. ISBN 81-7505-016-0.
337. N/U.
338. N/U.
339. N/U.
340. N/U.
341. N/U.
342. N/U.
343. N/U.
344. N/U.
345. Consciousness and the Absolute: The Final Talks of Sri Nisargadatta Maharaj, edited by Jean Dunn, The Acorn Press, 1994. ISBN 0-89386-041-7.

346. Living Reality: My Extraordinary Summer with "Sailor" Bob Adamson, James Braha, Hermetician Press, 2006. ISBN 0935895-10-8.
347. N/U.
348. N/U.
349. What is Neo-Advaita?, James Swartz, https://www.advaita.org.uk/discourses/trad_neo/neo_vedanta_swartz.htm.
350. N/U.
351. N/U.
352. N/U.
353. N/U.
354. N/U.
355. N/U.
356. N/U.
357. The Living Gītā: A Commentary for Modern Readers, Sri Swami Satchidananda, Integral Yoga Publications, 1988. ISBN 0-932040-27-6.
358. The Bhagavad Gītā: A Transcreation of The Song Celestial, Alan Jacobs, O-Books, 2003. ISBN 1 903816 51 3.
359. N/U.
360. Atma Darshan: At the Ultimate, Sri Atmananda, Advaita Publishers, 1983. ISBN 0-914793-16-0.
361. Atma Nirvriti: Freedom and Felicity in the Self, Sri Atmananda, Advaita Publishers, 1983. ISBN 0-914793-05-5.
362. N/U.
363. Introduction to Vedanta: Understanding the Fundamental Problem, Swami Dayananda, Vision Books, 1989. ISBN 81-7094-037-0.
364. N/U.
365. N/U.
366. N/U.
367. Simply This, Liz Jones, Simply This Publishing, 2005. ISBN 0-9549428-0-9.

368. N/U.
369. N/U.
370. N/U.
371. N/U.
372. Ātmabodha: Self-Knowledge. Translated and commentary by Raphael, Aurea Vidya Foundation, Inc., 2003. ISBN 1-931406-06-5.
373. N/U.
374. N/U.
375. N/U.
376. N/U.
377. N/U.
378. N/U.
379. A-U-M: Awakening to Reality, Dennis Waite, Mantra Books, 2015. ISBN 978-1-78279-996-2.
380. N/U.
381. N/U.
382. N/U.
383. The Vivekacūḍāmaṇi of Śaṅkarācārya Bhagavatpāda, John Grimes, Motilal Banarsidass Delhi, 2004. ISBN 81-208-2039-8.
384. N/U.
385. N/U.
386. The Muṇḍaka Upaniṣad with Śaṅkarabhāṣyam, compiled by Divyajñāna Sarojini Varadarājan, 2010. No ISBN.
387. *Srimad Bhagavad Gītā* (three volumes), A. Parthasarathy, self-published, 1992. No ISBN.
388. The Crest Jewel of Wisdom: Viveka-Chudamani, translated by A.J. Alston, commentary by Hari Prasad Shastri, Shanti Sadan, 1997. ISBN 0-85424-047-0.
389. A Collection from Sankara's Commentaries on the Prasthāna-Traya, Swami Kritarthananda, Ramakrishna Institute of Culture, 2016. ISBN 978-93-81325-86-5.
390. N/U.

391. N/U.
392. The Transparency of Things, Rupert Spira, Non-Duality Press, 2008. ISBN 978-0-9558290-5-5.
393. A Collection: Talks and Essays of Swami Dayananda, Vol. 1, Sri Gangadhareswar Trust, 2004. No ISBN. (And there have since been two further volumes.)
394. Vedānta: The Solution To Our Fundamental Problem, D. Venugopal, Bharata Vidya Bhavan, 2012. ISBN 978-81-7276-457-9.
395. N/U.
396. Bhagavad-Gītā, with the commentary of Śaṅkarācārya. Translated by Swami Gambhirananda, Advaita Ashrama, 2003. ISBN 81-7505-041-1.
397. N/U.
398. Confusions in Advaita Vedanta: Knowledge, Experience and Enlightenment, Dennis Waite, Indica Press, 2022. ISBN 978-93-81120-29-3.
399. Viveka-cūḍāmaṇi of Śrī Śaṅkarācārya, translated by Swami Turiyananda, Sri Ramakrishna Math, 1991. ISBN 81-7120-405-8.
400. The Thousand Teachings of Sankara, translated by A.J. Alston, Shanti Sadan, 1990. ISBN 0-85424-041-1.
401. White Fire, Mooji, Mooji Media Publications, 2nd edition, 2020. ISBN 978-1-908408-35-8.
402. N/U.
403. N/U.
404. Śaṅkara on Enlightenment (A Śaṅkara Source Book Volume 6), compiled and translated by A.J. Alston, Shanti Sadan, 2004. ISBN 0-85424-060-8.
405. Chāndogya Upaniṣad: With the Commentary of Śaṅkarācārya, translated by Swami Gambhirananda, Advaita Ashrama, 2006. ISBN 81-7505-100-0.
406. N/U.
407. N/U.

408. The Laughing Jesus: Religious Lies and Gnostic Wisdom, Timothy Freke & Peter Gandy, O-Books, 2006. ISBN 978 1 905047 819.
409. N/U.
410. N/U.
411. N/U.
412. N/U.
413. Painting the Sidewalk with Water, Joan Tollifson, Non-Duality Press, 2010. ISBN 978-0-9566432-1-6.
414. N/U.
415. N/U.
416. How to Attain Enlightenment, James Swartz, Sentient Publications, 2009. ISBN 978-1-59181-094-0.
417. The Bhagavad Gita, Winthrop Sargeant, State University of New York Press, 1994. ISBN 0-87395-830-6.
418. Śrīmad Bhagavad Gītā, Kailash Nath Kalia, New Age Books, 2008. ISBN 978-81-7822-306-3.
419. Bhagavad Gītā Home Study Course, Swami Dayananda Saraswati, Arsha Vidya Research and Publication Trust, 2011. ISBN 978-93-80049-39-7 (set of nine volumes).
420. Bhagavad Gītā, Nitya Chaitanya Yati, D.K. Printworld, 1993. ISBN 81-246-0010-4.
421. Brahma Sūtras According to Śrī Śaṅkara, Swami Vireswarananda, Advaita Ashrama, 2008. ISBN 978-81-85301-95-2.
422. Brahma-Sūtras: Sanskrit Text and Commentary by Śaṅkarācārya. English Translation and Notes by George Thibaut, Bharatiya Kala Prakashan, 2004. ISBN 81-8090-040-1 (two volumes).
423. The Brahmasūtra and Their Principal Commentaries: A Critical Exposition, B.N.K. Sharma, Munshiram Manoharlal, 1974. ISBN 978-81-215-0032-6 (three volumes).
424. Brahmasūtra-Catuḥsūtrī-Śāṅkarabhāṣyam, with Sanskrit text, Transliteration, Word for Word Meaning, English

Translation and Annotation, S. Sankaranarayanan, Chinmaya International Foundation, 2015. ISBN 978-93-80864-33-4 (two volumes).

425. Śaṅkara's Upadeśasāhasrī, Sengaku Mayeda, Motilal Banarsidass, 2006. ISBN 81-208-2770-8 (two volumes).
426. N/U.
427. N/U.
428. N/U.
429. N/U.
430. The Elusive Obvious, Roger Linden website, http://www.rogerlinden.com/.
431. N/U.
432. Presence: The Art of Peace and Happiness, Rupert Spira, Non-Duality Press, 2011. ISBN 978-1-908664-03-7. (This is Volume 1; Volume 2 is 978-1-908664-04-4.)
433. N/U.
434. The Realization of the Absolute, The 'Naiṣkarmya Siddhi' of Sri Sureśvara, translated by A.J. Alston, Shanti Sadan, 1959. ISBN 0-85424-021-7.
435. Pañcadaśī of Sri Vidyaranya Swami. English Translation by Swami Swahananda, Sri Ramakrishna Math, 1967. No ISBN.
436. Insights into Vedanta (Tattvabodha), translation and commentary by Swami Sunirmalananda, Sri Ramakrishna Math, 2005. ISBN 81-7823-229-4.
437. A Śaṅkara Source Book, 6 Volumes, compiled and translated by A.J. Alston, Shanti Sadan, 1989. ISBN 0-85424-061-6.
438. Introduction to Vedanta, Dr. K. Sadananda, Srath-Visual Press, 2017. ISBN 978-0-9991704-0-3 (paperback).
439. N/U.
440. N/U.
441. Enlightenment: The Path Through the Jungle, Dennis Waite, O-Books, 2008. ISBN 978-1-84694-118-4.
442. Eternity Now, Francis Lucille, Truespeech Productions, 2019. ISBN 978-1882874002.

443. Standing as Awareness, Greg Goode, Non-Duality Press, 2009. ISBN 978-0-9563091-5-0.
444. The Direct Path: A User Guide, Greg Goode, Non-Duality Press, 2012. ISBN 978-1-908664-02-0.
445. N/U.
446. N/U.
447. The Essence of Enlightenment, James Swartz, Sentient Publications, 2014. ISBN 978-1-59181-277-7.
448. N/U.
449. N/U.
450. N/U.
451. N/U.
452. N/U.
453. The Deepest Acceptance: Radical Awakening in Ordinary Life, Jeff Foster, Sounds True, 2012, 2017. ISBN 978-1-62203-865-7.
454. N/U.
455. The Garland of Guru's Sayings, Sri Murugunar, translated from Tamil by Prof. K. Swaminathan, Sri Ramanasramam, 1990.
456. Non-Duality: The Groundless Openness, Douwe Tiemersma, Mantra Books, 2012. ISBN 978-1-78099-289-1.
457. Enlightenment Is Not What You Think, Wayne Liquorman, Advaita Press, 2009. ISBN 978-0-929448-22-0.
458. N/U.
459. N/U.
460. N/U.
461. N/U.
462. N/U.
463. N/U.
464. N/U.
465. N/U.
466. Taittirīyopaniśad with Śaṅkarabhāṣyam Vol. 2, Divyajñāna Sarojini Varadarājan, Selva Nilayam, Coimbatore, 2014. No ISBN.

467. Back to the Truth: 5000 Years of Advaita, Dennis Waite, O-Books, 2007. ISBN 1-905047-61-4.
468. 'Confusions in Advaita Vedanta': Book Review, M. Giridhar, *Mountain Path,* Vol. 60, No. 3, July-September 2023.
469. N/U.
470. Sri Guru Ramana Prasadam, Mukavai Kanna Muruganar. Translated from the Tamil by Robert Butler, Lulu, 2011.
471. Ramana Maharshi's Forty Verses On What Is: The Ultimate Truth On Being as You Actually Are, a compilation of the writings and talks on Uḷḷadu Nāṟpadu by Michael James. Compiled and edited by Sandra Derksen, BeVision, 2023. ISBN 9798853101487.
472. The Path of Sri Ramana, Part One: The Jñāna aspect of the teaching, Sri Sadhu Om, Sri Ramana Kshetra, 1971. No ISBN. © Michael James.
473. N/U.
474. N/U.
475. N/U.
476. Confusions in Advaita Vedanta: Ignorance and Its Removal, Dennis Waite, Indica Press, 2025?. Still to be published at time of writing.
477. Maharshi's Gospel: Books 1 and 2: Being Answers of Bhagavan Sri Ramana Maharshi to Questions put to Him by Devotees, Sri Ramanasramam, 2002. ISBN 81-88018-02-3.
478. N/U.
479. Being: The Bottom Line, Nathan Gill, Non-Duality Press, 2006. ISBN 978-0-9551762-2-7.
480. N/U.
481. N/U.
482. Maurice Frydman - A Jnani and A Karma Yogi, Dr. N.K. Srinivasan. Downloadable from https://www.scribd.com/document/97304328/Maurice-Frydman-a-Jnani-and-a-Karma-Yogi#.

483. The Voice of Śaṅkara (Journal of Kāñcī Kāmakoṭi Pīṭha), Vol. 28, No. 1, Thus Spake Śaṅkara, R. Balasubramanian. Download from https://www.kanchimatamkudanthai.org/voice-of-sankara-journal.
484. Embracing the Now: Finding Peace and Happiness in What Is, Gina Lake, Endless Satsang Foundation, 2008. ISBN 978-0-6152-4068-8.
485. Right Here, Right Now: Seeing Your True Nature as Present Awareness, John Wheeler, Non-Duality Press, 2006. ISBN 978-0-9551762-3-4.
486. That is That: Essays About True Nature, Nirmala, Endless Satsang Foundation, 2010. ISBN 9781453759738.
487. I Hope You Die Soon: Words on Non-Duality, Richard Sylvester, Non-Duality Press, 2006. ISBN 978-0-9551762-1-0.
488. N/U.
489. N/U.
490. N/U.
491. N/U.
492. N/U.
493. N/U.
494. Reflection on Brahman: Brahmānucintanam, Śrī Śaṅkara Ācārya, School of Practical Philosophy, 2017. ISBN 978-0-646-96913-8.
495. An Introduction to Non-Duality, Non-Duality Advaita Liberation, Richard Sylvester, https://richardsylvester1.wordpress.com/.
496. Seeing and Not Seeing, Tony Parsons, https://www.theopensecret.com/seeing-and-not-seeing.
497. N/U.
498. N/U.
499. N/U.
500. N/U.
501. N/U.

502. The Outrageous Myths of Enlightenment, Stephen Wingate, Atma Publishing, 2006–2010. ISBN 13: 978-0-9787254-0-2. Download from https://vdoc.pub/download/the-outrageous-myths-of-enlightenment-5btajg1s3ur0.
503. Look At Yourself, John Sherman, SilentHeart Press/RiverGanga Foundation, 2010. ISBN-13 978-0971824676.
504. N/U.
505. N/U.
506. N/U.
507. N/U.
508. Awakening to Infinite Presence: The Clarity of Self-Realization, Robert Wolfe, PDF Book Edition (Original Print Publication ISBN-13 978-1-937902-23-0), Karina Library Press, 2016. Download from https://livingnonduality.org/.
509. N/U.
510. Never Mind: A Journey into Non-duality, Wayne Liquorman, Advaita Press, 2004. ISBN 0-929448-21-9.
511. N/U.
512. N/U.
513. N/U.
514. N/U.
515. The Art of Freedom: A Guide to Awakening, Michael Damian, O-Books, 2017. ISBN 978-1785355936.
516. Noticing What You Already Know: And That You Already Know It, Robin Dale, Wyrd Publications, 2005. ISBN 0734036108.
517. Seeds for the Soul, Chuck Hillig, Black Dot Publications, 2003. ISBN 1-55395-844-6.
518. N/U.
519. An Introduction to Awareness, James M. Corrigan, BookSurge, 2006. ISBN 1-4196-4889-6.
520. N/U.
521. Non-Traditional Modern Advaita Gurus in the West and Their Traditional Modern Advaita Critics, Phillip Charles

Lucas, Nova Religio: The Journal of Alternative and Emergent Religions, Vol. 17, No. 3 (February 2014), pp. 6–37. Download http://www.jstor.org/stable/10.1525/nr.2014.17.3.6. This is now serialized at my website, beginning at https://www.advaita-vision.org/non-traditional-modern-advaita-gurus-in-the-west-and-their-traditional-modern-advaita-critics/.

522. Neo-Advaita or Pseudo-Advaita and *Real* Advaita-Nonduality, Timothy Conway, https://www.enlightened-spirituality.org/neo-advaita.html.
523. Talks on Upadesa Saram (Essence of the Teaching) of Ramana Maharshi, Swami Dayananda, Sri Gangadhareswar Trust, 1987. No ISBN.
524. Wondrously Free: Nonduality; This is Already Paradise, Rosemarijn Roes, Boekscout, 2022. ISBN 978-9464503067.
525. Consciousness – Not such a Hard Problem, Dennis Waite. https://www.advaita-vision.org/consciousness-not-such-a-hard-problem-1-of-2/.
526. N/U.
527. Accomplishing the Accomplished, Monographs of the Society for Asian and Comparative Philosophy, No. 10, Anantanand Rambachan, University of Hawaii Press, 1991. ISBN 0-8248-1358-8.
528. N/U.
529. The Advaita Library. An extensive, categorized (and often reviewed) listing of some 1500–2000 books related to Advaita (not updated since around 2014), Dennis Waite. http://www.Advaita.org.uk/library/library.html.
530. Heart Whispers, Wayne Austin, Camelot Press, 2004. ISBN 978-0974987712.
531. Why Advaita Works, Dennis Waite, Watkins Mind Body Spirit, Issue 35, Watkins Books, Autumn 2015.
532. Radical Awakening with Ramana, Jill V. Mangino, Vision Magazine Article, November 2001. http://radicalawakening.org/awakening/vision.html.

533. N/U.
534. Osho International Online, Individual Transformation For Contemporary People. https://booking.osho.com/.
535. Home Page of website, Joan Tollifson, August 23. https://www.joantollifson.com/.
536. 'The Transparency of Things' by Rupert Spira, Book Review by Dennis Waite. https://www.advaita.org.uk/discourses/teachers/transparency_waite.htm.
537. 'Standing as Awareness: The Direct Path' by Greg Goode, Book Review by Dennis Waite. https://www.advaita.org.uk/discourses/teachers/awareness_greg.htm.
538. Oregon Issues First Psilocybin Therapy Treatment Center License, A.J. Herrington. https://www.forbes.com/sites/ajherrington/2023/05/08/oregon-issues-first-psilocybin-therapy-treatment-center-license/.
539. What Is Enlightenment?, Andrew Cohen, Volume 1, No. 1, January 1992. Download from https://s3.eu-central-1.amazonaws.com/wieoldissues/wie_en_weboptimized/EN_Vol01_01.pdf.
540. What Is Evolutionary Enlightenment?, Andrew Cohen, https://www.andrewcohen.com/evolutionary-enlightenment/.
541. Getting off the Wheel: A Conceptual History of the New Age Concept of Enlightenment, Bas J.H. Jacobs, Numen – International Review for the History of Religion, June 2020. https://brill.com/downloadpdf/view/journals/nu/67/4/article-p373_2.pdf.
542. Deciphering The Hidden Meaning: Scripture And the Hermeneutics of Liberation in Early Advaita Vedānta, Aleksandar Uskokov, Department of South Asian Languages and Civilizations, Chicago, Illinois, 2018.
543. The Meaning of Sāṅkhya and Yoga, Franklin Edgerton. The American Journal of Philology 45 (1): 1–46, 1924.
544. The Path to Self-Knowledge, Ing Jiri Vacek, Mountain Path, Vol. 29, Aradhana Issue, June 1992.

545. N/U.
546. The Leela Foundation. https://leela.org/what-is-satsang/.
547. Vasant Swaha. https://vasantswaha.net/who-is-swaha/.
548. David Spero Autobiography. https://davidspero.org/about/.
549. Non-Duality Cartoons, Bob Seal. https://advaitatoons.blogspot.com/search/label/non%20duality.
550. Pure Silence, Teachers, Gurus, Priests, Lamas, Rabbis, and others, Mark McCloskey. https://www.puresilence.org/teachers.htm.
551. Radiance of Being: A Blog on Nonduality, Rodney Stevens. https://radianceofbeing.blogspot.com/.
552. RASA Transmission International, Inc., Spiritual Life Coaching with RASA for Rapid Non-Dual Awakening (Enlightenment).https://www.rasatransmissioninternational.com/.
553. Living Enlightenment: A Call for Evolution Beyond Ego, Andrew Cohen, New Age Books, 2002. ISBN 81-7822-142-x.
554. Nonduality: Fred Introduces The Living Method's Brand New Teacher! https://awakeningclaritynow.com/nonduality-fred-introduces-the-living-methods-brand-new-teacher/.
555. The Teacher is Everywhere..., Jeff Foster, Newsletter, 25th January 2024.
556. Is Guru Required For Self Knowledge, Guru Purnima Lecture by Swami Paramarthananda, transcribed by Sri VLN Prasad, Arsha Avinash Foundation. Download from https://arshaavinash.in/index.php/download/is-guru-required-for-self-knowledge-swami-paramarthananda/#.
557. Everyone has Self-Knowledge, the Self is ever-realised | Sri Ramana Maharshi, Tom Das, April 24, 2023. https://tomdas.com/2023/04/24/everyone-has-self-knowledge-the-self-is-ever-realised/.

558. Do You Need a Guru? Understanding the Student-Teacher Relationship in an Era of False Prophets, Mariana Caplan, Thorsons, 2002. ISBN 0 00 711865 1.
559. Halfway Up the Mountain: The Error of Premature Claims to Enlightenment, Mariana Caplan, Hohm Press, 2001. ISBN 0-934252-91-2.
560. A Tradition of Teachers: Śaṅkara and the Jagadgurus Today, William Cenkner, Motilal Banarsidass, 1983. ISBN 81-208-1763-x.
561. Gems from the Ocean of Devotional Hindu Thought, V. Krishnamurty, Readworthy, 2011. ISBN 978-93-5018-015-0.
562. Spiritual Enlightenment: The Damnedest Thing, Jed McKenna, Wisefool Press, 2002. ISBN 0-9714352-3-5.
563. Vedānta Prabodha, Swāmi Paramānanda Bhāratī, Jñānasamvardhani Pratiṣṭānam, 2014. No ISBN.
564. Śrī Śaṅkara's Vivekacūḍāmaṇi. English translation of The Sanskrit Commentary of Śrī Candraśekhara Bhāratī of Śṛṅgeri, Bharatiya Vidya Bhavan, 2022. ISBN 978-81-7276-420-3.
565. The Philosophy of the Bhagavadgītā, S.M. Srinivasa Chari, Munshiram Manoharlal Publishers Pvt. Ltd., 2005. ISBN 81-215-1101-1.
566. Pure Presence Conferences, Bill Free. https://pure-presence-productions.mykajabi.com/home.
567. Bodhi Avasa: There Is But One Being In All Things And This One Is You. https://bodhiavasa.com/.
568. The GURU Question: The Perils and Rewards of Choosing a Spiritual Teacher, Mariana Caplan, Sounds True Inc., 2011. ISBN 978-1-60407-073-6.
569. About Dolano, Satsang with Dolano. http://www.dolano.com/frm_page.htm.
570. What is Truth?, article by Éric Baret, Science & Nonduality. https://scienceandnonduality.com/article/what-is-truth/.
571. 52 Enlightenment Myths: Myths and Misconceptions About Enlightenment, Eric Putkonen, Awaken to Life with

Eric Putkonen, 2010. https://drive.google.com/file/d/15MZDppf5S11PSvqBJSlKV694P2c9IZON/view.

572. Thoughts on suffering, the spiritual path, and their resolution, Felipe Oliveira. https://nothingwronganymore.com/.
573. Conscious.TV, Halina Pytlasinska – Non–Duality, Interview with Renate McNay. https://conscious.tv/text/05.htm.
574. Wild Fig Solutions, About Me, Read My Journey to Here, Helen Amery. https://wildfigsolutions.co.uk/about-me/.
575. Helen Hamilton. https://www.helenhamilton.org/.
576. Meetings in Truth, Isaac Shapiro. https://isaacshapiro.org/isaac_1/.
577. Natural Awakenings: What Is Enlightenment?, Jac O'Keeffe. https://www.jac-okeeffe.com/natural-awakenings.
578. RE: Certainty of knowledge, post to Advaitin Group, 25th September 2011, Chittaranjan Naik.
579. Vital Aliveness: The Heart of Silence, What is Satsang?, Jeannie McGillivray. http://www.vitalaliveness.com/what-is-satsang/.
580. N/U.
581. Definition: Self-Realization, Jeff Vander Clute, 12th August 2023. https://jeffvanderclute.com/2023/08/12/definition-self-realization/.
582. Jim Newman – Satsang agenda. About Jim Non-Duality Meetings with Jim Newman. https://www.satsang.nl/nl/data/jim-newman.html.
583. N/U.
584. Awake Joy: The Essence of Enlightenment, Katie Davis, Awake Spirit Publishing, 2008. ISBN 978-0-9800912-2-9. Extract at https://www.advaita.org.uk/discourses/teachers/practices_davis.htm.
585. Surrender to Silence, Lisa Schumacher, Living From Love. http://www.living-from-love.com/conversations-2014---2017.html.

586. Embodied Awareness: Explorations in Truth, Louise Kay. https://www.louisekay.net/.
587. The Journey To Enlightenment: The Way Things Really Are, John R.E. Harger. Published by Author, 2010, www.lulu.com, ID. 8984587.
588. No Path To Enlightenment: The I before I am – exposing the illusion of your Self, Colin McMorran, Self-published, 2021. ISBN 9798712135448.
589. Liberation IS: The End of the Spiritual Path, Salvadore Poe, CreateSpace, 2015. ISBN 978-1522768111.
590. Eyes Wide Open: Cultivating Discernment on the Spiritual Path, Mariana Caplan, PhD, Sounds True, 2009. ISBN 978-1-59179-732-6.
591. N/U.
592. Enlighten Life Meditation Retreat, Madhukar Enlighten Life, Madhukar. https://madhukar.org/.
593. Illusory duality is an expression of eternal wholeness, Nic Higham. https://nisargayoga.org/illusory-duality-is-an-expression-of-eternal-wholeness/.
594. About satsang – What is satsang?, Nirmala. https://www.endless-satsang.com/about-satsang.
595. Natural – Satsang February 6, 2022, Reflections, SAT Temple, January, February, March 2023. https://reflections.satramana.org/Reflections_JanFebMar2023.pdf.
596. Are you the body?, Salvadore Poe. https://www.liberationis.com/blog/are-you-the-body/.
597. Maya, Salvadore Poe. https://www.liberationis.com/blog/maya/.
598. About Shakti. https://www.shakticaterinamaggi.com/shakti/.
599. Nonduality - Introduction, James Braha. https://jamesbraha.com/nonduality-advaita/.
600. Molten Lava, James Eaton. https://www.authenticliving.org.uk/molten-lava/.

601. The Daydream Unmasked, Jan Kersschot. https://www.advaita.org.uk/discourses/teachers/daydream_kersschot.htm.

602. Buddha at the Gas Pump, 094. Jeff Foster. https://batgap.com/category/nond/page/34/.

603. On Neo-Advaita, Jeff Foster – Life Without a Center. https://www.lifewithoutacentre.com/writings/on-neo-advaita/.

604. About Jeff Vander Clute. https://jeffvanderclute.com/about/.

605. One: Essential Writings on Nonduality, edited by Jerry Katz, First Sentient Publications, 2007. ISBN 978-1-59181-053-7.

606. The Attitude of the Witness, Jim Gilman. https://www.thesilentway.org/the-attitude-of-the-witness.

607. Nondualism Takes No Prisoners, Jim Newman. https://www.simply-this.com/essays.

608. There Is No After (or before) Awakening—Being Awake is NOW, Joan Tollifson, Right Now, Just As It Is! Newsletter, 20th August 2023.

609. Where are You Going?: A Guide to the Spiritual Journey, Swami Muktananda, SYDA Foundation, 1989. ISBN 978-0914602996.

610. Modern Psychology and Vedanta, Introduction – The Basics, John Baxter. https://non-dualpsychology.com/2023/04/modern-psychology-and-vedanta/.

611. Direct Immediate Knowing, Joan Tollifson. Substack Newsletter, 14th December 2023.

612. Arunachala Talks, Premananda, Open Sky Press Ltd., 2007. ISBN 978-0-9555730-2-6.

613. Embodied Nonduality, published in Undivided, an online journal at http://undividedjournal.com/?p=536. https://realizationprocess.org/wp-content/uploads/2018/12/EmbodiedNonduality.essay_.pdf.

614. Non-Duality Magazine: Interview with Karen Richards. https://evolutionarymystic.wordpress.com/2013/04/11/non-duality-magazine-interview-with-karen-richards/.
615. Interview 120 – Katie Davis, Buddha at the Gas Pump. https://batgap.com/katie-davis/.
616. Always Awakening: The Continuing Playful Exploration of Self-Inquiry & Life, Krishna Gauci. https://www.krishnasatsang.com/essay_always_awakening.htm.
617. Being: Conversations with Florian Tathagata, Florian Tathagata, 220 Publishing, 2006. ISBN 1-905479-01-8.
618. The Journey Is From Here to Here and the Only Time You Can Arrive Is Now, Leonard Jacobson. https://www.leonardjacobson.com/.
619. Time and Timelessness, Leonard Jacobson. https://www.leonardjacobson.com/blog?tag=enlightenment.
620. Cultural Robots, Enlightenment For No One, Maury Lee. https://nomaury.blogspot.com/2023/12/cultural-robots.html.
621. Happiness and the Art of Being, Michael James, Trafford Publishing, 2007. ISBN 978-1-4251-2465-6.
622. The Birth of the Lion: Dialogues of Self-Inquiry, OM C. Parkin, Advaita Media, 1998. ISBN 3-936718-02-4.
623. Reality, Peter Brown, The Open Doorway. https://www.theopendoorway.org/reality.
624. Transmission, Peter Brown, The Open Doorway. https://www.theopendoorway.org/transmission.
625. 'I' is a Door, Philip Renard, Zen Publications, 2017. ISBN 978-93-85902-66-6.
626. The Mind Keeps You in Darkness, Papaji's Avadhuta Foundation. https://avadhuta.com/the-mind-keeps-you-in-darkness/.
627. Is it not old fashioned to be with a guru?, Advaita Vedanta, Prajnaparamita. https://www.prajnaparamita.nl/en/texts-from-prajnaparamita/advaita-vedanta-2/.

628. You Are No Thing: Recognising Your True Nature, Randall Friend, Non-Duality Press, 2009. ISBN 978-0-9558290-7-9.
629. Dṛgdṛśyaviveka. Attributed to Śaṅkara. Translated from the Sanskrit, and Commentary, by Raphael, Aurea Vidyā, 1983. English Translation, 2008. ISBN 978-1-931406-09-3.
630. No You and No Me: The Loving Awareness in Which All Arises, Richard Linchitz, Non-Duality Press, 2011. ISBN 978-1-908664-00-6.
631. Divine Romance, Satsang with Shri Rishi Rajivji. Download from https://www.rishirajiv.org/uploads/images/Transcription%20of%20Satsang%20on%20Divine%20Romance.pdf.
632. The Selected Sayings of Robert P. Meizer, being the best of bobby. https://mu.thelemistas.org/bobbymeizer/rpmeizer/index.html.
633. The Ten Thousand Things, Robert Saltzman, New Sarum Press, 2018. ISBN 978-1999353506.
634. Being Lived, Roger Castillo. https://www.rogercastillo.org/.
635. The Ego is a Sneaky Caterpillar, Unbroken Self. https://www.unbrokenself.com/the-ego-is-a-sneaky-caterpillar/.
636. The Ultimate Revolution, An essay on fresh observation, Rupert Spira. https://rupertspira.com/non-duality/blog/philosophy/the_ultimate_revolution.
637. 'The Transparency of Things' by Rupert Spira, Book Review by Dennis Waite. https://www.advaita.org.uk/discourses/teachers/transparency_waite.htm.
638. Journey Beyond: A Non-Dual Approach (three volumes), Acharya Dr. Kuntimaddi Sadananda, Notion Press, 2019. ISBN 978-1-64650-544-9, 978-1-64650-546-3 and 978-1-64650-548-7.
639. Ancient Wisdom for Modern Management, T.R. Ramachandran, Tattvaloka Publications, 2006. No ISBN.

640. Make It Happen, Chinmaya Mission Home Study Courses. https://www.chinmayamission.com/what-we-do/courses/postal-e-vedanta-courses/make-it-happen-2/.
641. What is Primal Yoga?, Satyananda. https://www.satyananda.org/PrimalYoga.
642. Dark to Light, What if this is all an illusion?, Sheilan. https://infinitelivingteachings.wordpress.com/2020/07/24/dark-to-light/.
643. Stephan Bodian 2nd Interview Transcript, Buddha at the Gas Pump. https://batgap.com/stephan-bodian-2nd-interview-transcript/.
644. The Phenomenon, Stuart Schwartz. https://www.advaita.org.uk/discourses/teachers/phenomenon_schwartz.htm.
645. Free Spirit: A Guide to Enlightened Being, Sundance Burke, Awake Spirit Publishing, 2007. ISBN 978-0-9800912-3-6.
646. The Supreme Self: The way to enlightenment, Swami Abhayananda, O-Books, 2005. ISBN 1-905047-45-2.
647. Resident Teacher, Ajatananda Ashram, Swami Atmananda Udasin. https://ajatananda.org/about-ashram-rishikesh/swami-atmananda-udasin-2/.
648. When the Drop becomes the Ocean: A journey to the Ocean, to the Divine. On the Upanishads, the Ancient Wisdom of India, Swami Dhyan Gite, Lulu.com, 2021. ISBN 979-1716546623.
649. Inviting the World, International Centers of Divine Awakening, Swami Premodaya. https://www.i-coda.org/teaching/#quotes.
650. Swami Sarvapriyananda Transcript, Buddha at the Gas Pump. https://batgap.com/swami-sarvapriyananda-transcript/.
651. Articles and Thoughts on Vedanta, Sri Sri Satchidanandendra Saraswathi Swamiji, Adhyatma Prakasha Karyalaya, 2015. No ISBN.

652. Consciousness, Timothy Schoorel. https://www.advaita.org.uk/discourses/teachers/consciousness_schoorel.htm.
653. Is everything really consciousness?, Tom Das, Liberation and Non-Duality. https://tomdas.com/2016/11/11/is-everything-really-consciousness/.
654. N/U.
655. N/U.
656. About Tom, Present Being Awareness, Tom Fitzgerald. http://www.tomfitzgerald.org/about/index.html.
657. Tom Thompson, The Awakened Heart Center for Conscious Living. https://www.theawakenedheartcenter.com/tom-thompson.html.
658. Spiritual Humanism vs Neo-Advaita – A 3-way discussion between Möller de la Rouvière, Tony Parsons and Alan Stoltz, https://www.advaita.org.uk/discourses/trad_neo/humanism_moller.htm.
659. Traditional not two-ness is better than Neo not two-ness???, Tony Parsons, The Open Secret. https://www.theopensecret.com/traditional-not-two-ness.
660. The Dream of Separation, Tony Parsons, The Open Secret. https://www.theopensecret.com/dream-of-separation.
661. What is a Teacher?, Unmani Liza Hyde. https://www.die-to-love.com/about/what-is-a-teacher/.
662. Danger – Sort of, Vince Flammini. https://vinceflammini.com/3-principles-living/.
663. Path to Enlightenment, Vishrant. https://www.vishrant.org/teachings/.
664. N/U.
665. What Happens in a Radical Awakening Session?, Radical Awakening and the Opening to Heart Consciousness, (Yukio) Ramana. http://radicalawakening.org/awakening/session.html.
666. Empathic Ground, The Realization Process™, Zoran Josipovic. https://realizationprocess.org/empathic-ground/.

667. Topic of the Month – Becoming, Sitara, October 2014. https://www.advaita-vision.org/topic-of-the-month-becoming/.
668. Defining Enlightenment, The Dawn Within, Alain Joly. https://thedawnwithin.com/defining-enlightenment/.
669. Life Beyond Belief: Everyday Living as Spiritual Practice, Alice Gardner, Awake Publishing, 2008. ISBN 978-0-9792435-0-9.
670. The Mind is a Problem Factory, Don't Eat the Menu, Alicia St. Rose. https://donteatthemenu.com/mind-problem-factory/.
671. N/A.
672. N/A.
673. The Game of Distinctions, September 30th, 2013, Blog Archive. http://www.anamikaborst.com/blog.html.
674. Books and Essays by Ananda Wood, Advaita Vision. https://www.advaita.org.uk/discourses/ananda_wood/ananda_wood.htm.
675. Ananta Kranti – About. https://www.ananta-kranti.com/about.
676. Analysis of Quotes by Ramana Maharshi and Nisargadatta Maharaj, Yes Vedānta: Knowledge of the Seers, Andre Vas. https://www.yesvedanta.com/analysis-of-quotes-by-ramana-maharshi-and-nisargadatta-maharaj/.
677. Manifest Nirvana, Meeting Truth – Supporting the Nondual Community. https://meetingtruth.com/Group/manifest-nirvana.
678. You Are He: Commentaries on the Teaching of Shri Ranjit Maharaj, Andrew Vernon, Golden Day, 2005. ISBN 978-0615156033.
679. Awake: It's Your Turn, Introduction, Angelo DiLullo, SimplyAlwaysAwake.com, 2021. ISBN 978-1737212324.
680. How does Māyā operate? How is the Self concealed from itself?, Teachings of Sri Annamalai Swami. https://sriannamalaiswami.org/recorded-teachings/.

681. Approach, Annette Knopp. https://www.annetteknopp.com/approach.
682. Drop it All, Even "What is Truth?", Annette Nibley. https://www.advaita.org.uk/discourses/teachers/truth_nibley.htm.
683. Inner Knowing, Awakening Coach Aruna Byers. https://www.awakeningcoach.com/inner-knowing.
684. Pure Presence Conferences. https://pure-presence-productions.mykajabi.com/home.
685. None to enlighten, There Is But One Being In All Things And This One Is You, Bodhi Avasa. https://bodhiavasa.com/none-to-enlighten/.
686. The Seeking, There Is But One Being In All Things And This One Is You, Bodhi Avasa. https://bodhiavasa.com/the-seeking/.
687. Come and Go, The heart of presence is love, Wild Animal Zen, Kip "Bok" Wood. https://wildanimalzen.com/teachings2.
688. Meeting Truth, Brian Piergrossi. https://meetingtruth.com/Teacher/BrianPiergrossi.
689. My Life, Bruce Joel Rubin. https://www.brucejoelrubin.com/mylife.html.
690. What happens when the body dies?, The Awareness Foundation Teaching the Wholeness of Life, Burt Harding. http://www.burtharding.com/writings/articles/what_happens_when_the_body_dies_-44.html.
691. Interview with Canela Michelle Meyers, Jerry Katz. https://www.nonduality.com/hl4435.htm.
692. A Thunderstorm in the Open Sky: On Suffering and Freedom, An Interview with Catherine Ingram by Peter Moore, Quest Journal, 1994. https://www.catherineingram.com/thunderstorm/.
693. Ajata / No Creation, Satsang with Cee, January 4th, 2003. No longer available for download.

694. Who is Chad?, The WAY Project: Who Are You?, Chadwick Johnson. https://chadwick-johnson.wixsite.com/theway/whoischad.
695. Simply Being, Charlie Hayes, CreateSpace, 2012. ISBN 978-1479347537.
696. The Natural State: A Collection of Teachings by "Non-Duality Teacher" John Wheeler. https://johnwheelernonduality.wordpress.com/.
697. Nonduality by Colin Drake, The Words of a Mystic... https://mysticson.blogspot.com/2010/09/nonduality-by-colin-drake.html.
698. Awakening and Realization, Darryl Bailey. https://www.darrylbailey.net/awakening/.
699. Big Bangers 'n' Mash in The Wonder of This, David Brockman, Beyond Description Publishing, 2007. ISBN 978-1847997401. Extract at https://www.nonduality.com/hl2987.htm.
700. Lighthouse of the Impossible, Autobiography, David Spero. https://davidspero.org/about/.
701. Are You Ready?, Dolano. https://www.friendsofdolano.org/post/are-you-ready.
702. Éric Baret – (unpublished?) interview by Paula Marvelly.
703. Oneness is the Reality, Multiplicity is the Concept, the Edge, Eric Putkonen, September 1st, 2018. https://www.edgemagazine.net/2018/09/oneness-is-the-reality-multiplicity-is-the-concept/.
704. Notes on Being, Felipe Oliveira, 2006. Book in PDF format. No idea where it came from!
705. Advaita Vedanta Quotes and Nonduality Quotations, Floyd Henderson. https://advaitaquotes.blogspot.com/.
706. About Francis Lucille. https://www.francislucille.com/about/.
707. Email discussion between myself and Francis Lucille on the topic of ajāti vāda (non-creation), 19th January 2000.

708. Interview 208 – Fred Davis, Buddha at the Gas Pump. https://batgap.com/category/nond/page/27/.
709. The Book of Undoing: Direct Pointing to Nondual Awareness, Fred Davis, CreateSpace Independent Publishing, 2013. ISBN 978-1484015629.
710. Bringing Nondual Reality Into Everyday Life, Sacred Space for Awakened Living, Dr. Gail Brenner. https://gailbrenner.com/2020/10/bringing-nondual-reality-into-everyday-life/.
711. The Pearl Within Your Emotions: Part V – Self-Worth and the Open Heart, November 27th, 2023, Gangaji. https://gangaji.org/blog/self-worth-and-the-open-heart.
712. True Apperception, Gautam Sachdeva. https://www.gautamsachdeva.com/writings/true-apperception/.
713. Non Duality is not a subject or object, Gilbert Schultz. https://seeing-knowing.com/blog/non-duality-is-not-a-subject-or-object/.
714. The Direct Path: A User Guide, Greg Goode, Non-Duality Press, 2012. ISBN 978-1-908664-02-0.
715. Non Duality, Good Film, 2023. https://good.film/title/movie/1148771/non-duality.
716. Rozengeur en prikkeldraad, Hans Laurentius, Samsara, 2020. ISBN 978-9493228207.
717. Revealing Your Aligned Expression, The Enlightenment Event, Wild Fig Solutions, Helen Amery. https://wildfigsolutions.co.uk/2024/01/03/the-enlightenment-event-feb-to-nov-24/.
718. Core Teaching 2 – Self-inquiry, Helen Hamilton. https://www.helenhamilton.org/uploads/4/0/0/9/4009977/core_teaching__2_-_self_inquiry.pdf.
719. Quotes, Isaac Shapiro. https://isaacshapiro.org/quotes-1/.
720. Unity Consciousness: The Experience of Oneness, Jac O'Keeffe. https://www.jac-okeeffe.com/challenge-page/unity-consciousness-course.

721. What is satsang?, Jan Koehoorn. https://www.jankoehoorn.nl/.
722. Beyond Knowledge, Jean Klein, Non-Duality Press, 2006. ISBN 978-0-9551762-8-9.
723. The Heart of the Unknown, Jeannie McGillivray. http://www.vitalaliveness.com/125/.
724. About, Kenneth Madden Non Duality. https://www.kennethmadden.net/about.
725. Everything that arises here is an opportunity for Freedom, Neelam. https://neelam.org/read/.
726. How do you know if you are Enlightened?, Nukunu. https://nukunu.net/how-do-you-know-if-you-are-enlightened/.
727. Darshan, OM C. Parkin. https://www.om-c-parkin.de/en/teaching-and-activities/darshan.
728. Consciousness Is All: The Magnificent Truth of What You Are, Peter Dziuban, Peter Francis Dziuban, 2020. ISBN 978-0998652474.
729. Conscious Immortality (Conversations with Sri Ramana Maharshi Recorded by Paul Brunton), Ramana Maharshi, Sri Ramanasramam, 2013. ISBN 978-8182881785.
730. Dissolving into Nothing, Wake up… You Are Dreaming, Randall Friend. https://avastu0.blogspot.com/.
731. Illusion vs. Reality, Shri Ranjit Maharaj, transcribed by Robert Wolff, Sadguru Publishing, 2023. ISBN 978-1737660774.
732. Powerful quotes from Sri Ranjit Maharaj, Tom Das. https://tomdas.com/2019/06/11/powerful-quotes-from-sri-ranjit-maharaj/.
733. No Me and No You: Guest Teaching by Rick Linchitz, Fred Davis. https://awakeningclaritynow.com/no-me-and-no-you-guest-teaching-by-rick-linchitz/.
734. Untamed Spirit, Celestial Song, Sandy Jones. https://celestialsongspirit.blogspot.com/p/untamed.html.
735. From Onions to Pearls: A Journal of Awakening and Deliverance, Satyam Nadeen, Hay House Inc., 1999. ISBN 978-1561705870.

736. Satyam Nadeen, Nonduality.com. https://www.nonduality.com/satyam.htm.
737. The Characteristics of Wakefulness, What Does It Mean to Be Spiritually Awakened?, Steve Taylor, Psychology Today. https://www.psychologytoday.com/intl/blog/out-of-the-darkness/202401/what-does-it-mean-to-be-spiritually-awakened.
738. Stop Seeking and Relish It: Guest Teaching by Suzanne Foxton, Fred Davis. https://awakeningclaritynow.com/stop-seeking-and-relish-it-guest-teaching-by-suzanne-foxton/.
739. Scientist's Search for Truth, Swami Virajeshwara, Hamsa Ashramam, 2005. ISBN 978-8190082709.
740. Vedanta: the Solution, Serialization of the book by D. Venugopal. Also downloadable as a PDF file. https://www.advaita-vision.org/vedanta-the-solution-part-1.
741. Books by Swami Paramarthananda, Arsha Avinash Foundation. https://arshaavinash.in/index.php/books-by-swami-paramarthananda/.
742. Vivekachudamani, Transcription of talks by Swami Paramarthananda. https://arshaavinash.in/index.php/books-by-swami-paramarthananda/#.
743. Book Review: 'Awakening to the Dream: The Gift of Lucid Living' by Leo Hartong, Matthew West. https://www.indicamoksha.com/book/awakening-to-the-dream-the-gift-of-lucid-living/.
744. 'Perfect Brilliant Stillness,' David Carse – Brief review by myself at https://www.indicamoksha.com/book/awakening-to-the-dream-the-gift-of-lucid-living/; sample chapter at https://www.advaita.org.uk/discourses/teachers/vision_carse.htm; two more reviews and a long response from David at https://www.advaita.org.uk/discourses/trad_neo/stillness_carse.htm.

745. Maha Yoga (Book PDF Download), Tom Das. https://tomdas.com/2021/05/30/maha-yoga-book-pdf-download-the-upanishads-in-the-light-of-the-teachings-of-bhagavan-ramana-maharshi/.
746. Tamil, Telugu and English Publications, Sri Ramanasramam. https://www.gururamana.org/Resources/english-tamil.
747. Māṇḍūkya Upaniṣad with Kārikā and Sankaracharya's Commentary (two volumes), Divyajñāna Sarojini Varadarājan, Arsha Vidya Gurukulam, 2022. No ISBN.
748. The Teaching of Sri Atmananda Krishna Menon, Ananda Wood. https://www.advaita.org.uk/discourses/atmananda/atmananda1.htm.
749. Direct Path vs Traditional, Q. 508–512. https://www.advaita-vision.org/q-508-direct-path-vs-traditional-pt-1/.
750. Peace Beyond Understanding ... Zoom with Jim, Jim Dreaver. Email, 4th October 2023.
751. Your questions answered – Sacred Exhaustion and more, Jeff Foster. Email, 30th August 2023.
752. The Circle, Dave Eggers, Penguin, 2013. ISBN 978-0-385-35139-3.
753. Details of Traditional and Western Satsang Teachers. https://www.advaita.org.uk/teachers/teachers.htm.
754. Disciples of Ramana Maharshi – Lineage Chart. https://www.advaita.org.uk/teachers/ramana_parampara.htm.
755. Navnath Sampradaya: Disciples of Nisargadatta Maharaj – Lineage Chart. https://www.advaita.org.uk/teachers/navnath_sampradaya.htm.
756. Disciples of Atmananda Krishna Menon – Lineage Chart. https://www.advaita.org.uk/teachers/atmananda_parampara.htm.
757. Invitation to join Live Zoom session with Br. Pratyagatma Chaitanya on Sunday, April 21, 2024. AVRPT News. Email received 19th April 2024.

758. Three Faces of Advaita, Aja Thomas, Blog around 2012. https://www.advaita.org.uk/discourses/trad_neo/advaita_aja.htm.
759. The Myth of Self-Enquiry, Jan Kersschot. Non-Duality Press, 2007. ISBN 978-0955399961.
760. GRP + Love Heals Everything, Jim Dreaver. Email promoting Zoom session, 8th November 2023.
761. Call Me to My True Names, Jivanjili. (Translated from Dutch by Google.) https://www.jivanjili.org/index.php/nl/artikelen/roep-mij-bij-mijn-ware-namen.
762. Silent Presence, Satsang with Ganga Maa Vol. 1, Edited by David Godman, Hridaya Kshetram Trust, 2024. No ISBN?
763. Personal email from Dhanya Moffitt. July, 2024.

Index

Recent bestsellers from MANTRA BOOKS are:

The Way Things Are
A Living Approach to Buddhism
Lama Ole Nydahl
An introduction to the teachings of the Buddha, and how to make use of these teachings in everyday life.
Paperback: 978-1-84694-042-2 ebook: 978-1-78099-845-9

Back to the Truth
5000 Years of Advaita
Dennis Waite
A demystifying guide to Advaita for both those new to, and those familiar with this ancient, non-dualist philosophy from India.
Paperback: 978-1-90504-761-1 ebook: 978-184694-624-0

Shinto: A celebration of Life
Aidan Rankin
Introducing a gentle but powerful spiritual pathway reconnecting humanity with Great Nature and affirming all aspects of life.
Paperback: 978-1-84694-438-3 ebook: 978-1-84694-738-4

In the Light of Meditation
Mike George
A comprehensive introduction to the practice of meditation and the spiritual principles behind it. A 10 lesson meditation programme with CD and internet support.
Paperback: 978-1-90381-661-5

A Path of Joy
Popping into Freedom
Paramananda Ishaya
A simple and joyful path to spiritual enlightenment.
Paperback: 978-1-78279-323-6 ebook: 978-1-78279-322-9

The Less Dust the More Trust

Participating in The Shamatha Project, Meditation and Science

Adeline van Waning, MD PhD

The inside-story of a woman participating in frontline meditation research, exploring the interfaces of mind-practice, science and psychology.

Paperback: 978-1-78099-948-7 ebook: 978-1-78279-657-2

I Know How To Live, I Know How To Die

The Teachings of Dadi Janki: A warm, radical, and life-affirming view of who we are, where we come from, and what time is calling us to do

Neville Hodgkinson

Life and death are explored in the context of frontier science and deep soul awareness.

Paperback: 978-1-78535-013-9 ebook: 978-1-78535-014-6

Living Jainism

An Ethical Science

Aidan Rankin, Kanti V. Mardia

A radical new perspective on science rooted in intuitive awareness and deductive reasoning.

Paperback: 978-1-78099-912-8 ebook: 978-1-78099-911-1

Ordinary Women, Extraordinary Wisdom

The Feminine Face of Awakening

Rita Marie Robinson

A collection of intimate conversations with female spiritual teachers who live like ordinary women, but are engaged with their true natures.

Paperback: 978-1-84694-068-2 ebook: 978-1-78099-908-1

The Way of Nothing
Nothing in the Way
Paramananda Ishaya
A fresh and light-hearted exploration of the amazing reality of nothingness.
Paperback: 978-1-78279-307-6 ebook: 978-1-78099-840-4

Readers of ebooks can buy or view any of these bestsellers by clicking on the live link in the title. Most titles are published in paperback and as an ebook. Paperbacks are available in traditional bookshops. Both print and ebook formats are available online.

Find more titles and sign up to our readers' newsletter at www.collectiveinkbooks.com/mind-body-spirit. Follow us on Facebook at facebook.com/OBooks and Twitter at twitter.com/obooks